W9-AQV-740

BUST

Greece, the Euro, and the Sovereign Debt Crisis

MATTHEW LYNN

BLOOMBERG PRESS
An Imprint of
WILEY

Copyright © 2011 by Matthew Lynn. All rights reserved.

Published by John Wiley & Sons, Inc., Hoboken, New Jersey.
Published simultaneously in Canada.

No part of this publication may be reproduced, stored in a retrieval system, or transmitted in any form or by any means, electronic, mechanical, photocopying, recording, scanning, or otherwise, except as permitted under Section 107 or 108 of the 1976 United States Copyright Act, without either the prior written permission of the Publisher, or authorization through payment of the appropriate per-copy fee to the Copyright Clearance Center, Inc., 222 Rosewood Drive, Danvers, MA 01923, (978) 750-8400, fax (978) 646-8600, or on the Web at www.copyright.com. Requests to the Publisher for permission should be addressed to the Permissions Department, John Wiley & Sons, Inc., 111 River Street, Hoboken, NJ 07030, (201) 748-6011, fax (201) 748-6008, or online at http://www.wiley.com/go/permissions.

Limit of Liability/Disclaimer of Warranty: While the publisher and author have used their best efforts in preparing this book, they make no representations or warranties with respect to the accuracy or completeness of the contents of this book and specifically disclaim any implied warranties of merchantability or fitness for a particular purpose. No warranty may be created or extended by sales representatives or written sales materials. The advice and strategies contained herein may not be suitable for your situation. You should consult with a professional where appropriate. Neither the publisher nor author shall be liable for any loss of profit or any other commercial damages, including but not limited to special, incidental, consequential, or other damages.

For general information on our other products and services or for technical support, please contact our Customer Care Department within the United States at (800) 762-2974, outside the United States at (317) 572-3993 or fax (317) 572-4002.

Wiley also publishes its books in a variety of electronic formats. Some content that appears in print may not be available in electronic books. For more information about Wiley products, visit our web site at www.wiley.com.

Library of Congress Cataloging-in-Publication Data:

Lynn, Matthew.
    Bust : Greece, the euro, and the sovereign debt crisis / Matthew Lynn.
      p.   cm.
    ISBN 978-0-470-97611-1 (cloth); ISBN 978-1-119-99068-0 (ebk);
    ISBN 978-1-119-99069-7 (ebk)
      1. Financial crises—Greece—History—21st century. 2. Debts, External—Greece—History—21st century. 3. Greece—Economic conditions—1974–
4. Greece—Economic policy—1974– 5. Economic stabilization—Greece—History—21st century. I. Title.
    HB3807.5.L96 2010
    330.9495—dc22
                                      2010042208

Printed in the United States of America
10 9 8 7 6 5 4 3 2 1

Miami Dade College Library

To my mother

Contents

Introduction

May Day in Athens

I t had been a long time since the *Hammer & Sickle*, the Marxist symbol of the unity of workers and peasants, had been flown anywhere
in Europe with anything approaching pride. But on May 4, 2010, as
the protests in Greece over the austerity package imposed on the country by the European Union and the International Monetary Fund gathered force, members of the Greek Communist Party stormed the Acropolis
and draped a huge banner across its famous old stones. The slogan,
"Peoples of Europe Rise Up," was etched into the banner, and, next
to the words, in stark, blood-red graphics, the crossed implements that
were formally adopted as the official flag of the Soviet Union way back
in 1924.

The Acropolis is the most potent symbol of Greek culture; indeed,
it is one of the foundation stones of Western civilization, a monument
that reminds all of us of the common intellectual and cultural heritage
we all share. Over the next 24 hours, across all the news networks, the
protestors' flag was broadcast as a backdrop as reporters filed reports on
the riots rampaging through Athens.

There could be no better way of illustrating what was happening,
both on the streets and in the financial markets. On one level, ordinary Greeks were venting their anger and frustration over an economy
that appeared to have gone off the rails as suddenly and violently as a
train accelerating into a crash. On another, a wider conflict was being
played out. The riots were about far more than just a few budget cuts

1

in one smallish country far from the center of the world economy. They were about whether a whole economic and political system created over three generations was sustainable. Or whether, groaning under a mountain of debts and a mess of ill-thought-through dreams and aspirations, it was about to collapse under the weight of its own contradictions.

It was no exaggeration to argue that the postwar economic system established in Europe was breaking apart in front of people's eyes. And the Hammer & Sickle drove that point home with the kind of unrelenting clarity that would have bought a smile to the corpse of the man who had approved the design, Vladimir Lenin.

Early May 2010 in Athens was to prove an extraordinary few days. Violent, brutal, and passionate, on the streets of the Greek capital, all the fault lines and conflicts within the global economy were about to be played out in vivid Technicolor.

The drama had been brewing for the past two years. In the wake of the credit crunch, following the collapse of the American investment bank Lehman Brothers, the financial markets had frozen. There was a sudden and terrifying collapse in world trade: In response, governments everywhere had massively increased their budget deficits in an attempt to steady economies that looked to be on the verge of tipping into a replay of the Great Depression of the 1930s. But as 2009 turned into 2010, and as the fears of another depression eased, the markets started to worry about something else. The cure was starting to look even worse than the disease. And the buildup of sovereign debts, and whether those debts could ever possibly get repaid, was suddenly the issue everyone was worrying about.

There were a dozen different countries the bond dealers could have picked on. But it happened to be Greece. Over the course of the past few weeks, the country's Prime Minister, George Papandreou, had been taught a painful lesson in the harsh realities of global finance: When the money runs out, so do your options. The capital markets were no longer interested in buying Greek bonds. Their neighbors and allies in the euro area showed little interest in helping out, either. The country's debts were proving quite literally impossible to finance. Already, the Greeks had been forced to appeal for outside help. Now the European Union and the International Monetary Fund had landed in Athens with the promise of a rescue package. But the price they would demand would be a heavy one: cuts on a brutal and massive scale, an end to the easy-money culture that had taken root in Greece over the past decade, and a shocking assault on the living standards of ordinary people. That was the price that would have to be paid, and it was no longer negotiable.

As May 1 dawned, it was already clear that this was to be a pivotal weekend in Greek history. The nation that had been the birthplace of modern *democracy*, which had indeed created the word itself, did not have a great track record of implementing the ideals for which it had been the cradle. Between 1946 and 1949, it had been the scene of a vicious civil war between rival armies backed by the forces of left and right. The country was left in ruins. It struggled to rebuild itself, and managed to miss out on the postwar reconstruction of Europe. In 1967, a group of reactionary, socially conservative military leaders staged a coup, creating a buffoonish, at times ridiculous, "Regime of the Colonels" that lasted until 1974. This was a country with a long history of settling its divisions with riots and bloodshed. It had happened plenty of times in the past. And now it looked to be happening again.

May Day has always been a crucial date in the European calendar. As the International Workers' Day, it is the traditional moment for trade unions and leftwing political parties to mobilize their forces and challenge the capitalist order. It is, as well, the month of revolution. The convulsions that shook much of Europe in 1968 started in that month. Perhaps the start of spring turns people's minds to the possibility of creating society afresh. Whatever the truth of that, officials from the International Monetary Fund and the European Union could have hardly chosen a worse moment to descend on the Greek capital demanding cuts.

The trouble started on the Saturday night, May 1. As Labor Day rallies gathered to march through the city, scuffles broke out with riot police armed with shields and batons. Nineteen people were arrested. The former president of the Greek Parliament, Apostolos Kaklamanis, was targeted by demonstrators, and both missiles and abuse were hurled at him before the police managed to extricate the surrounded politician and get him safely away to the hospital.

On the Sunday night, there were signs of more trouble brewing when a bomb exploded outside a branch of the British bank HSBC in central Athens. A small, homemade device, put together by enthusiastic amateurs from gas canisters and petrol, it wasn't powerful enough to do much more than damage the front of the building. It was, however, a warning of worse to come over the next few days. Meanwhile, far away in Brussels, Luxembourg Prime Minister Jean-Claude Juncker, a veteran of European Union negotiations and the current president of the euro group that represented the interests of the nations sharing the single currency, had called an emergency meeting of euro-zone finance ministers for 5 P.M. Athens time on the Sunday evening. Their task would be to endorse whatever deal the *troika*, the group of European Union, European Central Bank, and IMF officials, had managed to hammer out with the Greek government over the course of the weekend.

Against the backdrop of simmering violence, a deal was finally welded into shape. The euro-zone finance ministers agreed on a $146 billion package that would enable the Greek government to limp through the next few months. In return, the Greek government agreed to push through 30 billion euros of budget cuts, amounting to 13 percent of GDP. Of the bailout package, 10 billion euros would be set aside for helping out the country's battered banking system. "I want to tell Greeks very honestly that we have a big trial ahead of us," Prime Minister Papandreou told his nation in a televised address on the Sunday evening after the deal was announced. "I have done and will do everything not to let the country go bankrupt." Ordinary Greeks would, he continued, have to accept "great sacrifices" to avoid "catastrophe."[1]

A solution to the crisis? That was far too much to hope for. To keep her own electors at home happy, German Chancellor Angela Merkel had played up the extent to which her government had toughed up the conditions attached to the loan. "This is an ambitious program that contains tough savings measures and on the other hand seeks to improve the efficiency of the Greek economy," Merkel insisted at a press conference in Bonn after the deal was agreed. "Three months ago it would have been unthinkable that Greece would accept such tough conditions."[2]

For the Greeks, the idea of a German Chancellor imposing painful austerity measures on their country was more than many could tolerate. This was, after all, a country that had suffered terribly under German occupation during World War II. Three hundred thousand people had died of starvation in Athens during the winter of 1941–1942 as the Nazi occupying regime requisitioned food and fuel to send back to the Third Reich. And in towns such as Kalavryta, German troops had executed almost the entire adult male population (they left only 13 male survivors and children) in reprisals for attacks by the Greek resistance. Too many Greeks had been raised on stories of German brutality for Merkel's language to be anything other than provocative.

There was little sign that the Greeks were willing to accept their fate, at least not without violent, bitter protest. Giorgos Delastik is a popular columnist in the country, writing for *To Ethnos,* a mass-market daily controlled by the Bobolas family of industrialists. "Today, people across the country woke up to a palpable atmosphere of tension in the wake of the government's announcement of a fresh package of austerity measures including major wages cuts, which will prompt a significant decline in living standards," he wrote in an incendiary column published on May 3.

> Civil servants and pensioners will be worst affected, but private sector workers will also lose out. Perhaps the most galling aspect of this latest development is the fact that Prime Minister George Papandreou announced the austerity package under orders from the foreign powers that have now assumed control of our country: the International Monetary Fund and the European Union.[3]

He warned his readers that Greece faced a bleak future of unparalleled austerity:

> There is no denying the utter disregard for social progress in these austerity measures, which are worse than anything that Greece has seen in more than a century . . . the GDP of our country is set to fall by a record 4 percent in 2009, the most dramatic decline in 50 years—a slump only exceeded by a 6.4 percent drop in 1974 prompted by the joint effect of the oil crisis and

the invasion of northern Cyprus by the Turkish army, which followed the fall of the military junta. And worse still, they will have no positive impact on Greece's public debt, which is set to increase from 115 percent in 2009 to 140 percent in 2014.

That was just one small snapshot of the mood right across Greece. As the emergency rescue package was unveiled, the civil service union called an immediate general strike. Greeks are used to strikes, and they are used to far-left communist and anarchist groups stirring up trouble. But this was different. Ordinary people were willing to march out into the streets themselves, protesting what they believed was an unfair and unjust package imposed on them by outsiders.

It was on May 5, as the scale of the pain about to be inflicted on the Greek people became clear, that the violence turned raw and ugly. The crowds chose their spots well, gathering in places which were, for most ordinary Greeks, filled with the symbolism of past conflicts.

The first demonstrators flocked to Sintagma Square. With the Parliament building directly behind it, the square is a popular meeting place and a hub for the Athens Metro. The English translation of its name is Constitution Square, and it acquired its name from the constitution that Greece's King Otto was forced to grant his people in 1843 after a popular and military uprising. (Otto was born Prince Otto Friedrich Ludwig of Bavaria, another reminder of the unhappy history of German meddling in Greek affairs.) Throughout modern Greek history, the Square has been the arena for voicing protest and anger against the reigning powers. Other protestors gathered around Athens Polytechnic, the site of a student uprising against the military dictatorship in 1973: At least a dozen people were killed in that year, and many more were injured in violent clashes that eventually turned out to be the catalyst for the downfall of the military junta. Now, once again, the Polytechnic students were out on the streets, and the Communist Party organizers were finding a willing audience for their recruiters. It was not hard to imagine that the IMF-EU junta, as some of the protestors already referred to it, might go the same way as the colonels of an earlier generation.

As the day progressed, the mood started to turn uglier. Protestors, aware that the world's media had descended upon Athens and that their actions would be broadcast around the world, attempted to storm

Parliament, ready to take the building by force if necessary. Many no doubt had learned the story of Lenin's assault on the Winter Palace in October 1917, a grand, theatrical coup that set the stage for the Bolshevik revolution. Capture the right building at the right moment, and you can take possession of an entire country. The riot police stood firm, however. Demonstrators rushing up the steps of the building chanted "thieves!," their voices carrying on the breeze to the politicians inside. With batons, shields, muscle, and tear gas, the police lines repulsed wave after wave of attacks. Paving stones were ripped up, and improvised petrol bombs were hurled toward them in a brutal assault of flame and concrete, but the police stood resolute. The protestors threw up barricades and set cars on fire. One building was incinerated, and the fire-fighters managed to pull four people to safety at the last moment before they died in the flames.

On Stadiou Avenue, a road leading up toward the Square, protesters firebombed the Marfin Bank. Twenty people were working inside that day. As the flames took hold, most of them managed to escape. But three of the staff tried to make their way up to the roof to avoid suffocation. Their way was blocked, and as the flames kept rising higher and higher, it was too late for the fire-fighters to do anything for them. All three died in the blaze. The riots had claimed their first casualties. As news spread around the city of the deaths, an angry mob started to gather around the burned-out building. When the owner of the bank arrived on the scene, he was accused of forcing his workers to stay at their posts despite the general strike called by the trade unions.

More protests were rising up around the country. In Salonika, 50,000 people marched through the streets destroying dozens of banks and shops in Greece's second largest city. Over many hours demonstrators fought running battles with the police. Anarchists occupied the city's labor center. In Patras, around 20,000 protesters were joined by farmers driving tractors and garbage truckers on their vehicles, as flaming barricades were erected along the central streets of the city. There were fierce clashes between protestors and the police. In Ioannina, the protesters attacked banks and shops, prompting the police to respond with tear gas, while in Corfu, protesters occupied the County Headquarters. The Administrative Headquarters of Naxos and the City Hall of Naoussa all came under attack. Although the riots and demonstrations eventually fizzled out, for a moment the anger of the country appeared revolutionary in its potency.

As the debris was cleared up, Greece awoke the next morning asking itself tough questions: "Can a society self-destruct?" asked the Greek daily newspaper *Kathemerini*, posing the question in big, bold capital letters. "Of course it can, and it is certain that this will happen if we continue this way—when the state and society allow some nihilist hooligans to burn the city and murder three working citizens."

It was a good point, and one that could well be posed more widely. After all, it wasn't just Greece that was being put to the test as the rioters rampaged across the capital and through the streets of all of Greece's major cities. It was the *euro*, a currency still only just over a decade old. And it was the European Union, the foundation of peace and prosperity across the continent for the past half-century.

The euro was created by an economic elite convinced that they were creating a better, more harmonious, and more efficient Europe. But now it was being defended with tear gas and truncheons. That was certainly not the way it was meant to be.

As the burned-out cars were cleared away, it was obvious to anyone that Greece was bust. It faced a generation of grinding austerity, political turmoil, and resentful poverty. But the euro was broken as well, and with it the idea of the EU, or at least one centralizing version of it.

On May Day in Athens, the edifice had cracked. That, as we shall discover over the rest of this book, had been a long time coming. Arrogance and hubris had caught out a generation of political leaders that had pushed too hard and too fast for political and monetary union.

But broken it was. And, as we shall also discover, it will be impossible to put it together again.

When the rioting stopped, the Hammer & Sickle was no longer flying over Europe. A day after it was put up, the banner draped across the Acropolis urging the people of Europe to rise up had been removed. Tourists could once again wander amid the ancient stones. But a kind of revolution had taken place. The euro no longer looked like the future of anything. Sovereign debt was dominating discussion in the world markets. And that was a transformation—and one that was to ready to dominate the continent, and indeed the global economy, for much of the coming decade.

Chapter 1

Now We Are Ten

On January 13, 2009, Jean-Claude Trichet, president of the European Central bank, traveled to the Strasbourg to give a lecture celebrating the tenth anniversary of the euro. It was a pleasant, downbeat occasion. Over much of its short existence, Europe's single currency had been a bitterly contested, viciously fought-over creation. Over prolonged European summits it had been argued over savagely by a whole generation of political leaders. Careers had been made and broken. Referenda had been played out across Europe, and, as the votes were counted, the fate of the project regularly hung in the balance. As preparations were made for its introduction, the global financial markets poured endless buckets of scorn on its prospects for success. As the notes and coins were introduced from Bavaria to Lombardy, from Catalonia to Provence, shopkeepers turned up their noses at this strange, foreign money, a garishly colored imposter creeping into their tills. And as it made its debut on the markets, it was treated much as the new fat boy might be at a rough school: an object to be kicked around and bullied, mainly for the amusement of the bigger and nastier children.

And yet, even at the tender age of 10, it appeared to be approaching a kind of calm, middle-aged serenity. If it was possible for a currency to pull on a cozy pair of slippers, make a cup of hot chocolate, pull itself up by the fire, and start reading the gardening supplement in the newspaper, then that is what the euro would be doing. And that mood was very much reflected in the tone of Trichet's speech to the European Parliament that afternoon.

"For decades, the single European currency was merely an idea shared by a few people. Many others said that it could not be done, or that it was bound to fail," said Trichet.

> Today, the single currency is a reality for 329 million citizens. The creation of the euro will one day be seen as a decisive step on the long path toward an "ever closer union" among the people of Europe.
>
> Since the introduction of the euro, fellow Europeans have enjoyed a level of price stability which previously had been achieved in only a few of the euro area countries. This price stability is a direct benefit to all citizens. It protects incomes and savings, and it helps to bring down borrowing costs, thus promoting investment, job creation and prosperity over the medium and long term. The single currency has been a factor of dynamism for the European economy. It has enhanced price transparency, increased trade, and promoted economic and financial integration within the euro area and with the rest of the world.[1]

Indeed so. Trichet is in many ways the perfect Mr. Euro. A smooth, articulate French intellectual, he speaks with the calm authority of a fiercely intelligent technocrat. You could interrogate the man for weeks and not force him into a single error, slip, or gaffe. Over a career spent pushing for the closer integration of the European nations, he sometimes appears to have transformed himself into a living embodiment of the ideals he strives to articulate: a kind of Franco-German unity turned, with surprising success, into flesh and bone. Like all French political and intellectual leaders, his speeches and press conferences are often elaborately erudite, laden with cultural, historical, and literary references. In the manner that only French officials can achieve, he is never afraid to make the connections between poetry and central banking (Goethe and Dante turn out to be among the influences on the European Central Bank's decisions on interest rates, in case you were wondering). But he has also assumed a Teutonic rectitude and sternness. He is never shy about imposing a very German view of financial conservatism on Europe. He discusses thrift and balanced budgets as matters of morality as well as economics and bookkeeping, in a way that plays better in Bavaria or Saxony than it does anywhere else in Europe. He is well aware that money is as much a matter of national identity as a medium of exchange, and perhaps more so. The euro could have no better champion.

In his lecture, he pointed to three key achievements of the first decade since the euro was introduced, first as a financial currency in 1999 and then in the form of physical notes and coin in January 2002.

First, it had overcome the credit crunch. Plenty of people had been warning that the euro didn't have the strength to survive any kind of significant shock to the global economy. And yet only a few months earlier, following the collapse of the American investment bank Lehman Brothers, the financial system had gone into meltdown. Banks had been going bust all around the world. In the case of Iceland, a whole country had gone pop. Trade had collapsed at a faster rate than at any time since the Great Depression of the 1930s. The great container ships that sailed from Shanghai to Rotterdam laden with the mass-produced consumer goods that were the physical manifestation of globalization were suddenly tethered empty to the docks. And yet, even though the ships were empty, the euro had sailed through the crisis unscathed. Whatever the problems weighing down on the global economy—and there were plenty of them, no question about that— no one was suggesting that the euro was one of them.

Next, the economic union that had been the primary goal of the euro had been summoned brilliantly to life. Price stability had been achieved, and the economies of Europe had been drawn closer together. Raw materials harvested in Sicily could be sent to the Rhineland to be manufactured, then trucked to Burgenland in Austria or to the Algarve in Portugal, for sale, and the goods could be paid for, accounted for, and taxed all in the same, uniform unit of money. The result was a Europe that was far more dynamic, more prosperous, more open, and more innovative, Trichet argued.

Finally, it was getting bigger all the time. Whereas its critics claimed the euro would quickly collapse, and while the British, the Swedes, and the Danes snootily declined to take part at the beginning of the grand experiment, fearing it was doomed to inevitable failure, instead this was turning into a club that everyone wanted to join. When the euro was launched a decade ago, Trichet reminded his audience sharply, it had 11 members. As of the first of January 2009, it was the common currency of 16 nations. If the natural impulse of any organism is to survive, replicate itself, and enlarge its territory, then the euro was by that measure a triumphant success.

"Ladies and gentlemen, during its first years of existence, the euro had to face major trials: the establishment of a sound and credible central bank and the creation of a stable new currency inspiring confidence," he concluded with a flourish. "These challenges were overcome successfully and the euro is today firmly established. Hence, this is certainly a time for celebration."[2]

On January 8, Trichet was singing from a similar hymn sheet, this time at a ceremony to mark the arrival of Slovakia in the euro-zone. In Bratislava, the Slovakian capital, on January 8, the European Central Bank welcomed the second of the former Soviet bloc countries into the club of nations that shared the single currency. It was, once again, a remarkable testament to the power of the euro. Two decades earlier, Slovakia had been part of a communist empire that stretched from the borders of Austria and Germany all the way to Vladivostok in the Far East. Now it was able to share its currency with the rest of Western Europe. "Robert Schuman stated in his founding declaration that Europe will be made through concrete achievements which create tangible solidarity among its people. European monetary union is a concrete achievement, and the euro is a tangible sign of solidarity among its people,"[3] said Trichet in his remarks welcoming Slovakia into monetary union.

It was, in truth, a historic achievement, and one built against the odds. As it celebrated its tenth birthday, the euro could be celebrated not just with rhetoric, but with, just as Schuman demanded it should be, tangible, demonstrable achievements.

"It is absolutely conceivable that the euro will replace the dollar as [the] reserve currency, or will be traded as an equally important reserve currency,"[4] former chairman of the Federal Reserve, Alan Greenspan, told the German magazine *Stern* in 2007. According to a study by Harvard University's Jeffrey Frankel and Menzie Chinn of the

University of Wisconsin for the U.S. National Bureau of Economic Research, the euro could surpass the dollar as the world's most important currency by 2022. They looked at the way the dollar gradually replaced the British pound in the years before World War I and found that something very similar was happening right now. The United States was declining in global importance, it was running an evermore reckless fiscal policy, and it was failing to hold the line against inflation. For all those reasons, the rest of the world would gradually despair of holding dollars and start looking for a safer alternative.

As the years rolled by, and as the euro established itself more firmly in the minds of investors, that view was gaining steadily in credibility. OPEC, the powerful cartel of oil producers, started to make noises about pricing oil in euros rather than dollars. The Chinese, who use the vast trade surpluses run up by the country's exporters to accumulate massive foreign exchange reserves, started to talk by the middle of 2009 about holding more of their assets in euros rather than dollars. The Russians, whose oil reserves meant they were steadily building up financial reserves in the same way the Chinese were, shifted some of their holdings out of the dollar and into the euro. Whichever way you looked at it, the European currency was gaining ground over the American one.

Nor was that a mere matter of continental machismo (although there would be plenty of politicians, particularly in Paris, who would regard every inch of territory the euro gained on the dollar as another step forward for the forces of civilization against the forces of barbarism). There are huge economic advantages to having the world's reserve currency. Right now, everyone has to hold dollars because that is the money used for world trade. Every time people buy some of those dollars, they are, in effect, making an interest-free loan to the United States. Moreover, the government of the world's reserve currency has huge financial firepower. A U.S. Treasury bill is the benchmark safe asset for the financial markets. When there is a crisis, everyone buys T-bills: It is the acme of safety. That makes it very easy and very cheap for the U.S. government to issue lots and lots of debt that, in effect, the rest of the world has little choice but to buy. Reserve currency status acts as a kind of tax the United States is allowed to impose on the rest of the world. But if the euro could oust it from that position, then some of those benefits would accrue naturally to Europe and its citizens, rather than to the United Sates. It would be Frankfurt that would tax the rest of the world, not Washington. Europeans would become richer, and Americans poorer, and, best of all, they wouldn't even have to do any more work. It was a prize well worth striving for.

The growing importance of the euro in the capital markets, however, was only one component of the single currency's success. In plenty of other ways, the euro was doing well enough to make its founders proud of their creation. Inflation was low and steady right across the vast continental economy the euro now covered. Government bond markets functioned smoothly: Portugal could borrow money just as easily and almost as cheaply as the Netherlands or Germany, despite the fact those countries had vastly better credit records. The capital markets functioned more smoothly. There were signs that trade was increasing between countries as companies no longer had to factor in the risk of the currency markets moving against them when they made goods in Eindhoven and sold them in Turin. What had started out as a great and risky experiment, and one that plenty of people had predicted would collapse when it faced its first real test, was turning into a huge success. By 2009, the euro was becoming boring, normal, a part of everyday life. It was part of the atmosphere, like the oxygen we breathe. It was *just there*. That was everything its founders could have hoped for.

But, in truth, the tenth birthday party was premature in its toasts of success. That speech in Strasbourg was to be the last chance Trichet would have to celebrate very much. Even as the words were delivered, a crisis was brewing that would, in the year that followed, threaten to blow the single currency to pieces.

It would be a crisis that would expose the flaws built into the very foundations of the euro itself.

■ ■ ■

A continental currency, with a dual metallic and fiduciary base, resting on all Europe as its capital, and driven by the activity of 200 million men: this one currency would replace and bring down all the absurd varieties of money that exist today, with their effigies of princes, those symbols of misery.[5]

The notion of a single European currency, like all bad ideas, has been around for a very long time. That sentence was written by the great French writer, Victor Hugo, author of *The Hunchback of Notre Dame* and *Les Misérables*, among many other works, in Actes et Paroles, which was published in February 1855.

Nor, as it happens, was Hugo the first person to think of it. The patchwork of currencies across Europe, each with its own rules and territories, has long been a puzzle to reforming, liberal minds. Napoleon Bonaparte had proposed a single currency for the whole of Europe, under French leadership, naturally enough. John Stuart Mill, the great philosopher of Victorian improvement, advocated a single European currency as part of the inevitable march toward a single global money. Winston Churchill, far more of a believer in melding European nations together than later leaders of the British Conservative Party, endorsed a single currency as part of his wider vision, put forward in a famous speech in 1946, of a "United States of Europe" to be built out of the rubble and ruins of World War II.

A single currency had long been a dream of politicians, and indeed of some economists. It had even been tried a couple of times already. The Latin Monetary Union was created 1865, and comprised France, Italy, Belgium, Switzerland, and, rather surprisingly, Greece as well. Based on both silver and gold, it made each member's currency legal tender within every other state. The idea, much like the euro, was to promote trade among the members, while also serving as a stepping stone to a full monetary union. The central bank of the states in the union was meant to coordinate monetary policy among them. It lasted until 1927, but was running out of steam long before that, as the will to coordinate policy between the members lost momentum. It collapsed when both France and Italy, under huge pressure to reinflate their domestic economies, started issuing paper money that was backed by neither silver nor gold.

Another attempt was made with the Scandinavian monetary union, which linked the currencies of Denmark, Sweden, and Norway. It lasted from 1873 to 1920, and for a period involved intense cooperation among the central banks of the three different nations. And, of course, on a global scale the gold standard, which held sway right through the Industrial Revolution and lingered on in a diluted form until Richard Nixon took the dollar off gold in 1971, was a form of single currency. Every paper currency based on gold was convertible into every other one, depending on the price of the precious metal. So they were, in effect, all the same money, and it certainly wasn't possible for central banks just to print more currency whenever they happened to feel it might be necessary.

But it was only during the 1970s and 1980s that the idea of a single currency for the European Union started taking real, tangible shape. And it is worth pausing to review how it came about for the simple reason that it is the debates and arguments that led up to the creation of the euro, and the compromises between different visions, that in the decade to come will inevitably lead to its unraveling.

In the 1970s, French President Valery Giscard d'Estaing and his German counterpart Helmut Schmidt faced the inflationary turbulence of that decade with a determination to create a closer union between France and Germany. With the gold standard finally abandoned, and with all the world's major currencies floating against one another, exchange rates were moving violently against one another. Both leaders were well aware that this was crucifying their manufacturers. When German companies exported to France, they had no way of knowing what they would end up being paid, or whether they would make a profit, and vice versa. It was causing chaos. And there wasn't much point in taking down trade barriers between the countries of the European Union if they were still reluctant to trade with one another because of turmoil in the foreign exchange markets. The response of both men was the *Snake*, and it was to prove a formative event in the creation of the euro.

Created by the members of what was then still known as the European Economic Community (the more grandly titled European Union was not to be established until much later), it was in some respects a mini-version of the Bretton Woods system of managed exchanged rates that had lasted from the end of World War II until Nixon's decision to take the dollar off the gold standard in 1971. Under Bretton Woods, most of the world's major currencies were pegged to the dollar, and the dollar itself was pegged to gold. Devaluations were periodically allowed as a way of coping with economic shocks, but, by and large, currency rates remained stable against one another over long periods of time. Under the Snake, the European countries attempted to replicate that system for one another. Although the currencies floated against one another on the foreign exchange markets, each member agreed to limit, by market intervention if necessary, the fluctuations of its exchange rate against other members' currencies. The maximum permitted divergence between the strongest and the weakest currencies was 2.25 percent. The agreement meant that the French government, for example, would ensure that the value of the French franc would experience only very limited fluctuation against the Italian lira or the Dutch guilder, but that there was no commitment to limit or smooth out fluctuations against the U.S. dollar, the Japanese yen, or any other currencies that were outside the agreement. The idea was that while there might be frantic volatility against other major currencies, the European currencies would never move very much against each other. That would encourage trade among the members of the EU. And it would also mean that the different European currencies that belonged to the Snake would start to behave as a single block. If the deutschmark started to move up against the dollar, then so would the pound and the franc and the lira, because all the different currencies were in effect linked to one another. It was the euro in the making.

The trouble was, it didn't work very well. Britain and Ireland tried it for a month, and then, with the typical hesitancy of the Anglo-Saxons over any European project, gave up and withdrew. The French found it too hard to stay the course, and so did the Italians. Only the Germans, with typical determination, remained members all the way through to the end of the system, which lasted until 1979. Countries stayed in when it was easy to maintain membership, but generally opted out as soon as the exchange rate mandated by the system became difficult to defend. It wasn't, as it turned out, much of a protection against anything, because everyone always abandoned it as soon as the going got difficult.

The flaw in the system was simple. It was set up to fight the currency markets. The only way, for example, that the franc–deutschmark rate could be defended was if the Bank of France intervened to buy francs as soon as currency traders started selling them. But that quickly became ruinously expensive (to the central bank, that is; it was fabulously profitable for foreign exchange traders). The central bank was always going to lose money on the trade. By 1979, the system had become a joke: It was merely a way of transferring wealth from taxpayers to bankers. There was no point in carrying on with it.

With the collapse of the Snake, a fresh generation of European political leaders had another go at stabilizing exchange rates within the European Union. This time it was called the European Monetary System. Launched soon after the Snake collapsed, the EMS was a more serious and hardheaded approach to the issue. It created a new currency unit called the ECU (standing, not very imaginatively, for the European Currency Unit). The ECU was a basket of each member's currencies, weighted in terms of the respective size of their economies. Each member of the system undertook to manage the value of its currency against the value of the ECU. It worked in much the same way as the Snake in that it stabilized exchange rates between the member states of the EU, while allowing them to fluctuate against the rest of the world's currencies. It was, however, easier to defend. The standard maximum exchange-rate fluctuation permitted for each EMS currency was 2.25 percent. However, there were wider bands for weaker members, such as Italy from 1979 onward, Spain from 1989 onward, and the UK from 1990 onward. The system was also subject to frequent realignments of the grid, which had a tendency to make a mockery of the whole structure of the EMS. The trouble was there wasn't a huge amount of stability in the system when any one country might suddenly need to revalue the rate at which its currency was traded against the notional ECU. Rather like the Snake, it worked only when times were good. But, of course, when times were good, you didn't really need it. What you wanted was a system that could stand up to storms and shocks in the global economy, and the European Monetary System certainly wasn't that.

The system blew apart after the British joined. In 1992, with a deep recession in the UK, currency traders were selling the pound. The Bank of England was finding it impossible to defend the rate against the ECU (and in effect against the German deutschmark) mandated by the system. The German central bank, the Bundesbank, showed no inclination to help out by intervening in the markets on behalf of the pound, or by adjusting its own interest rates to bring them more into line with British ones. After a desperate battle with the markets, which cost the Bank of England billions of pounds in foreign exchange reserves, the British were ignominiously forced out of the system. Soon afterward, the trading bands for the EMS were widened to 15 percent. It was, in effect, dead. If currencies can fluctuate by 15 percent against one another, they are not fixed in any meaningful sense of the word.

The Snake and the EMS were both quite rightly regarded as failures. They had foundered on two main rocks. Any attempt to fight the foreign exchange markets was always doomed to ultimate failure. And any attempt to tie together very different economies was always going to produce strains and tensions that would in the end tear the system apart: It was the attempt to bind the very different British economy into the EMS that was to prove its downfall. But, as we have already noted, you can't keep a bad idea down. While some people might have concluded that any attempt to manage exchange rates between the members of the European Union was doomed to failure, the EU's political and bureaucratic elite drew precisely the reverse lesson. Their verdict was that the next time around they would try even harder, creating a single currency that was completely impregnable to attack by the currency markets, and that would bind the economies of its members together so tightly that they would in effect congeal into one harmonious economic whole, much as the economy of the United States did under its own single, continental currency, the dollar.

And so the idea of the euro was born.

■ ■ ■

On the banks of the river Meuse, which runs through France, Belgium, and the Netherlands before emptying out in the North Sea, the town of Maastricht is a historic tourist destination in the Dutch province on Limberg. It is famous both for its university and for its elegant stone streets. But these days it is probably better known as the city in which the euro was born.

On February 7, 1992, the leaders of the European Community gathered to sign what became known as Maastricht Treaty. Under the leadership of the energetic Frenchman Jacques Delors, the Treaty was the most decisive step yet taken toward a single government for the whole of Europe. The Treaty established the European Union as a political as well an economic union. And it committed the members to full monetary union. It laid down the criteria for membership, the essential rules that would govern the single currency, and a timetable for their introduction. There were still plenty of hurdles, but after the signing of the Maastricht Treaty the die was cast. Europe was committed to merging its old currencies, and there was no turning back.

When the treaty was signed, there were 12 members of the newly restyled European Union. British Prime Minister John Major, mindful of the fiercely anti-European mood of the Conservative Party back in the UK, had negotiated an opt-out for the British: They could join if they wanted to, but were under no obligation to do so. The Danes, who also tend to be suspicious of centralizing schemes cooked up in Paris and Brussels, hitched a ride with the British, and secured an opt-out of their own. But once the Treaty was ratified, the rest of the EU's members were formally committed to merging their old national currencies into one new one. The timing could be negotiated. So could the details of the new money. The ultimate goal could not.

But what kind of single currency? Nobody had ever attempted a project of this scale or ambition before. True, there had been earlier attempts at monetary unions in Europe, as we saw earlier in this chapter. The United States created a single currency with the dollar, a currency that replaced the old state-issued money that existed prior to the Declaration of Independence. Some would argue, with much merit, that it was only with the establishment of the Federal Reserve in 1913 that the United States moved to creating a genuine single currency for the entire country. Yet those were experiments of a completely different order. The European currency mergers of the nineteenth century were small, practical, local affairs. And anyway, with a foundation in gold and silver, they were already part of a global monetary system. The United States was a single country when it created its currency. It may have been a federal republic with a weak central government. But it would be absurd to imagine that Massachusetts and Texas, for all their obvious differences, were not recognizably part of the same country, in a way that France and Portugal, or the Netherlands and Spain, were simply not. In truth, this was the first serious attempt to create a single currency for a diverse continent. The scale of the ambition was breathtaking. So, too, were the challenges the new currency would soon face.

"There is no example in history of a lasting monetary union that was not linked to one state," argued Otmar Issing, chief economist of the German Bundesbank back when the euro was first being put together in 1991.[6]

Issing was absolutely right. Economists have been studying currencies since the dismal science was first invented. One feature they shared in common was absolutely clear. They were always and everywhere linked to a strong and unified central government: one that could raise taxes, distribute wealth between regions, borrow money on the global capital markets, and authorize a central bank to issue paper money. They weren't based on loose, optimistic confederations, with no significant revenue-raising powers, no ability to move funds around the region, and, when you looked at it closely, no genuinely popular mandate. Of course, that wasn't to say it wasn't possible. It was just that it hadn't been tried before.

As the euro was created, there were two views on whether it needed to be backed by an effective central government in Brussels. One said that the central authority would come in time. Indeed, the euro would be an instrument that would summon a single European super-state into being. Ever since the French politician Jean Monnet had founded the European Iron & Steel Community, the forerunner of today's European Union, in 1951, the federalist dream of uniting Europe had progressed by stealth. No one had ever said their goal was creating a strong, centralized government in Brussels: They pushed some other agenda, which ended up creating a stronger European government, as if it was a by-product of something completely different. The euro very much fitted into that pattern. It could be sold as a simple technocratic adjustment, a minor economic reform to make life easier for the accounting departments of companies that exported stuff around Europe and to save tourists the bother of swapping currencies if they had to change trains in Brussels. Once it was created, it would become gradually clearer and clearer that, to make it work, you needed common tax policies as well, and then common spending plans on top of that, until pretty soon you ended up with something that looked identical to a central government in Brussels. And by then it would be too late to do anything about it: The consequences of trying to unravel the single currency, once established, would be too horrific for anyone to contemplate.

The euro would have nudged Europe toward a fully centralized super-state.

An alternative view was that a currency could float above national governments. The Nobel prize–winning economist, Robert Mundell, is sometimes known as "the father of the euro," and with good reason. Mundell pioneered the concept of what became known in economics as an *optimal currency area:* that is, a geographic region where economic efficiency was optimized by sharing a single currency. Sometimes that would happen to be a single country, but quite often it wouldn't be. So, for example, it is easy to imagine that the Netherlands and Belgium could form a natural currency union, so similar are the two economies, while Italy, with its vast differences between the wealthy, industrialized north, and the rural, poverty-stricken south, probably wouldn't. The concept was a powerful impetus behind the creation of the euro. If you could demonstrate that Europe was an optimal currency area, then you wouldn't need a strong central government to try and iron out the differences between regions. The euro would function per-fectly well as the currency for all of them without one.

But it depended on what kind of euro you had: a strong or a weak one? And what kinds of rules would govern it? Those were issues that would be fought out in the years to come as the ground rules for the new currency were established. And they were battles that, as we shall see later, were to determine in due course whether the single currency would last for generations as its founders hoped and dreamed it would. Or whether it would buckle and then break when the first financial storms started to blow up around it.

■ ■ ■

On the surface, there was a smooth timetable laid out for the progress toward the euro. In stage one, the candidate members were to set strict targets for borrowing, inflation, and growth. The architects were well aware that you couldn't suddenly merge very different economies. And you couldn't even merge quite similar ones if they happened to be at different stages of the economic cycle. Once countries shared a single currency, that meant they also shared a single central bank and the same interest rate. If one economy was contracting and another was suffering from rising inflation, then it would be impossible for a single central bank to mitigate one while controlling the other. You had to get all the economies moving in sync, and then hold them there, to have any realistic prospect of making the euro work.

Stage two was the detailed planning for the new currency. The central bank had to be created, staffed, and policies and objectives set for it. Even a name for the new currency had to be chosen. There were plenty of suggestions. To the Italians, the term *florin* seemed a natural choice, harking back to the coins that circulated in medieval Florence. The Greeks argued that the word *drachma* had the virtue of unmatched longevity, if not stability. To the French, ecu seemed the most obvious name: An ecu was not just the European Currency Unit, the immediate forerunner of what became the euro; it was also a thirteenth-century French coin. There was even a suggestion that each country keep the name of its own currency, but prefix it with the word *euro*, so that the "euromark" would circulate in Germany, and the "eurofranc" in France, and so on. Among German bankers, there was a joke that any currency that ended with a vowel was always a disaster: the lira, the drachma, the peseta, or the escudo, for example. Proper currencies ended with a consonant: the pound, the dollar, the yen, or, since you happen to mention it, the mark. On that logic, they favored the "euromark" as the name for the new money.

That, however, like every name that included part of the old currencies, or was rooted in one particular language, seemed to miss out on the spirit of the new money. It wouldn't have severed the link, psychologically at least, between the old national currencies and the new European one, which would inevitably make it far too easy to go back to the old ones if that was what people wanted to do one day. And that was not what the founders intended at all. The euro was designed to be irreversible, and everything about it had to suggest solidity and permanence. In the end, in 1995, it was decided to go for the simple word euro. It was the first four letters of the continent's name. And it was the one word every European could pronounce easily enough, if not always in the same way.

But it was not matters such as the name that really counted, nor whether you put Beethoven or Picasso on the banknotes. Those were all relatively trivial issues. What really counted was the plumbing: the way the central bank would work, and the way it would govern the huge new economic empire that it would take charge of. Behind the scenes, a fierce battle was being fought for the type of euro that would be created. A hard, stern, anti-inflationary currency, modeled on the German deutschmark, and with a central bank built in the image of the old Bundesbank? Or a soft, political bank, much closer to the old Bank of France, firmly under the control of the politicians? That was the crucial choice that had to be made.

One victory was won over the location of the ECB. Frankfurt won out over Paris and Brussels, and indeed, rather implausibly, London. According to a theory fashionable in the late 1990s, the location of the central bank played a crucial role in determining which cities emerged as important financial centers. It was never a very compelling explanation. After all, the Federal Reserve was based in Washington, but the American banks were 200 miles away in New York. Even so, it stoked the argument, with the British and the French insisting they needed the ECB headquarters in their capital to preserve the status of their financial center. The British had no plans to join the euro, so their new Prime Minister at the time, Tony Blair, never had much of a claim. Brussels already had more than enough European Union buildings to be getting on with. Paris was a more serious contender. It had the backing of the French, and they always win more battles in the European Union than they lose. But in the end, Frankfurt was the more important financial center. And only basing the new central bank there would convince the global money markets, the audience that really counted, that the ECB meant serious business.

There were other battles to be fought as well. The French wanted one of their own men, Bank of France Governor Jean-Claude Trichet, to be the first president of the new European Central Bank. The Germans were proposing Dutch banker Wim Duisenberg. In EU political dogfights, the Dutch tend to be used as proxy Germans, allowed to take up senior roles when the Germans feel bashful about grabbing them for themselves.

But, in reality, the issues of the headquarters and the presidency were just metaphors for a much larger and far more important battle. The key fault-line was emerging, as might be suspected, between France and Germany. The Germans wanted a strictly disciplined currency. They wanted the central bank to be completely independent of any form of political interference. They wanted hard, inflexible limits on how much debt any member of the single currency could run up. And they wanted there to be no bailouts between member states.

The French wanted something different. They didn't express it as a "weak currency." That wouldn't have sounded quite right. But they did express it as putting the central bank under firm political control. They demanded an "economic government" for Europe to be built into the creation of the euro. At a summit to discuss progress toward monetary union in 1996, then–French Prime Minister Alain Juppe hammered home the historical differences between the French and German approaches to economic management. "We don't want a technocratic, automatic system that will be exclusively under the control of the European Central Bank," he told the *Frankfurter Allgemeine Zeitung* in December 1996. During that month, Juppe and French President Jacques Chirac called for an EMU Advisory Council to be created alongside the ECB, with the power to advise on interest rates. That proposal was fought off by German Finance Minister Theo Waigel.

In fact, that only set up a more heated argument, this time over the Growth and Stability Pact, an agreement on economic management that each member of the new currency was to be made to adhere to. The proposal was very clear. The Germans wanted each euro member state to be limited to running a budget deficit of just 3 percent of GDP. The monetary logic was impeccable. A country with its own currency and its own central bank can, if it wants to, run just about any kind of budget deficit it happens to feel like. If it finds it can't borrow the money it needs to fund itself, then it can just order the central bank to print some more. This is not the completely cost-free exercise it might appear at first glance. Print too much money, and you will create hyperinflation and your currency will collapse in value. That is what happened in Germany in the 1920s. It is what has happened in countries such as Zimbabwe in the past few years. But it is still an important freedom. Within those constraints there is flexibility and room to maneuver. Countries with their own currencies can when necessary run far larger deficits and get away with it than countries with currencies that are pegged to some other monetary unit, or, indeed, that share their currencies with other nations.

The Bundesbank could see very clearly that once inside the euro, it couldn't work like that. The national central banks would continue to exist. There would still be a Bank of France, of Italy, of Spain, and of course a Bundesbank. But they would be pale shadows of their former pomp and splendor. Crucially, they would have no ability to issue currency. That would be the sole preserve of the European Central Bank in Frankfurt.

So what would happen if one member ran up big debts? Say it went on a wild borrowing spree, running up bills it could never meet, until ultimately it lost the confidence of the bond markets and could no longer pay its bills? The ECB couldn't be expected to print more and more euros to help it out. That would risk creating inflation, and if there was one thing the Germans were determined upon it was that the euro should be as stable and secure as the deutschmark it replaced. But neither could the other member states be expected to bail out that country, with soft loans extended to cover up its deficit. That, too, would never work. It would be grossly unfair if the states that were managing their finances responsibly were forced to subsidize the states that had been spending profligately. There would be no incentive for anyone to keep their national books in order. The situation would quickly descend into chaos, with every member living way beyond its means, then expecting its neighbors to bail it out or the ECB to print the money to finance its extravagance.

The situation was unthinkable. There needed to be strict rules to prevent it. And the answer was the Growth and Stability Pact. The 3 percent limit on budget deficits would stop national governments from running up excessive debts.

The trouble was, not everyone in Europe saw it the same way the Germans did. At a summit meeting held in the Irish capital Dublin on December 13 and 14, 1996, there was a furious battle between Germany's finance minister, Waigel, and his French counterpart, Jean Arthius. "The French and Germans had almost come to blows on the subject of the Stability Pact," reported the authoritative German newspaper, *Die Welt*, in its report of the behind-the-scenes machinations. "The bone of contention in the closing phase of the negotiations was above all Germany's request that the budgetary discipline demanded of euro-zone members be shored up by precise quantitative criteria. Most other countries were reluctant to agree to an automatic mechanism of this kind."

They certainly were reluctant. The German proposal seemed to many of the other members as if it was imposing too strict a limit on their independence of action. Governments would no longer be free to set their own fiscal policy: There would be a set of rules, enforced in Brussels, that would decide how much they could and could not spend. It was a huge compromise in national sovereignty, and one that many countries, the French in particular, didn't feel they had signed up for when they embarked on the euro project. Against that, the Germans argued that all they were giving up was the right to destroy the currency union through financial profligacy. It was of no more significance than the right most of us give up to carry submachine guns through the street: There may be some notional loss of freedom involved, but it is very clearly in the greater good.

In the end, Luxembourg Prime Minister Jean-Claude Juncker hammered together a compromise. Member states would stick to the Stability Pact, but they could invoke "a severe recession" as an excuse to run a larger deficit. How severe? A drop of 0.75 percent in GDP, which in the view of many economists would not really be a severe recession at all, but more a normal cyclical dip of the kind a healthy economy can expect to experience every few years. The European Commission would automatically launch an inquiry against a country that breached the Pact, except in cases where output fell by more than 2 percent a year, in which case the country could do pretty much whatever it wanted. And the French succeeded in getting the word *Growth* inserted in addition to what the Germans wanted to be called just the *Stability Pact*: They insisted that the euro had to be a currency that promoted economic expansion, and were already fearful that the entire project was being hijacked by a fiercely anti-inflationary Bundesbank. But, crucially, the German demand for stiff, automatic penalties for any country that broke the 3 percent deficit ceiling was dropped. The worst you would face was an inquiry from the European Commission. "As so often happens, there were only winners in the end," said Die Welt, delivering its verdict on the summit.

French President Jacques Chirac congratulated the German Finance Minister on his success in the negotiations and Theo Waigel too was manifestly pleased with the outcome. As the Dublin Euro-summit came to an end, the conference participants were only too happy to exchange compliments, in the warm glow of the press.[7]

But that rosy view of the outcome wasn't one that would survive in Germany for much longer. The country had bought into the single currency, in part as a quid pro quo for the rest of Europe accepting the reunification of Germany without any protest. While the euro looked like swapping a lot of weak Mediterranean currencies for a recreated deutschmark, Germans could live with that. But they had already had to water down the Stability Pact as well as fight off an effort by the French to install one of their own officials in the ECB presidency. And as the run-up to the launch continued, it became clear that fudges and compromises would have to be made all over Europe if the target date for the introduction of the euro was ever to be met.

The hard, inflexible euro turned out to be remarkable malleable. Italy announced a special "Europe tax" in its 1997 budget to allow it to just about squeeze into the Maastricht convergence criteria. France switched some pension assets from the state-owned France Telecom to get its public debt figures into better shape. Nor was there much sign of rigor in economic management. One of the most obvious consequences of the launch of the euro was that the market was about to get a lot tougher. Countries weren't going to be able to devalue their way out of trouble the way they had in the past. They would have to compete with the ruthlessly efficient Germans on quality and productivity. Their workers would have to hold down wages to make sure they remained competitive with their neighbors. And yet, what did the French do? The new Socialist government of Lionel Jospin introduced the 35-hour week, one of the most destructive economic policies of recent decades, and precisely the wrong preparation for the rigors that lay ahead in a monetary union with Germany.

As the legislation establishing the European Central Bank was written, there were some victories for the old Bundesbank. Monetary instruments and monetary control techniques were all closely modeled on the old German central bank, rather than any of its rivals around Europe. It was set an inflation target of below 2 percent per year over the medium term, about the same as the old Bundesbank target rate. It was declared illegal for any of the national governments to seek to influence ECB policy, an even stricter definition of independence than the old German central bank had enjoyed.

But they were drowned out by two important concessions. The European Union had not built in any significant penalties for breaching the deficit rules. And in the run-up to the launch of the euro, it had allowed government to blatantly fudge and fiddle with the convergence criteria.

Both were to prove very costly in the medium term, and, as events far away were to demonstrate a decade later, probably even fatal.

■ ■ ■

The great day dawned with a certain amount of nervousness. In the run-up to the launch of the physical euro, on January 1, 2002, the European Union, the European Central Bank, and the governments of the 11 countries that would make up the initial members of the currency union had been running campaigns to reassure their people that everything would go smoothly. The euro had already been up and running for two years, of course, but that was purely as a financial currency. Some digits in a banking computer system were a very different proposition from hundreds of millions of notes and coins filling tills and wallets right across the continent. And there was no way yet of knowing how that would play out.

The marketing campaigns varied from country to country. The Bank of Ireland sent out a free pocket calculator, with a special button for converting Irish pounds into euros, to all of the country's 1.4 million households. The Finnish central bank ran television ads featuring a friendly truck driver explaining how much easier it would be for him to crisscross the continent without having to change currencies constantly. In Belgium, the ads showed a small girl with her piggy bank. "Don't worry, little pig," she said, patting the little porcelain figure with her hand. "I will have to get all the francs out of you on January first to trade in for euros. But it won't hurt."[8] The ECB ran its own advertising campaign, in addition to each national one, evoking shared elements of

European heritage: from lederhosen-clad campers along alpine lakes to smiling couples at outdoor cafes looking out over the Mediterranean, all with the tagline underneath: "The Euro, Our Money" (or *Der Euro, Unser Geld, El Euro, Nuestra Moneda,* and so on).

The logistical challenges were formidable. Because the ECB was worried about the risk of counterfeiting, it didn't want to hand out any notes or coins in advance of the official handover. So instead 14 billion euro notes had to be printed and stored in readiness for the big day. Virtually every delivery truck in Europe—and thousands of military vehicles as well—were used to make sure that if you used an ATM anywhere in the euro-zone a minute after midnight on the opening day of 2002, you'd be given euros instead of francs, lira, or deutschmarks.

And yet, for the all the anxiety, and for all the chewed fingernails, after the fireworks had been released it all went perfectly smoothly. There was a two-month transition period during which both the new notes and the currencies they replaced would carry on being legal tender. But it didn't even take that long. At the end of the first week, the new currency had settled down, and most people appeared to accept it. The strikes threatened by bankers in France and Italy to protest at all the work had fizzled out. By the end of the first month, most of the old paper currencies had been handed back into the banks, from where they were either burned for fuel or else mulched down into agricultural compost. It was a slightly sad end for all those deutschmarks, francs, and lira, but at least it was environmentally friendly. And it would stop anyone from thinking you could get them out again, as they might if they were stored in a vault somewhere.

"The process of monetary union goes hand in hand, must go hand in hand, with political integration and ultimately political union," said the ECB's first president, Wim Duisenberg, in the European Parliament in the month before euro notes and coins were introduced. "EMU is, and was always meant to be a stepping stone on the way to a united Europe."[9]

Indeed it was. And at that moment it seemed to be going perfectly according to plan.

■ ■ ■

To mark the tenth anniversary of its founding, the European Union published a report on the currency's first 10 years. "EMU is a resounding success," it concluded, somewhat boastfully.

Ten years into its existence, it has ensured macroeconomic stability, spurred the economic integration of Europe—not least through its successive enlargements—increased its resilience to adverse shocks, and become a regional and global pole of stability. Now more than ever, the single currency and the policy framework that underpins it are proving to be a major asset.[10]

It was hardly an unbiased, or indeed an objective assessment. There were, of course, successes to be pointed to. The euro was a far larger currency than it had been when it was started: Greece had joined, so had Slovenia, Malta, and Cyprus. Inflation had been low and stable across the euro-zone: Inflation averaged just over 2 percent in the first decade of the euro, falling from 3 percent in the 1990s and a range of 8 to 10 percent in the 1970s and 1980s. There was more trade across Europe's old borders: Cross-border trade now accounted for a third of euro-zone GDP, compared with a quarter when the single currency was launched (although how much of that was due to the single currency itself and how much was due to the onward march of globalization was not really clear).

Financial markets were more integrated, companies could raise capital from anywhere in the continent, and the strength and stability of the euro allowed the economy to withstand whatever storms were blowing through the financial markets. "Today once again, the euro area appears protected from the worst of the present global financial turbulence," the report argued.

Meanwhile, the nations of the euro-zone were drawing closer together. "The environment of macroeconomic stability and low interest rates coupled with the support of the cohesion policy and its structural and cohesion Funds have created the conditions for accelerated catching up; the positive effects of sound economic policies have been reinforced by the development and integration of national financial markets with the rest of the euro area," it stated.[11]

Overall, it reported, 16 million jobs had been created in the euro-zone since the single currency was launched. Unemployment had fallen to 7 percent, the lowest rate in 15 years. Jobs were being created at a faster rate than in other mature economies such as the United States. The euro was taking a bigger share of the global money markets, establishing itself as the world's second most important currency after the dollar, and increasingly as the U.S. currency's challenger. Although growth had not been fantastic, and productivity hadn't really advanced, there was plenty to boast about.

Most important, however, was not the economics. It was the politics of the euro that really counted. "Although its objectives and achievements are predominantly economic, EMU has never been solely an economic project," the report concluded. "From the outset EMU was conceived as a crucial step in the process of EU integration."[12]

That was certainly the way the European elite saw it. The creation of the single currency was the most significant step forward in creating a single European state since the founding of the European Union itself. It was both an important symbol in itself of the transformation of what used to be a set of distinct nations into a single political and economic space, as well as a spur to further integration. Everyone was well aware that making the euro work would require more integration. But a huge amount had been achieved, and so long as the euro could establish itself, and so long as the single currency was seen as irreversible, then those questions could be answered later.

And yet, perhaps there had been too much fudging of the hard questions. "Independence of the central bank is a means to an end, to win Germany's approval for monetary union, but it is not the end of the story," said Michel Rocard, the former French prime minister, in 2007. "We will not be able to escape a situation taking place where the government will have to give orders to the central bank."[13]

That was certainly going to be true one day. The Germans appeared to have won many of the battles over the euro. They had fought for it to be a hard currency, modeled on the deutschmark. But they hadn't won every battle. The euro that was created had been compromised.

Fatally so? The answer to that question was taking shape many hundreds of miles to the south—in Athens.

Chapter 2

How to Blag Your Way into a Single Currency

In April 1997, then–Greek finance minister, Yannos Papantoniou, traveled to Brussels for a meeting of European Union finance ministers. The decision to create a common currency for the EU had already been taken. Only two years remained until the new money would come into existence, and only four years were left until the freshly minted notes and coins would replace the familiar francs, deutschmarks, lira, and pesetas for the 300 million people that would share the single currency. There was still plenty to do to make sure the launch was a success, and that the currency would feel as safe and secure as the money that it replaced. The central bank had to be created and staffed. Payment mechanisms had to be put into place. The rules governing the new currency had still to be created.

But one of the most important decisions was one that, on the surface, might appear simple. What would the money look and feel like? What would it say on the notes? As any economist or banker knows, a currency is, at the most fundamental level, a confidence trick. Money is just paper with some colored ink and some solemn-sounding pledges printed on it. People have to believe it is worth something for it to have any value. And if that belief ever evaporates, then the money is soon completely worthless. The new euro notes and coins would have to be designed with a ready-made aura of authenticity and durability.

They would need to look and feel as old and as permanent as the notes there were replacing. Otherwise, there was little hope of people ever feeling comfortable with them.

At the meeting, Yannos Papantoniou argued with his fellow finance ministers that the notes shouldn't just have Latin lettering on them. They should have Greek letters as well. The response from German Finance Minister Theo Waigel was withering. Only Latin characters would be acceptable, he pointed out with Teutonic condescension. "Poor, small, semi-agricultural Greece is in no position to start making demands about the kind of money that should circulate in mighty industrial powers such as France and Germany," he told his Greek counterpart. "What makes you think you will ever be in the euro?"[1]

It was a fair point, even if not a very polite one. At the time that discussion was taking place, the debate on the rules that the euro should follow was still taking shape. But the Germans, as we saw in the previous chapter, were already clear on one point. This should be a hard currency, a worthy successor to the indomitable deutschmark, the rock on which Germany's postwar reconstruction had been built. There would be no better way of alarming the hardworking, thrifty citizens of Hamburg and Munich than putting some Greek lettering on the banknotes they suddenly found in their pockets. Waigel, like all the German finance ministers to come after him, would fight for the solidity of the euro. And in due course, like all his successors, he would lose.

"I fought hard, and placed a bet with him then and there—and I won," recalled Papantoniou later.[2]

Indeed he did. Over the course of the next four years, Papantoniou was to be the man who steered Greece into the euro, ultimately in the face of fierce resistance from Germany and the other northern European nations.

But was it the right decision, both for Greece or for the rest of the euro-zone? Or was Greek membership of the euro, as Theo Waigel and much of the rest of the German industrial and economic establishment realized at the time, a catastrophe in the making?

To begin to get to grips with that question, you have to understand something about Greece's history, its economy, and how it ever got into the position of contemplating a currency union with Germany and France in the first place.

■ ■ ■

The story of postwar Greece is the story of two families, the Karamanlises and the Papandreous. Most countries have political dynasties. Politics exists in the blood of some families, and in some the patriarchs are so powerful that the rise of their offspring is impossible to resist. But in Greece, power has been divided up between the Karamanlises and the Papandreous as if it were their own personal heirloom. George Papandreou, the grandfather of the current prime minister, held the same office three times, the first term beginning in 1944 and the last one ending in 1965. The father of the current Prime Minister, Andreas Papandreou, dominated Greek politics through the 1970s and 1980s and brought it close to something modeled on Soviet-style socialism. So a Papandreou was Greek prime minister in the 1940s, 1960s, 1980s, 1990s, and now in the 2000s as well. When it is not a Papandreou occupying the highest office in the land it is usually a Karamanlis. Constantine Karamanlis was the other towering figure of postwar Greek politics: First taking office in the 1950s, then again in the 1960s, he returned to power in the 1970s. The dynasty was taken over by his nephew, Kostas Karamanlis, who served as Prime Minister from 2004 to 2009, and would end up being the man who took much of the blame for creating the mess that Greece was ultimately to find itself in.

There is something almost medieval about the way power is switched from one family to another. It is closer to the kind of family politics that Machiavelli wrote about than modern mass democracies. And that reflects the kind of country that Greece has been for the past century. Although many Europeans and Americans like to think of Greece as the birthplace of modern culture, science, and democracy (and of course it is), from the Middle Ages onward it has been a very different country from the Greece of classical civilization. It has one foot in the West, another in the East. It is part of the Balkans more than it is of Western Europe. The Greek Orthodox church is as close to the Russian version of Christianity as it is to the Catholic or Protestant versions of the creed that dominates the rest of the European Union. And, by the standards of northern Europe, it has always been a relatively poor and backward place.

All the southern European countries were, as twentieth-century French economic historian, Fernand Braudel, put it, defined by "traditionalism and rigidity."[3] That was largely the result of the geography of the Mediterranean Sea. The relatively poor quality of Mediterranean soils, which made it hard to grow crops, favored large agricultural holdings, and they were, naturally enough, under the control of a few wealthy families. That created a rigid, inflexible social order in which the middle classes developed much later than in northern Europe. Arguably, the kind of prosperous, entrepreneurial middle class that created modernity in northern Europe never really emerged in the south. When those countries did industrialize much later on, they switched straight to state-dominated corporations and autocracy. So it is probably no great surprise that for the past half-century Greek politics has been dominated by the Karamanlises and the Papandreous: It has always been a country under the control of a few wealthy families, and even as a member of the European Union, and then of the euro, its history has remained a far more powerful force than the new currency.

Although it had been the center of the European world in the classical era, in the pre-modern and modern era the center of Europe's civilization had moved decisively north. To many historians it is no coincidence that all of the European Union's great centers of power—Brussels at its heart, Strasbourg, where the Parliament sits, and Frankfurt, which plays host to the European Central Bank—are grouped around the city of Aix-la-Chapelle (or what is now Aachen, in Germany). That was the capital of Charlemagne's empire, and the king of the Franks and creator of the Holy Roman Empire was arguably the first of the great European unifiers, as well as the figure who decisively tilted the balance of European power and influence from the south to the north. The Low Countries, stretching up into the Rhineland and across to northern France, are the hub of what became modern European civilization. Open to the Atlantic, and not enclosed like the Mediterranean Sea, the land was rich and fertile, and the abundance of protected rivers and inland waterways were ideal for what were to become nations that could trade, not just with one another, but with the whole world. Even the thick, dense forests of Germany provided a natural defense against attack.

The divide in wealth, culture, and temperament between northern and southern Europe was not, therefore, a temporary phenomenon, something that could be reversed with some simple macroeconomic meddling. It had deep roots in the soil, societies, and histories of the nations that make up the continent. Against that background, integrating northern and southern Europe into a single currency was always going to be a formidable challenge. But, of all the southern European countries, even including Spain, Greece's was always the most difficult case of all. Cut off by the Carpathian Mountains from the mainstream of northern Europe, for much of the past millennium it was dominated by the Byzantine Empire based in Constantinople. Indeed, modern Greece owes as much to Byzantine and Turkish despotism as it does to Periclean Athens. Indeed, probably more.

Moreover, this was a country with a record of financial stability that was, to put it kindly, decidedly mixed. Dionysius the Elder, born in about 432 B.C., was the ruler of the Greek city of Syracuse, located in what is modern Sicily, and for a time ruled much of what is now Greece and the Adriatic. His approach to financial management is well told in an essay published in 1929 by the Harvard economist Charles Bullock. After running up vast debts to finance his lavish court, his military campaigns, and spectacles for the common people, Dionysius found himself perpetually short of money. He'd already borrowed as much as could from the long-suffering citizens and could borrow no more. So instead, he forced all his subjects to hand over all their money on pain of death. Once all the drachma coins had been handed in, he simply restamped each one-drachma coin as a two-drachma coin, and used those to pay off his debts. Simple.

Modern Greece wasn't much better. "From 1800 to well after World War II, Greece found itself virtually in continual default," note Carmen M. Reinhart and Kenneth S. Rogoff in their book on the history of financial crises, *This Time Is Different*.[4] After the formation of the modern Greek state in 1829, the country proceeded to default on its debts 1826, 1843, 1860, and 1893. It was hardly an inspiring record. In fact, according to Reinhart and Rogoff's calculations, Greece has spent a greater percentage of the years since independence (or from 1800 onward) in default than any other European country: It has been in default for 50 percent of those years, compared to the next-worst country, Russia, which has been in default for 39 percent of that time.

Indeed, it has a worse record than any Latin American country, with the exception of Ecuador and Honduras.

What kind of economy and society was it that was to join the single currency in 2001? In truth, not a very healthy one, nor one that would, on the surface at least, look remotely prepared for the rigors of competing with German and French industry on a level playing field.

Greece was occupied by the Nazis during Word War II, and suffered terribly under a brutal regime imposed on the nation by Berlin. In that respect, however, it was not really any different from the rest of Europe. The whole continent suffered terribly during the war, nowhere more so than Germany itself. By 1945, Europe was on its knees, economically, politically, and socially. Ravaged by two world wars, and split between a shakily democratic west, and a socialist, totalitarian east, it was exhausted and bankrupt. And yet while the rest of the continent got on with steadily rebuilding itself, Greece never quite managed to get back on its feet. By the 1950s, the British were celebrating the end of austerity; the French were laying the foundations of their postwar technocratic prosperity, even though their political system was wobbly (*les Trente Glorieuses* as the years from 1947 to 1973 are known to French economic historians); the Italians, in the north at least, were embracing industrialization for the first time; and even the shattered Germans, thanks to the *wirtschaftswunder*, or economic miracle of the postwar years, were turning themselves into the model of wealth, peace, and responsibility that became West Germany. Greece, however, despite its best effort, never quite managed to climb on board the bus. While the rest of Europe rapidly modernized, it remained backward and chaotic.

One cause was an accident of history. Greece held a pivotal position between Eastern and Western Europe as the Cold War started to unfold. The country had always had a powerful Communist Party, the KKE, and one that was rigidly obedient to whatever line was coming out of Moscow. After the War, Stalin was turning the states of Eastern Europe and the Balkans into satellites of the Soviet Union. Albania, Bulgaria, and what was then still Yugoslavia, each right on Greece's borders, all fell under Soviet control. Greece was not that high on Stalin's list, but there is little question that a major Mediterranean nation would have been a useful addition to the Soviet Empire, and that if a puppet communist regime could have been installed in Athens without too much trouble, it would have been. But the British and the Americans, aware of the country's strategic importance, poured enough men and money into the country to make sure that didn't happen. Instead, postwar Greece collapsed into a vicious civil war between the former communist partisans and the forces loyal to democracy and the monarchy.

It was, in some ways, the first of the proxy conflicts that were to characterize the Cold War: a foretaste of the much larger, more savage wars still to be fought in Korea and Vietnam. For the Greeks, however, it was still a brutal conflict, and one that was to leave a legacy for many years to come. George Papandreou, the grandfather of the current prime minister, had formed a government in exile in Italy and led the democratic forces. As the Nazi forces withdrew from Greece, there was a lull in the conflict while World War II was wrapped up in northern Europe, but by 1946 the fighting had started again. Over 1947 and 1948, the communists, mostly organized into informal, guerrilla bands, much as the North Vietnamese were to be 20 years later, were gaining territory and power right across northern Greece, moving south out of the border country next to Macedonia and Bulgaria. Whether the government in Athens would have ever been able to regain control of the whole country by itself is a moot point. It could be debated for generations. In the end, however, power politics intervened. In 1949, Yugoslavia's Marshall Tito broke with Moscow, and the camps and bases in Yugoslav-controlled Macedonia were closed to the Soviet-dominated Greek communists. Without support from across the border, the KKE's challenge for power slowly faded, and the insurgency was laid to rest.

The civil war left a terrible legacy, however. While the rest of Europe had been struggling with reconstruction, Greek had still been fighting Greek. There were terrible casualties on both sides, and some 30,000 Greek children had been forcibly evacuated to the Soviet bloc, many of them never to return. There was a legacy of bitterness, conspiracy, and violence that was to scar Greek society for a generation and that still influences it today.

In the 1950s, Greece moved back to normality. The premierships of Karamanlis slowly restored the nation. King Paul, who had assumed the throne in 1947, had given the country an air of stability, although the monarchy was by no means popular. And yet the economy remained in ruins, dependent as much on generous U.S. aid as anything else. Prewar, Greece's main export had been tobacco grown for the German market, but it was to be a long time before the Germans would recover sufficiently for that market to revive. Even so, it limped forward and under Karamanlis took its first tentative steps toward joining the mainstream of European nations when, in 1962, it signed a Treaty of Association with what was then still the fledgling European Economic Community.

The decision to try to link itself to the EEC was part of what Karamanlis liked to call "Greece's European Destiny." It was that vision again, the same one that was to be heard when Greece wanted to join the euro: making the country a Switzerland of the south. As usual, however, the nobler sentiments involved in that ambition also involved a huge numbers of subsidies. The 1962 treaty provided for loans to Greece subsidized by the community of about $300 million between 1962 and 1972 to help increase the competitiveness of the Greek economy in anticipation of Greece's full membership in the EEC. It was the first bailout of Athens organized in Brussels—although, as we shall see, it was to be far from the last.

That path to modernity was to be rudely interrupted by the Greek Army. In 1967, a group of colonels staged a coup and installed a military junta that was to rule as a dictatorship until 1974. Georgios Papadopoulos led the "Regime of the Colonels," as it was known to the rest of the world. Like most juntas, the Colonels were a good advertisement for not putting military officers in charge of anything more complex than a tank brigade. Authoritarian, reactionary, and backward-looking, they took control of a country that was making some attempts to reinvent itself for the postwar world and led it straight back toward a Victorian autocracy.

The 1960s were a crucial decade for the postwar world. Old barriers were broken down, new industries were created, new types of culture came to the fore, and the barriers between the sexes started to be dismantled. It was the decade in which the modern world began to be created. The Colonels turned their backs on all of that. Their policies verged on the absurd. Pop songs were banned, replaced by martial music. Long hair on men was outlawed. The press was censored, and so were films and books. It was a repressive, boorish regime, and one that gave a younger generation of Greeks no space to establish themselves. It was dedicated to turning back the clock: a common enough instinct but one that is never very successful, even in the short term.

One Greek industry did start to flourish: tourism. The package holiday was one of the great inventions of the immediate postwar years. It was particularly popular in Britain and Germany, allowing millions of middle-class and then working-class families to escape their own dreary weather for two weeks of Mediterranean sunshine. It was the first time traveling abroad had been available to anyone but a wealthy elite. Spain and Greece were the two natural destinations: They had plenty of sunshine, beaches, and lots of cheap labor, and that was all you really needed to get into the package holiday business. New hotels started to spring up across the Aegean islands. Even by the early 1970s, tourism was becoming a major component of the Greek economy (and it is still, along with shipping, one of its two major industries). But the bumbling Colonels managed to make a mess even of that, squandering all the newfound wealth the package holiday business was bringing into the country. By 1973, inflation had hit 30 percent, the economy was in ruins again, and a year later, amid street protests and riots in Athens, the junta had been deposed. Karamanlis returned to power as prime minister, slowly steering the country back toward some kind of normality.

During his second spell in power, Karamanlis achieved his lifetime ambition of steering the country into the EEC. A treaty of accession was signed in 1979, preparing the country for membership in 1981. Karamanlis himself gave up the premiership and became president. But during this second spell in power his economic policies were only a little more enlightened than those of the Colonels he replaced. Large chunks of the economy were nationalized, including many of the banks, as well as the transport systems: The national airline, Olympic Airlines, for example, was taken under government control. Much of the rest of the Greek economy, even if it remained nominally under private control, was placed under the leash of tight state regulation. At precisely the moment when Greece should have been modernizing its economy to cope with the rigors of free competition with the rest of the European Union, it was hurtling in the other direction.

Worse was to come. After an experiment with military dictatorship in the 1960s, in the 1970s Greece flirted with full-scale socialism.
In 1981, under a restored democracy, it elected Andreas Papandreou
as prime minister. As a general rule, there is probably no single class
of person you'd less want to be in charge of an economy than an
academic economist: That, unfortunately for Greece, was precisely
Papandreou's background. After studying at Harvard, Papandreou held
professorships in economics at Berkeley as well as at other universities in the United States and Sweden. Throughout his premiership, he
traded on his expertise in economics, portraying himself as the expert
who could lead the nation to prosperity. There was, however, to be
precious little evidence of it during his time in office.

Papandreou campaigned against the military junta, and had been
one of the highest-profile of the exiled leaders during the regime of
the Colonels. His Pasok party rode to power on a wave of enthusiasm. But Papandreou wasn't really a social democrat in the mould of
the German SPD or the British Labour Party. He was far more hard-
line than that: It would be wrong to describe him as a fully fledged
Marxist-Leninist but he was certainly not a man who believed in capitalism or the free market as the way to steer Greece toward a more
prosperous future.

In the early 1980s, the tide of global opinion was shifting rapidly
toward the liberal right. Margaret Thatcher had been elected prime
minister of Britain, and Ronald Reagan president of the United States.
Most of the developed world—with the sole exception of France,
which had just elected the socialist Francois Mitterrand—was about to
embark on a decade of deregulation and privatization. The free market
was about to be let rip. Yet, once again, Greece was about to move in
the opposite direction. It turned left at a time when everyone else was
moving right.

The results were both predictable and catastrophic. Wages and
pensions were pushed up sharply. The trade unions were strengthened.
The state-controlled banking system was used to prop up industries that
didn't make any money and almost certainly never would. In 1980, the
state had controlled 30 percent of Greek GDP, but by 1990, that share
had risen to 45 percent: It was one of the fastest rates of expansion of
the state ever seen within the European Union. By the middle of the

decade, as anyone apart from the expert economist in charge of the place could have predicted, the country was bust. Inflation was raging out of control—it touched an annual rate of 25 percent, close to the point where money ceases to have any real meaning—and the trade balance was sinking ever further into the red. In response, Papandreou was forced into an austerity package. The drachma was devalued by 15 percent; importers were forced to lodge between 40 and 80 percent of the value of their imports at the Bank of Greece (a pretty good way of stopping anyone importing anything into the country), taxes were increased, and a system of wage and price controls was introduced. The European Union helped out with an emergency loan, which tided the country through a difficult time, but although the stabilization program stopped the economy from collapsing completely, it didn't do anything to reform an economy that was struggling to find a niche in the global marketplace it could feel comfortable with.

Greece was starting to find a pattern. A new government comes in, it embarks on an extravagant spending program, then the economy crashes, and there is an austerity budget and an EU bailout.

Over the next couple of decades it was to become a very familiar script.

■ ■ ■

The drachma—meaning *handful* in ancient Greek—was among the world's oldest currency. The standard silver coin of the classical Greek empire, it is believed to have been first minted in about 650 B.C. in what is now western Turkey, and was originally worth a handful of arrows. In ancient times, it was produced separately by the city states that made up the Greek empire, but the coins could be used from city to city much as the different national euro coins can be today. Trade and conquest spread the currency throughout the known world— it was the money that Alexander the Great used as he pushed his armies toward India. Archaeologists have dug up drachmas as far away as Afghanistan. It also served as the model for another coin, the dirham, which is still used as an expression for currency throughout the Islamic world today.

Although its ancient history was illustrious, the modern drachma was a rather less successful currency, and not one that anyone could be particularly proud of. The great free-market economist, Friedrich Hayek, once wrote about how moving to the London School of Economics from Vienna he could still use British coins with Queen Victoria's head on them that had been minted almost a century earlier. To him, that was a perfect physical expression of the safety and security of a currency that was vital to a properly functioning market economy. The more stable the currency was, the more stable society would be—and the more successful as well.[5]

The drachma, however, was not the kind of currency that Hayek had in mind. It had been first reintroduced in 1832 soon after the establishment of the modern Greek state. It was reorganized when Greece joined the ill-fated Latin Monetary Union in 1868, then again after that experiment in merging different national currencies together collapsed after Word War I. The German occupation, however, put paid to that currency. The Nazis were looting the country and, anyway, the economics of National Socialism were always a catastrophe, creating widespread shortages and terrible inflation in every country unfortunate enough to be occupied by the Third Reich. By 1944, the Bank of Greece was issuing 100 billion drachma notes, and even they didn't buy you very much. After the Germans went home, there wasn't much choice but to do what plenty of other governments had done when faced with a worthless currency: Scrap it, and start again.

The second modern drachma was issued in 1944, with the old notes switched for new ones. Amid the chaos of the civil war, it wasn't much more successful than the last one had been, and pretty soon 50,000 drachma notes were needed to complete the shopping. In 1954, with the nation at peace again, the Bank of Greece had another go. The third modern drachma was created, with a thousand of the old ones replaced by a single new one. Greece joined the postwar Bretton Woods system of managed exchange rates, pegged around the dollar. At the start the rate was pegged at 30 drachma to one U.S. dollar. It didn't exactly hold that value. By the time the euro replaced the drachma, the rate was 400 to the dollar, a depreciation of more than 10 times in value. Still, at least the currency had survived a military junta and several bailout packages from its neighbors, which was more than its immediate predecessors had managed.

It was no great surprise, though, that most Greeks were about as happy to get rid of the drachma as you would be to see the end of a nasty rash. Polling through the 1990s showed a steady 70 percent–plus support for joining the new single European currency. The Greeks wanted in. The interesting question was always going to be whether the rest of Europe would let them join the club.

Greece in the 1990s, by its standards, had achieved some measure of political stability. The Socialist Pasok Party maintained its grip on power, first under Andreas Papandreou up until 1996, and then under his successor, Costas Simitis. From the time the idea was first mooted in the early 1990s, Greece was an enthusiastic supporter of the euro. It wanted the single currency, voted in favor of it on every possible occasion, and indeed planned to be one of the founding members.

In 1993, with the Maastricht convergence criteria still newly written, the Greeks were busily submitting reports to the officials in Brussels vetting members for eligibility, pressing their own claims to be members of the club. A convergence plan submitted by Greek Economics Minister Stefanos Manos in that year was approved by the European Commission. The plan was not "overly optimistic," insisted Manos when some journalists and commentators suggested it might be a little on the hopeful side. Greece would be ready to participate in full economic and monetary union by 1997, he insisted.[6]

It didn't quite work out like that. Greece was not even a member of the revamped exchange-rate mechanism, a crucial precursor to euro membership. Nor, as the 1990s progressed, did it show many signs of the kind of steady, slow progress toward stable convergence with its more powerful northern neighbors that would have made signing up for euro membership a realistic option.

In June 1994, the drachma came under speculative attack on the markets. Interest rates were forced all the way up to 500 percent as the central bank fought to stabilize the currency. That was only a short-term measure, but even afterwards the rate only came down to 26.5 percent, hardly a level that was likely to encourage investment. Public debts running at 110 percent of GDP were the main cause of the 1994 crisis. In response, Finance Minister Yannos Papantoniou presented a five-year plan to bring the Greek economy in line with the criteria for euro membership set out in the Maastricht Treaty. The plan saw inflation falling to 3.3 percent in 1999 from an estimated 1994 average of 10.8 percent. Public debt would be bought down by the sale of state assets and a crackdown on tax evasion—lines that the financial markets had heard before, and that it would hear plenty of times more over the next few years. Needless to say, the targets were not met.

In happened again in 1997, the year when the Greeks had optimistically hoped to be merging their currency with Germany's, and when the finance minister was placing optimistic bets on its eventual membership in the single currency. Amid a series of speculative attacks in the foreign exchange markets, the currency started to wobble, then fall in value. In November that year, the Bank of Greece was forced to intervene in the market, spending $2.5 billion of valuable foreign exchange reserves to prop up a currency that was facing a wave of selling against the deutschmark. At one point, the central bank had to raise interest rates from 10 to 150 percent to try to stop the drachma going into freefall.

There were plenty of words you could use to describe that economy. Stable, however, was not among them. Greece was still a country at the mercy of the global capital markets and vulnerable to constant speculative attacks.

Convergence was more than just a matter of interest and exchange rates. It was about the real economy as well. The trouble was, there wasn't much sign of Greece moving much closer to the European mainstream on that measure, either.

One feature of the Greek economy during the 1990s, the crucial years running up to the adoption of the euro, was the relentless expansion in the size of the state. Taxes as a percentage of GDP were 34.5 percent in 1990, a relatively low and competitive figure by European standards. They had risen to 40 percent by 1995, and then all the way up to 44 percent by 2004. State spending throughout that period remained at around 50 percent of the economy: The difference was that in the early 1990s, the Greeks weren't making any serious effort to match government revenue to spending, while in preparation for the adoption of the single currency they did at least make some notional effort to bring the two figures back into line. A budget deficit that amounted to a staggering 15 percent of GDP in 1990 had closed to around 6 percent of GDP a decade later: still double what the Growth and Stability Pact mandated, but not as bad as it had been.

Even so, the failure of successive Greek governments to balance the books meant that public debt was exploding as a percentage of GDP. The outstanding stock of public debt came to 74 percent of GDP in 1990. By 2004, that had soared to 102 percent. It was very hard to describe this as a country that showed any willingness to get it debts under control or set its economy on a path to reasonable growth.

Indeed, the closer you looked at the statistics, the harder it was to see anything very modern about the Greek economy—and certainly not at the point where it was preparing to merge its economy with the innovative, technological powerhouses to its north.

Take research and development as a percentage of GDP. For a modernizing, dynamic economy, that can be a crucial figure. To grow more prosperous you need lots of small high-tech companies making pharmaceuticals or software or machinery. They need to be research intensive. How else are firms going to maintain a competitive edge over rivals in the rest of the world? And yet in 2000 Greece was spending only 0.7 percent of its GDP on R&D, compared with an EU average of 1.9 percent. That is, it was spending at around a third of the rate of its new competitors.

It wasn't inventing anything very much. In 2000, patents per 10,000 residents in Greece stood at 0.4. The EU average was 2.3. In 2000, there were merely six personal computers for every thousand residents in Greece. The average for the EU for that year was 27. Technology-driven firms, measured by their contribution to total output, accounted for just 6.7 percent of the Greek economy. The EU average was 19.6 percent. Skill-intensive industries accounted for just 4.4 percent of the Greek economy. In the EU as a whole, they accounted for 14 percent of output. The fast-growing computing and information technology industries made up just 2.2 percent of the Greek economy in 2000. For the whole of the EU, they accounted for 7.7 percent of the economy.

On any measure you cared to look at, Greece was lagging way behind the mainstream euro-zone economies. It was trapped within a backward-looking time bubble, reliant on agriculture, shipping, tourism, a few basic industries, and most of all massive state spending to keep its economy afloat.

But once it was inside the euro, it wasn't going to be able to compete with countries like Germany by devaluing its currency anymore. Nor could it print money, nor rely on subsidies. It would have to survive by making products the rest of Europe wanted to buy at prices they wanted to pay. If there was a plan for achieving that, the Greeks were keeping it to themselves.

In Germany, there were plenty of people opposed to letting Greece into the euro. Theo Waigel, the finance minister, was far from the only influential German who harbored doubts about whether Greek membership was a step too far. Pretty much the entire European Union establishment was approaching the single currency cautiously. They were well aware that melding different economies together into a single economic zone was a huge undertaking, and one fraught with danger. Get it right, and Europe would have taken a huge and probably irreversible step toward a full political union. Get it wrong, and a blow would be delivered to the EU that was so severe the entire edifice might well come tumbling down.

As we saw in the previous chapter, the euro was created with strict entry criteria. The purpose was to make sure that each economy was mature and stable enough to cope with the demands that membership would place on it. Every country had to have its government borrowing under control, and it had to have forced inflation out of the system. The euro was to be a rigorous economic regime. It wasn't a fitness club: a place you could join, then get in shape later. It was more like an athletics team: You needed to be in perfect condition before you were even allowed onto the field. That was the only way it could work.

In the run-up to the launch of the single currency, the official line from the politicians and central bankers was that the entry criteria were strict and inflexible. "It will be extremely important for the euro area to restrict entry to those countries which are ready in terms of their economic and anti-inflation policies," argued then-president of the German Bundesbank, Professor Hans Tietmeyer, a man who was without doubt the most important financial figure in Europe at the time the initial members were being decided.[7]

"In monetary union, all the participating countries must be in a position to stay the course unaided. They must be able to secure economic competitiveness and efficiency, above all, by virtue of their own internal efforts. If they are not in a position to do that, not only will they encounter difficulties themselves but other countries of the EMU area will, too,"[8] stated Tietmeyer in 1998.

The second most important figure in European financial affairs, the then-governor of the Bank of France, Jean-Claude Trichet, was speaking from the same script. In 1997, he was arguing fervently for a conservative approach to monetary stability. "The thrust of the spirit and of the letter of the Treaty is that everything is done to construct the euro area as an optimum currency area. First by ensuring that it incorporates economies that have already proved being convergent in the fiscal field as well as in the monetary and financial fields."[9]

Eventually that view prevailed. When the euro was launched in 1999, Italy was allowed in, despite plenty of doubts about whether it was really ready. So were Spain and Portugal, although there were question-marks about those two countries as well. The British chose not to apply. The Greeks, however, were turned down, judged not ready for membership of the single currency.

It was a crushing blow for the political and economic establishment in Athens. It had staked the country's future on steering it toward the mainstream of western European nations. It didn't really have a Plan B. The euro was meant to be the goal of a decade of economic planning, and at least some efforts at reform, even if they were fairly half-hearted.

Still, there was no point in arguing about it too much. Greece in 1999 clearly didn't meet the entry criteria. The budget deficit in the 1990s at one point soared to 16 percent of GDP, and outstanding debts ran to more than 100 percent of GDP. Inflation had been running at double-digit levels in the very recent past. As we have seen, the drachma was still subjected to regular speculative attacks on the exchange markets.

When the figures were checked, it didn't come close to the standards laid down. Greece didn't just fail by a little. It failed by a mile. The country was having enough trouble simply shadowing the deutschmark on the currency markets. It was impossible that any reasonable person could conclude that the two currencies should be merged.

And yet if the decision was tough on the Greeks, it wasn't much easier for the officials steering policy in Brussels and Frankfurt, either. The euro had never really been designed as an instrument of economic policy. It was, first and foremost, a political currency. It was a way of pushing the states of Europe toward closer integration, of centralizing power, and of turning the separate national economies into a single bloc. It was a grand, idealistic project.

But where did that stand if certain countries weren't allowed to join? It was one thing for the British, the Swedes, and the Danes to decline membership, but it was something quite different for countries to be turned down for membership. That raised all kinds of troubling questions. Could there be two different versions of the European Union, one for members inside the single currency and one for those outside? If the euro was a stepping stone to closer integration, how would the members outside keep up with the others if they weren't sharing the euro? Was there any point in a country like Greece being a member of the EU at all if it was not allowed into the single currency?

Those were all questions with no ready or simple answers. In reality, the euro had to include as many members of the European Union as possible, and certainly all those that wanted to join. A country might be turned down initially. But it couldn't be turned down permanently without threatening the legitimacy and viability of the entire project.

The euro was always planned as an expansionary currency, a monetary empire that would only grow and grow. "The euro area: How big will it be?" asked Nobel-prize winner Robert Mundell in 1999. The man who, as we have already seen, was regularly described as the father of the euro was in no doubt that it would only get bigger and bigger.

> My own prediction is that by the year 2002 the European monetary union will include its current eleven members plus Greece (which is already committed to join), Sweden, Denmark, and Britain. By 2005, Slovenia, the Czech Republic, Poland, Hungary, and Estonia will also be in. And by 2010, assuming all goes well and the monetary union is prosperous, no country in Europe will want to, or be able to afford to stay out. Thus, Slovakia, Croatia, Lithuania, Latvia, Romania, and Bulgaria will all join the monetary union.[10]

In that optimistic assessment, he was merely reflecting the mainstream view of Europe's establishment. "An enlarged EMU area will be positive both for the euro-zone area and for the countries joining," said Romano Prodi, then the European Union's Commissioner for Economic and Monetary Affairs (and now, of course, the president of the European Commission) in 2000.[11] So something would have to be done about the fact the Greeks had asked to join but been turned down.

The solution? Between them, Brussels and Athens would make sure that Greece would qualify for the euro by 2001—by any means necessary. "We must enter the euro with a clean sheet on all the criteria," said Yannis Papantoniou in 1999.[12] Well, that was a fair point. But there was something of the Freudian slip about the way Greek finance officials kept reassuring the world that they weren't planning to fiddle the numbers to make sure that Greece qualified for euro membership by the new 2001 deadline. Because, in truth, that was precisely what they were planning to do.

Between 1999 and 2001, something very mysterious—and indeed convenient—happened. The Greek economy completely transformed itself. Just like that.

The budget deficit came down to just 1 percent of GDP. Inflation dropped to just 5 percent. Public debt was still running at around 100 percent of GDP, but at least it wasn't going up as fast as it had been, and since it was now below that of both Italy and Belgium, which were already inside the euro-zone, it was going to have to use that as a reason for keeping Greece on the outside.

In March 2000, Greece formally applied to join the euro. "Today is an historic moment for the country," said Prime Minister Costas Simitis as he submitted the bid. "It opens a new era of security, stability and development."[13]

There wasn't really any reason to hold out anymore. Officials in Brussels or Frankfurt could stare at the numbers as long as they liked but unless they were about to accuse the Greeks of lying they couldn't argue Greece didn't meet the criteria for entry into the euro laid down in the Maastricht Treaty. At a summit in July in Portugal, the European Union's leaders looked at the application and duly approved it.

To most of Europe's elite, that was yet another step forward on the great, historic march toward closer union. "The arrival of Greece will not disrupt the monetary union," commented *Le Monde* smugly, as the drachma was finally consigned to history's dustbin.[14] The French left-liberal daily is probably the closest thing there is to an official mouth-piece of European integration, and its view was certainly one that was shared by the majority of officials and politicians in all the main capitals across the continent. Greek entry was another step forward in the process of European integration.

Not everyone was convinced, of course. A few people suspected this was only a step forward for the euro in the sense that putting your foot over the edge of an abyss is a step forward for an individual. "It's the oldest democracy in the world, but not the most stable country in monetary terms," commented Wilhelm Hankel, a professor at Frankfurt's Goethe University who had threatened to take German government to court for adopting the euro because of concern about the currency's weakness, in a story marking the final switchover from the drachma to the euro. "It would have been better to wait until Greece showed it was able to keep public finances and inflation under control long term."[15]

It would be another decade, however, before those kinds of warnings would get another airing. Against all the available evidence, Greece had been judged fit to join Europe's single currency. Everyone was assuming that would be a success, and warnings to the contrary were far from welcome at that point in time.

■ ■ ■

When Greece officially replaced the drachma with the euro on January 1, 2001, nobody was in the mood to mourn the demise of the world's oldest currency. A public holiday was declared for January 2, ushering in a week of celebrations as the country joined the club of rich European countries.

"Today is a landmark moment in the national aim of the Greek people on their way to increase our standard of living to that of the other European people; to achieve real economic and social convergence," said the prime minister of the day, Costas Simitis, marking the occasion with due fanfare.

Whatever regrets a few people might have had about losing a currency that Alexander the Great was familiar with were drowned out by the promise of riches to come. Economics might famously rule out the possibility of ever getting a free lunch, but the Greeks had just discovered the closest thing to a moussaka you didn't have to pay for yet discovered. Backed by an unexpectedly strong currency, with low interest rates set in Frankfurt, and with the implicit promise that whatever bills they might run would eventually be settled in Brussels or Berlin, Greece suddenly found it could borrow just about as much money as it wanted without having to worry too much about paying it back.

The early evidence was that that would be precisely what happened. When the financial markets reopened on January 3, 2001, after the Christmas and New Year break, Greek debt was suddenly in demand. Yields on Greek government bonds fell to an all-time low. In total, 2.7 billion euros of Greek debt was traded in a single day, about seven times the average amount. Investors who wouldn't have considered lending money in drachma were suddenly quite happy to do so in euros. The spread between Greek bonds and German government bonds, known as *bunds* in the financial markets, narrowed to just 55 basis points. In plain language, that meant that Greece could borrow money at a rate just slightly over 0.5 percent more than the German government paid for its money. The difference in risk between lending to Europe's most feckless government and its most responsible was vanishing overnight.

"Pre-euro, there were a certain number of investors who could not buy Greek debt," said a bond strategist at UBS in London quoted by Bloomberg as the drachma was abolished. "A number of investors who've been in for a long time are selling out. A switch in the investor base is taking place."[16]

Indeed it was. Greece was no longer a wacky fringe country, of interest only to brave speculators and emerging markets funds. At the end of a long journey, it was now right in the mainstream of European finance. It was a rock-solid, A-rated nation, as creditworthy as Germany.

It was the summation of everything a whole generation of Greek politicians had worked for. The bulk of the Greek establishment bought into the vision of the euro common among the Mediterranean countries that the single currency wouldn't be so much a form of money as a kind of catalyst. It would in a single act take what were in many ways still relatively backward, agricultural economies, dominated by the state- and family-controlled cartels, and, by a kind of alchemy that was never fully explained, transform them into modern, dynamic, liberal, technological powerhouses with the flash of a wand. It was as if Sicily could morph into Switzerland over night.

Yannos Papantoniou presented an articulate elaboration of that view in a talk he gave to the London School of Economics in May 2005. At the time, Greece was still basking in its membership of the euro. The economy was booming, and debt was under control. Inflation was low, and employment high. A country that had long felt itself patronized by the richer economies of northern Europe could feel it had joined the richer men's club. It was going up in the world and, like everyone who can feel their social status gradually rising, was enjoying the ride immensely.

"Euro entry removed monetary and exchange-rate instability," he told his audience of bankers and economists that day.

> And, together with the very considerable decline in inflation and interest rates, provided economic policy with additional flexibility, stronger acceleration in credit growth and domestic demand. Greece's membership in the euro-zone is the most critical element in our efforts to bridge the gap with our European partners, created by decades of economic retardation.[17]

Taken together with the successful staging of the Olympic Games in Athens in 2004, the arrival of Greece in the euro-zone, for a politician such as Yannos Papantoniou, completed the process of hauling the country into the twenty-first century. "Greece completed a cycle of substantial modernization over the previous decade," he continued in his LSE lecture. "Overcoming the economic instability and stagnation of the previous era, it managed to consolidate its finances, reduce inflation, accelerate growth and promote structural changes conducive to create a friendlier environment for enterprise and investment."

What lay ahead, he argued, was "a new, dynamic phase for the Greek economy, based more on knowledge and modern structures," while "Greek society" would become "more extrovert and cosmopolitan, adopting a more international perspective." With that achieved, he concluded, a "bolstering of national self-confidence" would be the natural result.

It was quite a claim. The euro was not just a way of swapping one set of banknotes for another. Nor was it a way of just re-jigging payment systems so that they worked more efficiently. It was, as we saw a little earlier, a catalyst: an element that you could drop into the mix that would create a chain reaction that transformed one substance into another.

Of course, the opinion of one Greek socialist politician doesn't matter very much. A certain allowance has to be made for the inevitable rhetoric of public speeches.

But it is worth quoting at length precisely because it is a well-articulated encapsulation of the intellectual worldview that captured a whole generation of Mediterranean politicians. You could hear precisely the same views in Portugal, Spain, or Italy. They would be repeated again in Latvia, Slovenia, Poland, the Czech Republic, and Hungary, the former Soviet bloc countries queuing up to join the euro just as soon as their economies were ready. Membership in the single currency would catapult them to modernization in a single step. Old economic structures would be swept aside in a single stroke, new ones created overnight. It was a bold, exciting vision, and one that was particularly appealing to politicians of the center-left: The notion of revolutionary change, steered by the government, appeals to socialist and social democrat parties. It allowed them to ignore the hard realities and to avoid the tough questions. The practicalities of whether their industries could really compete with the far more experienced competitors of northern Europe were conveniently swept under the carpet. The issues of whether the figures were real, or whether they had just been invented to please the politicians, were stuffed behind the sofa. So long as the vision was compelling enough, so long as the journey was exciting, and so long as the goal was a noble one, all of that could be safely ignored.

It is a story that has been played out many times. Political elites become entranced with a noble ideal and lead their countries toward it, ignoring the obstacles in their path.

Usually the results are tragic. And, as we will see over the next few chapters, Greece was to prove no exception to that rule.

Chapter 3

At Club Med the Party Never Ends

In June 2006, the European Central Bank's governing council gathered in Madrid for its monthly meeting to decide interest rates. There was nothing unusual about that. The Bank regularly meets in different cities around the euro area. It is part of its policy of getting out into the different regions of its vast monetary empire, making sure it is seen to be in touch with the people, and not just a remote financial dictator locked away in a steel-and-glass skyscraper in Frankfurt.

Had they chosen to look around, however, it would have been a sobering lesson in the impact that the monetary union was having on what had been, up until the launch of the euro, one of the peripheral nations in Europe.

Fleets of limousines collected the council members from what was, in 2006, the gleaming new Richard Rogers–designed terminal at Madrid's Barajas airport, itself a lesson in the extraordinary boom that was taking place in Spain. The new terminal was one the largest in the world, covering 760,000 square meters across two buildings. It was designed around glass panes and natural light, and was created to handle up to 70 million passengers a year.

As they drove in the center of the city they would have seen a forest of cranes. Madrid was, in the middle of the decade, going through a huge building boom. More than 400,000 homes were built in the Spanish capital in the first half of the decade, in part to provide houses for the one million new immigrants who flocked to the city. There were more than three million more cars angrily clogging the city's streets. Madrid, by 2006, was one giant symphony of jackhammers and car horns.

Nor was that just true of the capital. Spain was suddenly home to the world's most expensive and most innovative architecture. The Guggenheim Museum Bilbao was built by American architect Frank Gehry, and had become an immediately recognizable landmark around the world. In 2006, the 57-story Torre Espacio was opened in Madrid, a spectacular modernist skyscraper to match any in the world, designed by the American architect Henry N. Cobb. Those were just the high-profile projects. All around the country, new buildings were going up at an exhilarating rate. Indeed, by 2006, Spain was consuming half the cement produced in Europe.

For the Spanish, joining the euro and ditching the century's old peseta had been nothing to regret. It had marked the emergence of the country from the dark years of the civil war of the 1930s and the stagnant decades of General Franco's dictatorship that followed it. By turning itself back into a democracy and then joining the European Union, it had rejoined the mainstream of modern European nations. When it signed up for the euro, it cemented its status as a modern, growing economy. And whatever doubts the Spanish might have had would have been easily set aside once they saw the tangible results of the new currency. One of the great economic parties in history was getting going and Spain was right at the center of the fun. It would take the most dismal of skeptics to rain on this parade.

According to International Monetary Fund figures, the Spanish economy expanded 3.3 percent in 2006, compared with 3.4 percent in 2005. Over the decade running up to that date, the Spanish economy almost doubled in size, and it had beaten the euro area's average growth rate for 11 straight years. From a relative backwater, Spain had closed the gap on the rest of Western Europe in the space of a single decade.

It was becoming an economy that was central to the performance of the whole of Europe. According to calculations by British economic consultancy Lombard Street Research, between 2003 and 2005,

39 percent of the growth in the euro-area economy came from Spain. Without it, the euro-zone would scarcely have expanded at all.

Spanish firms were pushing out into the rest of Europe and indeed into the rest of the world. Grupo Ferrovial, the massive engineering and building conglomerate that had built Madrid's new airport and Bilbao's spectacular museum, paid £10 billion in 2006 for BAA, the British airport operator that owns London's Heathrow among others. Abertis Infraestructuras paid 12 billion euros for the Italian roads operator Autostrade. Banco Santander, under the brilliant leadership of Emilio Botin, consolidated an iron grip on the Spanish banking market and then expanded out across Europe, taking control of Britain's Abbey National. At one point, it was the largest bank in Europe, measured by market value, overtaking the mighty Deutsche Bank of Germany and the massive BNP Paribas of France. The Spanish were suddenly everywhere, wheeler-dealing as if they were born to it. Indeed, of the five largest corporate deals struck in Europe during 2006, three of them involved a Spanish company on one side of the deal.

The peripheral countries in the euro-zone were known as the "Club Med" countries among economists: Spain, Portugal, Greece, and Italy were all on the Mediterranean Sea and were all Latin nations that had developed very differently from the industrial powerhouses of northern Europe. But, as we shall see in the rest of this chapter, once they were inside the euro-zone they started to catch up very quickly. Nowhere was that more true than in Spain.

But the boom was far from balanced, and even as the party was in full swing there were plenty of people to question whether it was really sustainable. In truth, Spain was going through a massive property bubble. Between 1990 and 2009, Spanish property prices rose by a massive 80 percent. To afford those houses, 50-year mortgages were becoming commonplace, offered with reckless abandon by mainstream Spanish banks. It wasn't quite as bad as Japan at the height of its property bubble toward the end of the 1980s, when banks were offering people hundred-year mortgages that would have to be paid off by their children or grandchildren. But it was getting dangerously close.

Even in 2006, if you chose to look beyond the gleaming new skyscrapers there were plenty of signs of danger to come. The country's inflation rate of 4 percent was the highest in the euro-zone. Spanish labor costs were rising all the time, making it less and less competitive against its rivals within the single currency. At 67 billion euros, its current account deficit for those years was the second biggest in the world after the United States in absolute terms, and the worlds' largest in relative terms, at a massive 7.4 percent of gross domestic product. Ordinary Spanish families were taking on more and more debt at more and more dangerous levels of interest; family indebtedness reached a record 115 percent of disposable income at the end of 2005, according to figures published by the Bank of Spain.

Spain was indeed growing at an impressive rate. But as an International Monetary Fund paper published in 2008 pointed out, the growth was not based in anything very solid. "Spain's significant GDP per capita growth stems mainly from an upward shift in the occupation rate (which must stabilize in the medium term) rather than from productivity growth, which—despite some recent acceleration—remains low," argued the IMF.[1] Translate that from economists' jargon and what the Fund was saying was something very simple. Given that national output is simply the amount of stuff that people produce multiplied by the number of people, there are really only two ways for an economy to grow. One is to get more people working, either by getting unemployment down, or by encouraging more women to work, or by extending retirement ages; the other is by making sure that each worker increases his or her own individual output.

The Spanish had some success with the former. An intensely conservative Catholic society under the Franco regime, as the country modernized and liberalized more women did indeed start working. They no longer just got married and stayed home to cook paella and look after the kids. So, there were more Spanish working. But the record on productivity, which is the only long-term sustainable basis of prosperity, was dismal. While Spain grew at average rate of 2.6 percent a year between 1996 and 2006, productivity growing at an average annual rate of just 0.2 percent. In Germany it was growing at 0.8 percent over the same period. In France it was growing at 1.3 percent, according to the IMF figures.

On that measure—the only one that really counts in the medium term—Spain wasn't really growing at all. It was actually steadily falling behind its big competitors in the euro-area. As each year passed, it was steadily becoming slightly less competitive with its neighbors, not more so.

Indeed, the closer you looked at the Spanish economic miracle, the stranger it seemed. It wasn't as if there were suddenly lots of new Spanish-made goods filling up shops around the world. When we read that South Korea is a booming economy, we can see the physical evidence for this all around us, from the Samsung televisions in our houses to the Hyundai cars on the streets. But Spain? True, Banco Santander was becoming pretty well known around the world. The fashion chain Zara, created by the Leon-born entrepreneur Amancio Ortega, was among the biggest global retail success stories of the past decade. But that was about it. There was very little evidence of a new generation of Spanish entrepreneurs taking on the world with amazing new products. Nor was there any real sign that the Spanish had done much in the way of hard work on reforming or liberalizing their economy. "Since the late 1990s, reforms of goods and services markets have been timid, even though competitive pressures appear limited in several sheltered sectors," argued an assessment of the economy published by the Organisation for Economic Co-operation and Development in 2005 right in the middle of the boom.[2]

In fact, as the OECD made plain, the Spanish economy remained fairly backward, characterized by outmoded, restrictive labor laws, planning restrictions, and cartels that stopped its industries from becoming genuinely competitive. It was as conservative and backward-looking in many ways as it had always been.

So what was really going on?

In reality, the Spanish were just taking on more and more debt. According to figures published by management consultant McKinsey, Spanish debt levels have been rocketing upward for two decades now. Taken together, public- and private-sector debt grew in Spain at a rate of 4.1 percent a year in the 1990s, already fairly high by international standards. Between 2000 and 2008, the first years after the euro was formally launched, the rate of growth of public and private debts rose by 7.4 percent a year. It was the fastest acceleration of indebtedness among any of the major developed world economies (the UK was second, but that is another story). Overall, the total outstanding debt for Spain stood at 366 percent of GDP at the end of 2008. That compared with 193 percent in 2000. Debt levels had doubled in just eight years since the euro was launched.[3]

Spanish households were running deeper and deeper into the red. In 2000, the average Spanish family had debts of 69 percent of their disposable income. By 2008, that had increased to 130 percent. It was an 88 percent rise in indebtedness in the eight years since the euro had been launched, the highest rate in the developed world. The United States, which we think of as being a debt-fueled country, saw a mere 33 percent rise in household debt levels over the same period, and even in Britain it was only 52 percent. In frugal Germany, household debts actually fell: The average German family owed less money as a percentage of its household income in 2008 than it did in 2000.

In effect, the entire boom was fueled by borrowed money, much of it coming from abroad. One way of measuring that was the trade gap, which gives us a snapshot of the difference between what the Spanish were consuming every year and what they were producing. During 2007 and 2008, as the boom reached its peak, the trade deficit was running close to 10 percent of GDP. In some months it was up to almost 12 percent of GDP. These were enormous figures, far higher than the trade deficits run up by the United States, about which far more fuss is made in the financial markets. As a result, external debts were skyrocketing. In 2002, Spain's foreign debts amounted to around 35 percent of GDP. By 2009, that figure had risen to 95 percent, according to figures published by the Bank of Spain.

There was no real mystery about why it was happening. Spain historically had had both high and volatile interest rates. If you were Spanish, borrowing money had been a high-risk and expensive business, best avoided. It was expensive, and if rates suddenly spiked up, as they frequently did, you might well be ruined. Since it started sharing its currency with France and Germany, however, its interest rates had been set in Frankfurt by the ECB. Rates were far lower than they had been historically. They were also far more stable. Spanish borrowers could look several years ahead and feel comfortable that they had a rough idea what interest rates were likely to be and make their calculations accordingly. The risk had been largely taken out of the equation.

More importantly, money wasn't just cheap. It was effectively free. The *real interest rate* is not the rate you are charged; it is the difference between that rate and the rate at which prices are going up. In 2006, for example, Spanish inflation was running at 4 percent a year. The interest rate set by the ECB was just 2.75 percent. So the real interest rate was actually negative, by 1.25 percent. The banks were effectively paying you to take the money off their hands and find a way of spending it for them.

It is hardly surprising that people were only too happy to oblige. They would be crazy not to. And yet, in fact, the Spanish economy was overheating. It was being pumped up by free foreign money. The consequences of that were to be dramatic, as we shall see later.

But if the Spanish economy was suddenly on steroids, it was nothing compared to what was happening in Ireland.

■ ■ ■

In early 2005, the Paris-based Organisation for Economic Co-operation and Development published a remarkable statistic. It put out a list of the five richest countries in the world, measured by per-capita income—the only really meaningful measure of how rich or otherwise people actually are. It was the first time the research organization for the world's developed nations had updated this particular ranking since 1999, and the list was in most respects much the same as usual. Switzerland was up there; so were the United States, and Norway, and Luxembourg.[4]

But there was also one new entrant: Ireland.

In Britain, plenty of jaws dropped to the floor in amazement, as indeed they did all around the world. Ireland was famous for plenty of things. Its literature and music were justly famous. So were its beer and whiskey, its people's easygoing nature, and the lush splendor of its countryside. But economic miracles? That wasn't what people associated with Ireland.

And yet here was the proof in plain black-and-white figures from one of the world's most respected sources of economic statistics. Measured by the income of the average person, Ireland had vaulted straight into the top league of the world's richest countries.

It had been happening for some time. On the surface, Ireland might look to be an unlikely member of the Club Med. There is certainly nothing very Mediterranean about the country's rain-soaked countryside or windy beaches. But it had this much in common with its southern neighbors: Compared to much of mainland, mainstream Europe, with which it was to merge its economy in the euro, it had started from a position of relatively backwardness.

At the end of World War II, Ireland was a rural, mainly agricultural economy. A century of domination as a colony of England, and mass emigration to the United States, had left it hollowed out. There were always plenty of smart Irish people but they weren't making their careers in Ireland. The most powerful forces in Irish society were the Church and the State. Neither of them was very interested in developing the economy.

Go back to 1960, and all the countries on the periphery of the European Union were starting from a similar position. Portugal was the worst placed, with a GDP per capita of 42 percent of the EU average. Greece was at 51 percent, Spain at 61 percent, and Ireland at 67 percent. So Ireland was not quite as badly off as some of the Club Med countries, but it was certainly a lot closer to the Portuguese economy than it was to the French or the Dutch.

Over the next three decades, it hardly improved its position at all. Fast-forward to 1990, and Portugal's GDP per capita was up to 65 percent of the EU average. Greece was at 67 percent, and Spain and Ireland were level at 78 percent. But during that decade that followed, Ireland started to pull decisively ahead. While Greece had fallen back slightly to just 65 percent of the EU average GDP per capita, and the Portuguese and Spanish had made marginal progress to 70 and 87 percent respectively, the Irish had shot ahead. By 2000, its per-capita income was 115 percent of the EU average. By 2005, the year the OECD rankings were produced, it had stretched its lead further to close on 120 percent.

Ireland was now a richer country than its old colonial master, Britain, a cause of much satisfaction in Dublin. It was richer than France or Germany. If you wanted to make international comparisons, it was richer than the United States as well. It was a remarkable transformation, and one that took the Irish themselves slightly by surprise. Swank, moneyed prosperity had never really been the way the country had seen itself. All the more striking was the way it had been achieved without any of the obvious advantages the other countries on the

OECD list of the five richest nations enjoyed. The Norwegians had lots of oil and not many people (always a good combination, as anyone in Saudi Arabia will tell you). Both Switzerland and Luxembourg were secretive financial centers, their banks the grateful recipients of vast quantities of the world's money, from which they could make an easy, prosperous living. The United States was the world's global superpower with the world's reserve currency. But Ireland didn't have any of those advantages. It was a small island, stuck out on the edge of Europe, without great transport links. True, it had a well-educated workforce, and its spoke English, the global business language of the modern world. But it was hardly uniquely blessed in those respects. Plenty of other countries had been dealt a similar hand of cards without managing to play them nearly so well.

Clearly, something had gone incredibly right for the Irish.

The evidence of the boom was available everywhere. Irish house prices rocketed into the stratosphere, and people were taking on more and more debt to get themselves on the property ladder. In 1994, the average residential mortgage in Ireland had been just one-and-a-half times the average industrial wage, but by 2004 that figure had grown to five-and-a-half times the average. Many of the properties were being purchased purely for speculation. The 2006 census, carried pretty much at the height of the boom, found that there were 250,000 empty houses in the country. That was an extraordinarily high number for a country with a population of just four million. Clearly, many people were simply buying up houses, leaving them empty for a year or two, and then planning to sell them when prices had risen by another 50 percent.

For the first time ever, migrants were flocking to Dublin to find work. In the 1980s, 300,000 Irish people, most of them under 40, and most with valuable skills, had left the country to find work. In the 1990s, and 2000s, that turned into net immigration of more than a 100,000 people a year. Indeed, by the middle of the past decade, the Irish building unions were staging street demonstrations to protest about the numbers of Polish workers coming to take their jobs. They showed a supreme indifference to both irony and history: For decades, Irish workers had been doing precisely that in other cities. But it was a measure of just how much the country had changed.

There was a new breed of the Irish super-rich, with fortunes mostly made from property development. Take Sean Dunne, for example. When he married his 20-years-younger second wife in 2004, Dunne chartered the Christina O, a yacht once owned by the late Greek shipping tycoon, Aristotle Onassis. Mr. Dunne invited 44 of his friends to join him and his new wife on a fortnight's honeymoon cruise. In 2005, Dunne paid £355 million for a seven-acre site in Dublin's smartest neighborhood and announced he was going to build a Trump Tower–style commercial and residential development. The whole project was to cost him £1 billion.

That was just one example among many. A report for the private bank Investec in 2008 estimated that there were some 450 people with more than 10 million euros in investable assets, excluding their primary home. Their combined wealth came to more than 67 billion euros, the report concluded. By 2006, four Irish tycoons made the *Forbes* list of the world's richest men: Fermanagh-based businessman Sean Quinn, with a fortune of $2.5 billion; Dublin-based John Dorrance, with a fortune of $2.7 billion; Independent News and Media Chairman Tony O'Reilly, with $1.4 billion; and financier Dermot Desmond, with a fortune of $1 billion.

It was a new, wealthy elite, something that Ireland hadn't experienced before. Ireland wasn't used to Donald Trump–style bling or extravagance. But as the boom gathered steam, they were getting familiar with it. A country of starving artists, rural farmers, and migrant building workers was now associated with mega-rich multimillionaires.

So what had changed? The Irish had got a lot of things right. After winning its independence from Britain, the new Republic had embarked on a 50-year experiment in the kind of state-dominated quasi-socialism that was popular with much of Europe's intellectual elite for most of the postwar period. Taxes were high, the state spent heavily, and markets were tightly regulated. The young, ambitious Irish took a look at their prospects of making their careers in Dublin, decided they weren't much good, and tried their luck in London or New York instead. But from the early 1990s onward, the Irish embarked on a radical experiment in free-market, pro-business economics. While Mrs. Thatcher, British prime minister during the 1980s, may have been, along with U.S. President Ronald Reagan, the most famous exponent of supply-side economics, the Irish in the decade that followed came up with the real deal.

Ireland had joined what was then still the European Economic Community in 1973, at the same time as Britain. It had received some help from the Common Agricultural Policy, which siphoned off community funds to help farmers, of which Ireland had plenty. And as one of the poorest states within the community at the time it joined, it received help from the EU's structural funds. Plenty of new roads were built with money from the European Union. But, whatever its critics might say, Brussels has never been a great source of cash. It simply doesn't have the central budgets available to lift up a whole country. And as the 1970s turned into the 1980s, the Irish realized they couldn't look to Europe to help them out. A younger generation of politicians and policymakers, untainted by the legacy of past battles with the British, were determined to pull up the country by its own bootstraps.

Under the coalition government that ruled from 1994 to 1997, Finance Minister Ruairi Quinn drove down state spending and taxes. Quinn might have been a Labour Party politician, on the left of the Irish political spectrum, but his father had been a successful car dealer and he knew a bit about how business worked, what allowed it to flourish, and what stopped it from working. Over his period in office, the overall tax burden for Ireland fell from 38 percent to 34 percent of GDP, or by 1.3 percentage points each year. It wasn't that difficult to achieve. Against a backdrop of an economy that was starting to grow, he held public spending steady, making sure it grew it a bit less than the overall economy every year. The overall government deficit of 2.1 percent of GDP in 1995 was turned into a surplus of 1.1 percent by 1997, and the overall total of outstanding government debt went down from 81 percent of GDP in 1995 to 63.6 percent in 1997.

But Quinn's most explosive move was a cut in the corporation tax rate. It was reduced to just 12.5 percent, less than half the standard rate charged on companies throughout the rest of Europe. Quinn had realized something pretty simple, although with powerful implications. Ireland wasn't, by itself, a great location for international companies looking for a base within the European Union. It had a few things going for it. The English language was a help: Most global executives speak some English. So, too, were the connections to the Irish

Diaspora, particularly in the United States: There were a lot of chief executive officers of S&P 500 companies with names like Kennedy or Fitzgerald or Doyle who would be more than happy to set up an office in the old country. There were some nice golf courses, which always helps get the Japanese on board.

But against that, it was a long way from the mainstream European markets. If you made stuff in Ireland, it was hard work to ship it to Portugal or Greece. And it wasn't an especially exciting place, certainly not in the 1980s and 1990s. Corporate wives in Seoul weren't going to get excited about the prospect of a five-year posting to Cork. On balance, sentimental factors don't play much of role in commercial decisions. They are made on the basis of transport costs, labor laws, and taxes. In the first 20 years of European Union membership, Ireland didn't see many big companies flocking to its shores. A few subsidies aside, it wasn't getting much out of its membership of the EU.

But once you added in the lowest corporate tax rate anyone had seen outside of a tax haven such as Monaco or Lichtenstein, suddenly all the calculations changed. Companies started moving to Ireland en mass. Corporations such as the computer manufacturer Dell placed their European headquarters in the country, bringing jobs and wealth to what had been largely agricultural regions. The impact on growth was immediate and dramatic. The year before Quinn became finance minister in 1993, Irish economic growth was 2.5 percent. By 1997, it had jumped to 10.3 percent.

Those were the kinds of rates that had previously been seen only by the emerging Asian economies such as South Korea and Taiwan. The Celtic Tiger, as it came to be known, had been created.

By the time the euro was created, the Irish had no doubts about giving up the Irish pound (or the "punt," as it was known locally). The link with the British pound had already been severed during the 1990s. The Irish were among the most enthusiastic pro-Europeans (although that started to change in 2001, when the country voted against the Nice Treaty). To most of the Irish, the European Union was about the modernization of their country. It allowed a small, independent state such as Ireland to find a place in the world, and gave the Irish a stage that allowed them to emerge from the shadow of Britain. There was nothing not to like about that—and they swapped their Irish punts for euros enthusiastically.

But the euro was not to work out the way most people thought it would. The new currency took an economy that was already growing fast and put rocket fuel into its tanks. The results were to prove catastrophic.

Ireland had no problem hitting the convergence criteria for monetary union. Its public finances were in great shape, inflation was under control, and the economy was growing strongly. But Ireland had lost the ability to set its own interest rates. Economic policy was now set not in Dublin, but in Frankfurt. Ireland was a small country a long way away from the rest of the Europe, and policymakers in the German financial center could hardly be expected to have house prices in Donegal uppermost in their minds when it came to making decisions that would impact an economy of more than 300 million people.

The result was that interest rates started to come down dramatically, to far lower levels than an independent central bank would have set. And hot money started to flood into the country.

In fact, rather like Spain, Ireland was about to embark on a massive debt-fueled party. According to McKinsey figures, Ireland's total debt relative to GDP more than doubled from 2001 to 2008, to more than 700 percent of GDP. Put that another way, and for every euro of wealth that Ireland created, it owed seven euros. Financial sector debt accounted for more than half of that, at 410 percent of GDP. All that money flooding into the country had created a massive, though artificial, property boom. By 2008, real estate accounted for 61 percent of Ireland's outstanding credit.[5]

The crash, when it came, and as it inevitably would, was always going to be horrific.

■ ■ ■

David McWilliams started his career with Ireland's central bank, but quickly found that he was so good at explaining the Irish economic miracle to global investors that he was hired by UBS and BNP Paribas. He was right at the heart of the flood of money that poured into the country, before returning home to write about the bubble and becoming the closest thing that Ireland, or indeed the world, has to a celebrity economist.

In the summer of 2010, he turned his hand to comedy and theater, performing in a 90-minute monologue at Dublin's Abbey Theatre. McWilliams's rather unlikely standup routine was in fact a brilliant exposition of how the economics of the euro worked out in practice.

Essentially, Irish banks borrowed from Germans—personified by McWilliams as "Gunter," the careful BMW accountant whose only eccentricity is an annual visit to a nudist colony in Croatia. The banks fed Gunter's cash to the Irish, who used it to build, buy, and sell property to each other, buy worthless apartments in Bulgaria, and send their children to private crèches with names like "Little Harvard." Now Gunter wants his money back, and Ireland can't pay.

It got a lot of laughs in performance, partly because like all good comedy, it contained a hard kernel of truth. In a very simple form, that is precisely what happened. In Spain, Ireland, Greece, Portugal, and, to a lesser extent, Italy, money was shipped out of the big northern European economies and directed toward the peripheral economies.

Greece, perhaps surprisingly, didn't have nearly such massive total debts as either Spain or Ireland. Total indebtedness stood at only 230 percent of GDP by 2008, according to McKinsey. But in many ways, that simply reflected the relative backwardness of the economy. Greece didn't have the kind of hard-sell financial services industry that could load up ordinary people with credit cards and mortgages. What it had was a government that went out and borrowed money, then spent it on behalf of the ordinary people, mainly by hiring them to do non-existent jobs. Greek government debt amounted over 100 percent of GDP by 2008, almost half the country's total debts (and that assumes you believe the published figures, which of course you shouldn't).

The more sophisticated the economy, the more hot money started to flow into it. To start with, it worked out pretty well. Interest rates across the euro-zone converged on a single rate set by the European Central Bank. The bond markets were happy to play along, and so were the banks. They pretended that the Greek government, a property developer in Malaga, and an industrialist in Cork were all as solid and reliable to lend money to as an old-established engineering firm in Düsseldorf.

But, of course, it was never really true. It was fantasy economics, creating fantasy prosperity.

As the years passed, ever-more extravagant debts were built up. One way of illustrating that was the trade balances between different countries. While Germany ran huge surpluses—often amounting to 13 billion euros a month or more—the Club Med countries were running bigger and bigger deficits.

Greek exports were merely around a third of its exports every month. The country wasn't even beginning to pay its way. The Spanish trade deficit, as we have already seen, at the peak of the bubble was running at more than 10 percent of GDP. In effect, the Spanish were consuming 10 percent more than they produced every year and financing that extravagance by borrowing money from Germany.

On the surface, as we saw in the previous chapter, the first decade of the euro had, by most conventional measures, been a resounding success. Inflation was steady, the currency was accepted everywhere, and there was growth, even if there was a lot more evidence of it around the euro-zone's periphery than within its core.

But appearances are always deceptive, and nowhere more so than in economics. It was a like a beautifully refurbished house. It looked terrific. But if you got a surveyor to check the foundations, the results were not always encouraging.

The euro-zone was becoming dangerously unbalanced. The core countries—Germany, France, Belgium, and the Netherlands—had relatively slow growth and low inflation. Prices rose far faster in the peripheral countries. In Ireland, for example, prices between 2000 and 2007 rose by 10 percentage points more than they did in the euro-zone as a whole, according to figures published by the London-based Centre for Economic Policy Research. In Greece, the figure was eight percentage points, and for Spain it was seven points. In Germany and Austria, however, inflation was four percentage points lower over the same period.[6]

Those figures might seem arcane, but they were in truth very important. Inflation is the main determinant of real interest rates. So, for example, if the ECB set rates at 4 percent, and your country had an inflation rate of 4 percent, then the real interest rate you were paying was zero. Since the peripheral euro-zone countries had far higher inflation rates than the core nations, they also had far lower real interest rates. In countries such as Ireland and Spain, money was, in effect, free. It wasn't some kind of strange coincidence that people borrowed huge sums of money and property prices soared into the stratosphere. It was a direct result of the euro and the policies of the European Central Bank. And it was the direct result of trying to shoehorn economies that had very little in common into the same monetary system.

The big differences in growth and inflation rates explained the huge trap gaps that opened up between the euro-zone countries. And those trade balances were evened out between countries through the banking system.

According to calculations by the Centre for Economic Policy Research, between 2000 and 2007, Portugal racked up a cumulative trade deficit equivalent to 71 percent of GDP. For Greece the figure was 67 percent and for Spain it was 46 percent. By contrast, for Germany over the same period the cumulative surplus was 26 percent. For the Netherlands it was 45 percent and for Finland it was 50 percent. In effect what was happening was that some countries were consuming much less than they produced (the colder places, as it happened), while others (mostly the hotter ones) were consuming a lot more stuff than they got around to making themselves.[7]

You could see that most clearly by looking at the composition of the German trade surplus. After the single currency was introduced, German exports to the rest of the euro-zone, and to the Club Med countries in particular, started to soar. German exports within the euro-zone doubled between the adoption of the euro in 1999 and the end of 2009—German exports to Italy have risen by three quarters and German exports to Greece have gone up by more than 130 percent—so that 40 percent of Germany's exports now go to its European partners.

Everything has to be paid for. And the way that the deficit countries paid for all the things they were buying from the surplus countries was by borrowing money through the banks. The result was that the financial system turned into a way of shuffling vast sums of money through the euro-zone. In Ireland, bank assets as percentage of GDP soared from 360 percent in 2001 to 705 percent in 2007. That was the most extreme example, but in just about every euro country, the banking system was growing rapidly as the economy struggled to cope with the imbalances the euro had created. For France, the bank assets as a percentage of GDP went from 229 percent in 2001 to 373 percent in 2007, in Italy the ration went from 148 to 220 percent, and in Spain from 177 to 280 percent.

"This created fragility and interconnectedness so massive that it became a macroeconomic problem when the global crisis hit in late 2008," Richard Baldwin and Daniel Gros argued in a paper for the Centre for Economic Policy Research published in 2010.[8]

Indeed it did. For all the appearances of stability, the euro-zone had in reality become dangerously volatile. Money was flowing wildly through the system and massive debts were being built up everywhere. In their classic book on the Watergate scandal, *All the President's Men*, American investigative journalists Carl Bernstein and Bob Woodward described how their source inside Richard Nixon's White House kept telling them to "follow the money." If you followed the money through the euro-zone, it became dangerously clear just how fragile the system had become. Statistics published by the Bank for International Settlements, the most reliable source of how money flows around the financial system, looked at how banks in the core of Europe (defined as Germany, France, Austria, Belgium, and the Netherlands) increased their exposure to the nations on the periphery (Greece, Ireland, Spain, Portugal, and Italy) over the first decade of the euro's existence. The numbers are striking. Their exposure to Spain increased by 550 percent; to Greece by 449 percent; to Ireland by 481 percent; and to Portugal by 320 percent.

The euro was in effect a massive scheme for recycling money from the core of Europe out to its periphery. Some amazing fortunes were created in the process. Lots of property developers made a lot of money and so did plenty of bankers. But the euro, at least in the Club Med countries, had also become a game of "Monopoly" turned into real life. It was paper, pretend money, in which properties changed hands for extravagant sums of money.

For a time, everyone was enjoying the fun. But it was never going to be sustainable in the medium term. At some point the party would have to come to an end. The euro had turned half the continent into creditors, the other half into speculators. The banks were playing middlemen, collecting extravagant fees, and racking up enormous debts on their balance sheets that were sustained only by the absurd valuations put onto property assets at the height of the bubble. The jackhammers and cement mixers were working nonstop to keep the illusion going. And yet the whole edifice was about as stable as a toddler on ice skates.

And it was in Athens that the debts started falling due.

Chapter 4

The Story of the Swabian Housewife

In December 2008, German Chancellor Angela Merkel traveled to Swabia, a province in the south of Germany, to give an address to her governing Christian Democrat Party. She was speaking in the immediate wake of the credit crunch. The investment bank Lehman Brothers had just collapsed in the United States. In its wake, the world's financial system had been shaken to its foundations. Over a few nervous, dramatic weeks, banks were collapsing by the day and governments around the world had been forced to throw billions at them in a desperate effort to keep their economies from simply freezing up.

But while other leaders talked up big government, and boasted about the way they were saving the global economy from ruin, Merkel had a different message for the party faithful who had gathered in Stuttgart that day. She talked of the *Verantwortung*, which is the German word for "responsibility." "As we are in Stuttgart, you should ask a Swabian housewife," Merkel told her audience, as she argued through the response of her government to a financial crisis that had hit the German banking industry almost as hard as the American or the British. "She would give us some short and correct advice, which would be this: 'You cannot live beyond your means in the long run.' We are not going to participate in this senseless race for billions."[1]

By invoking the story of the Swabian housewife, Merkel knew exactly what she was doing. Conservative female politicians have always been good at playing the matriarchal housekeeper, carefully taking care of the family's money, balancing the books, and making sure all the children have food to eat and shoes on their feet even when times are hard. Margaret Thatcher used to pull precisely the same rhetorical trick when she was the leader of the British Conservative Party in the 1980s. It plays wells to a center-right audience, composed mostly of middle-class professionals, entrepreneurs, and businesspeople, who believe in the church and the family and who value self-reliance and responsibility above all other virtues.

But the story of the Swabian housewife also has a particular resonance within Germany. And by telling it, indeed celebrating it, Merkel was very definitely invoking a very different sort of Germany from the country that the rest of Europe had grown used to during most of the postwar period.

Swabia, although it is hardly internationally famous, has one of the richest cultural heritages in the whole of Europe. The Swabians were historically a Germanic tribe from the Baltic Sea, who moved steadily west during the collapse of the Roman Empire before settling in southwest Germany. The Duchy of Swabia gave rise to two of the great European dynasties, the Habsburgs, who dominated the Holy Roman Empire, and the Hohenzollerns, who went on to dominate much of central and eastern Europe, most notably Prussia. Another Swabian family, the Welfs, went on to control Hanover, from where they ended up taking control of the British Royal Family. The Swabians, in short, are not people to be messed with lightly.

Nor are they any slouches in culture, science, or industry. Leopold Mozart, father of the composer, came from Swabia. So did Albert Einstein. Gottlieb Daimler created the modern motorcar there, and went on to set up a company to manufacture the new contraption with his friend Karl Benz.

But, within Germany, the Swabians are known for something else as well. Every country has a region, or a minority, that it singles out to make fun of. They tell jokes about their meanness and stinginess. In Britain, it is the Scots. In Germany, it is the Swabians.

In "The Seven Swabians," a story by the Brothers Grimm, they are depicted as frugal, serious, and prudish. That is their reputation within the country. So when Angela Merkel started referring so explicitly to the story of the Swabian housewife, she was partly making a point about good-housekeeping and the need to count the pennies. But she was doing something more interesting as well. She was asserting a very German sense of cultural identity, and doing so in way that most Germans hadn't seen before.

In a way that may not have been immediately clear to foreigners, every German knew precisely what Chancellor Angela Merkel meant when she started using the story to discuss the demands for a bailout of the banking system in the wake of the credit crunch. We work hard, live within our means, and help ourselves, she was saying. We expect everyone else to do the same.

By end of the first decade of the new century, Germany was changing. Twenty years after the reunification of East and West Germany, and 65 years on from the end of World War II, it was staring to become a normal country again.

For decades, Germany had immersed itself within the European Union as a way of coming to terms with its violent history. It shied away from ever asserting any kind of national self-interest. But, below the surface, a different Germany was emerging. A generation was coming to power to which the war meant very little.

The assumption had always been that the mighty German economy would provide the money to pay the European Union's bills. But when the global financial crisis broke, the ordinary German was not prepared to pick up the tab. Many Germans had opposed the introduction of the euro, fearing that they would end up subsidizing what they saw as lazy Mediterraneans, and that it would turn into a weak, inflationary currency—precisely what Germany suffered from in the Weimar Republic and that led to the rise of Hitler and the Nazis. Now they could see that billions were being spent to prop up a broken financial system.

As the financial crisis unfolded, and as most counties bailed out their banks, Merkel was the only major world leader to question the prevailing wisdom. Certainly she was the only leader to question

whether the tidal wave of borrowed money that appeared to be engulfing the world for much of the past decade was not in fact the cause
of the crisis, and whether it could really be fixed by just borrowing
more and more. "Excessively cheap money in the U.S. was a driver of
today's crisis," she told the German parliament in November 2008.
"I am deeply concerned about whether we are now reinforcing this trend
through measures being adopted in the U.S. and elsewhere and whether
we could find ourselves in five years facing the exact same crisis."[2]

Over the next two years, those warnings were to prove pro-
phetic. And the worst fears of most ordinary Germans were about
to be realized. The bill for the bailouts, in Europe at any rate, would
end up being put on their tab. And as it turned out, they didn't like
it one bit.

■ ■ ■

The story of postwar Germany, and certainly the events leading
up to the crisis of the euro that broke in 2010, can't be told without understanding something about the Bundesbank and the unique
role that it plays in German life. Every country has a central bank,
but they are mostly technocratic institutions of interest only to a few
economists, bankers, and financial journalists. The Americans treat
the Federal Reserve with mild suspicion, the British regard the Bank
of England with amused detachment, and the French look upon the
Bank of France with indifference. But the Bundesbank is different. It
is the guardian of a conception of Germany. It is more like a flag or an
anthem or an ideal than a bank: something to be respected, defended,
even sometimes to be fought for.

Surprisingly, for an institution so revered, the Bundesbank is not
even particularly old, although it had powerful antecedents. The old,
fragmented states that came together to create a unified German state
in the 1870s all had their own currencies. The German monetary system was unified under the control of the Reichsbank, set up in 1876.
The Reichsbank was largely subservient to the government. Since
Germany was on the gold standard, that didn't matter a great deal:
The *goldmark*, the currency of the German empire up until World War
I, was a reasonably stable currency by the standards of the Victorian
world.

But the German insistence on independent central banks and stable money, which we view as such an important part of the country's character these days, was largely unknown prewar. It is a modern invention and the product of bitter experience.

In 1914, with the outbreak of World War I, the link with gold proved unsustainable, and the Reichsbank introduced the *papermark*, a new currency based on nothing very much apart from the promises of the government. It was, of course, catastrophic. Even during the War inflation was rampant, but as the country struggled with the consequences of defeat and the vast cost of reparations imposed on it by the Treaty of Versailles, the Reichsbank colluded in the wild printing of money that led to the great German hyperinflation of the 1920s. Prices rose 16-fold in a single year. The papermark gave way to the *rentenmark*, and then to the *reichsmark*, which remained the German currency right through the Nazi era. The Reichsbank was nominally independent, but in practice, once the Nazis came to power, it was completely subservient to the Fascist regime. In 1937, it was made subject to Hitler's personal instructions, and in 1939, six of its directors were dismissed for objecting to the amount of money the Führer was borrowing to finance the war.

It would be wrong, of course, to blame the Reichsbank for hyperinflation, the rise of Hitler, and the outbreak of World War II. The causes were many, varied, and complex. But it would be fair to say it had played a role, even if only a minor one. A stronger central bank would have exerted greater monetary discipline. Maybe it would have stopped inflation taking off the way that it did. And maybe then . . . ?

Historical what-ifs are always impossible to answer, even if they make amusing intellectual games. But it is safe to say that the Reichsbank was a disgraced institution, and the new West German state that emerged after World War II needed to establish a system of economic management that was very different from everything that had gone before.

Postwar Germany was a chaotic place, devastated by defeat and split into different zones under the control of the British, the French, the Americans, and, of course, the Russians. Shortages of everything and the shattered state of its industry made another spell of hyperinflation virtually inevitable. The reichsmark couldn't survive it. By 1948, the Allies in charge of the western half of the country had created a central bank, the Bank Deutscher Länder, which minted a new currency, the *deutschmark*. That in turn paved the way for the creation of the Bundesbank in 1957.

The Bundesbank was created amid an intellectual climate that was in many ways unique and that stood in stark contrast to the consensus prevailing among the global economic and political elite in the 1940s and 1950s. Germany's postwar economic miracle, which saw it recover from the obliteration of much of its industry, and the loss of millions of its young men, to overtake the rest of the Europe and to become its richest, most successful economy, remains one of the great social transformations of recent history. Some people explain it as resulting from the innate industriousness of the people, and there is some truth in that. A country full of Germans is always going to be a hardworking, efficient place: They don't know any other way of doing things. Others explain it through the massive transfers of cash the United States poured into the country under the Marshall Aid program. There is some truth in that as well, although lots of American cash doesn't always transform a country (take a look at Iraq, for example). But none of them quite explain the extent of the transformation.

In reality, the Germany postwar economic miracle was an intellectual triumph as much as anything else. Most of the postwar world was in thrall to a mixture of Keynesian demand management and state-dominated industrial planning. At every level the state was meant to guide the economy, setting the level of demand, picking the industries of the future, and working with the trade unions and companies to plan what was produced and where. Faith in a free market to regulate the way things were made, bought, and sold had been shattered by the Great Depression of the 1930s. Nobody wanted to go back to the economic slumps and mass unemployment that characterized the run-up to the war. The state was seen as the guarantor of prosperity.

Except in West Germany, that is. Germans had seen precisely what the corporatist state had looked like. In their country it was called National Socialism. And they weren't in any mood to go back to that. If there was one thing that postwar Germans craved it was stability, freedom, responsibility, and prosperity, and they would listen only to economists who could address those values.

A small group of German intellectuals, led by two great liberal economists, Walter Eucken and Wilhelm Ropke, had, with great courage, opposed the increased socialization and central planning of the Nazi economy and developed the ideas of what they described as *ordo-liberalism*. It emphasized monetary stability, free entry to markets, private property, and above all maintaining fierce competition between companies as the key to economic success. Inflation, as Eucken explained, not only undermined the savings of ordinary families, it distorted the price signals that were central to the way an efficient market economy worked. Most Anglo-Saxon economists in the 1950s thought inflation wasn't really a problem, certainly not if it was predictable and relatively stable. But the Germans could see that that was nonsense: Inflation, as the 1920s had taught them, was an insidious cancer undermining society from the inside.

Likewise, the Anglo-Saxon economic establishment thought that state-sponsored cartels would easily outperform a chaotic mess of small, family-owned companies. Competition was dismissed as wasteful, advertising as trivial, and there was a widespread expectation that the planned economies of Eastern Europe would keep pace with their western rivals, and probably outpace them. The economic advisers to the Allies' provisional government thought that the coterie of economic advisers surrounding the great postwar West German Chancellor Konrad Adenauer, who held power from 1949 to 1963, were mad at best and evil at worst. Lord Balogh, the most eminent of postwar British economists and an adviser to the 1960s Labour prime minister, Harold Wilson, dismissed Germany's postwar economic policies as nutty, and forecast that East Germany would race ahead while West Germany would collapse into chaos. It didn't happen, of course. Quite the reverse. It was East Germany that stagnated while West Germany became the most prosperous, innovative economy in Europe, a model that within 30 years everyone else was trying to figure out how to follow.

It wasn't achieved without a struggle, however. The first president of the Bank Deutscher Länder was Wilhelm Vocke, a stern, puritanical banker whom Adenauer once referred to as "an over-cooled icebox." His conception of the new currency he was creating for West Germany was crystal pure. "Our task is to defend and secure with

all means the trust which the deutschmark and the Bank Deutscher
Länder have been able to achieve," he wrote in a letter to the chancellor in 1949. Over the next 10 years, there were constant skir-
mishes between the Bundesbank and the government over the way it
was running economic policy. To many of the members of the federal government, based in the new postwar capital in Bonn, the Bank
was too deflationary in its approach: They harbored sympathies with
its Keynesian critics who argued it was too obsessed with controlling
inflation and wasn't doing enough to promote growth. Indeed, at one
point in the early 1950s, it was proposed to bring the central bank
under the control of the government, abandoning its independence.

Time, however, was to prove its critics wrong. As West Germany
grew richer and richer, the power of the bankers grew along with the
GDP numbers and the trade surplus. Germans who'd lived through
the terrible suffering of the War, who'd seen their country shattered,
occupied, and divided, who had cousins living in what was effectively
a Russian colony in the East, and who had wondered whether they
would ever be able to live with the shame of the Holocaust, could
suddenly afford to buy nice new cars, furnish their houses with smart
furniture, and take summer holidays in Spain and Greece.

It was more—much more—than they could have possibly hoped
for in 1945. And the Bundesbank was central to that miracle. It delivered a strong, stable currency, something that the Germans had never
reliably experienced before. Within the Bretton Woods system of
managed exchange rate that lasted up until 1971, the deutschmark was
a rock of stability. The British government had to devalue the pound
against the dollar, the French the franc, and the Italians, hardly surprisingly, devalued the lira many times. But the Bundesbank never had
to devalue the deutschmark. In fact, as Germany started to rebuild its
economy and started to rack up big trade surpluses, it had to revalue
it—that is, the deutschmark went up in value against the dollar while
most other European currencies went down.

After the Bretton Woods system collapsed, most of the industrial
world experienced terrifying levels of inflation. Prices in countries such
as Britain were racing ahead at 20 percent a year or more in the mid-
1970s. It was getting close to the level at which a nation tips over into
hyperinflation, and the monetary system, in effect, breaks down. But

not in Germany. Throughout the inflationary 1970s and early 1980s, the Bundesbank remained committed to a disciplined control of the money supply. The result? The German inflation rate was the lowest of any member of the Organisation for Economic Co-operation and Development: Germany's inflation rate averaged just 4.9 percent from 1970 to 1979, and only 2.1 percent from 1980 to 1991. Relative to other countries that was an incredible performance. "During the turbulent 1970s and 1980s the Bundesbank established an outstanding reputation in the world of central banking. Germany achieved a high degree of domestic stability and provided safe haven for investors in times of turmoil in the international financial system," concluded a European Central Bank working paper on the success of the Bundesbank and the lessons it held for its Frankfurt-based successor.[3]

Indeed it did. It is worth dwelling on some of the figures. If you take the whole period from 1960 to 1998, the deutschmark had retained about 30 percent of its original value, compared with less than 20 percent for the U.S. dollar, the Canadian dollar, and the Japanese yen, about 13 percent for the French franc, about 8.5 percent for the British pound, and merely about 6 percent for the Italian lira, according to ECB statistics. The deutschmark was without question the world's most stable and successful currency for the bulk of the postwar period. In turn it had helped create what looked to be, by the close of the century, the world's most stable, secure, and prosperous economy.

There was no coincidence about that. As the founders of the *Wirtschaftswunder,* as the miracle economy is referred to in Germany, had quite correctly seen, a stable currency was not somehow the product of a successful economy: It was a foundation of it. Get the currency in good shape and the economy would come good as well. But get the currency wrong and there was little chance of the economy ever prospering. Indeed it might not even survive.

It is important to be aware of this very precise point. German views on economics, certainly since the end of World War II, have stood apart from the rest of the world (as well as from prewar Germany, of course). They have developed a very different intellectual tradition and found a very different way of building an economy. And, as hardly needs to be pointed out, they have been proved more often right than wrong.

The Bundesbank is part of that tradition and key to it. And its strength as an institution is derived from its position in German life and from its success in helping to create a Germany that is an infinitely happier, more successful, more contented place than anything that existed before. "I believe, however, that the extent of the powers of the Bundesbank does not depend primarily on this constitutional independence, but more fundamentally on the widespread respect and support afforded by the electorate," noted the British economist Sir Alan Walters, an adviser to Margaret Thatcher, in an essay published in the American quarterly journal *The National Interest* in 1994. "Germans appreciate that the Bundesbank defends their precious deutschmark and woe betide politicians who try to subvert this sacred trust."[4]

■ ■ ■

Given that legacy, it was hardly surprising that not everyone in Germany was happy about giving up the deutschmark and stripping the revered Bundesbank of its most fundamental powers. It is one thing to abandon a failed currency like the lira or the drachma. It is quite another to give up the most successful currency in the world.

On January 12, 1998, with the foundation of the new currency being put in place, four professors made a trip to Karlsruhe, a small city southwestern Germany, which is where the constitutional court for the German Republic sits. Wilhelm Hankel, Joachim Starbatty, and Wilhelm Nölling, all economists, had joined forces with constitutional legal expert Karl Albrecht Schachtschneider to mount a legal challenge to the euro. Over the course of a 352-page brief, the four men argued that the euro could not remain stable, because the economies of the participating countries were too different and the control mechanisms for the new currency were too weak. This would jeopardize German price stability and affluence. Over time, a monetary union would lead to a political union, ending German independence. It was, in short, unconstitutional.

The court didn't agree. The four professors were dismissed as fringe extremists. The former chancellor, Helmut Schmidt, described them in the influential news magazine *Die Spiegel* as "idiot savants with no sense of history." Later on one of the professors, Wilhelm Hankel, would describe the reaction the lawsuit received in the same magazine. "We were the Antichrists," he recalled.[5]

True, they were kicked around by the political and economic establishment. Most of the German elite had bought into the euro project 100 percent. The one weakness of the Teutonic mind, alongside its formidable strengths, is its lack of flexibility. Once Germany sets out on a course, it sticks with it, even when it becomes painfully clear that the consequences of its actions are likely to be catastrophic. The four professors may not have won their case, but they received huge publicity within Germany. They had touched a nerve, not with the elite, but among the ordinary people. Most Germans were wedded to their deutschmark in a way that other countries find hard to understand. They were embarking on a currency union, not with optimism, not even with hope, but with what could best be described as a grudging acceptance. It might be inevitable, but, rather like having a wisdom tooth removed, that didn't mean you were going to enjoy it.

The professors were in fact putting down a marker, and one that was of great significance. They were insisting that there was a German national interest that was quite separate and distinct from a European interest. That might seem a very everyday thought to most people in most other countries. It wouldn't strike anyone in France or Britain as at all odd. Indeed, it would seem completely obvious. But in Germany in 1998, it was still very much a minority, eccentric view.

As we shall see, however, it was a view that was to grow in strength over the next decade. And it was to explode once the Greek crisis erupted, with results that were to be shattering for the future of the single currency of which Germany was the most important member.

■ ■ ■

One of the most illuminating explanations of the way that Germany has changed as a nation over the past decade has been made by Jürgen Habermas. A sociologist and philosopher, Habermas is an influential intellectual in a country that takes its philosophy seriously. He was extraordinary professor of philosophy at the University of Heidelberg before taking up the chair of philosophy and sociology at the Johann Wolfgang Goethe University, Frankfurt, and his many awards include the Gottfried Wilhelm Leibniz Prize of the German Research

Foundation, the highest honor awarded in German academic life. Born near Düsseldorf in 1929, he came of age in postwar Germany and is one of the few German philosophers to grapple openly and honestly with the way that his country has come to terms with the legacy of World War II, Nazism, and the Holocaust. As his *Stanford Encyclopaedia of Philosophy* entry notes: "The Nuremberg Trials were a key formative moment that brought home to him the depth of Germany's moral and political failure under National Socialism."

In an article for the British newspaper, *The Guardian*, he described how a whole generation of German politicians and intellectuals had been willing to bury their national self-interest in the wider European project. "After the Holocaust, it took decades of concerted efforts— from Adenauer and Heinemann through to Brandt and Helmut Schmidt to Weizsäcker and Kohl—to bring the Federal Republic of Germany back into the fold of civilized nations," he noted.[6] This was, as he notes, far from an elite project. While the ordinary German still drank beer, and ate sausages, and flew the black, red, and gold flag with patriotic enthusiasm during every soccer World Cup, this genuinely was a country in which mainstream popular opinion had abandoned nationalism in a way that no other country had. There were no votes in tub-thumbing German nationalism, nor were there any newspaper sales, for the simple reason that it had no popular support.

"Within the constellation following the Second World War, the cautious pursuit of European unification was in the country's interests because it wanted to return to the fold of civilised nations in the wake of the Holocaust," Habermas remarked in an interview with the *Financial Times* published in early 2010.[7]

And yet slowly, in the wake of reunification, all that started to change. "The current German elites are enjoying the return to normality as a nation-state," argued Habermas in his article for *The Guardian*.

Having reached the end of a "long path to the west," they are certified democrats and can once again be "just like the others." What has disappeared is the anxiousness of a people, who were also defeated morally and compelled to engage in self-criticism, to find their bearings in the post-national constellation. The solipsistic mindset of this self-absorbed colossus in the middle of Europe can no longer even guarantee that the unstable status quo in the EU will be preserved.[8]

The analysis—and it was a hard one to disagree with—was that Germany had thrown off its postwar guilt. It had become "normal" again. To someone of Habermas's generation, that was something to be regretted. They had taken pride in creating a country that had in many ways moved on from the idea of a national self-interest. There was a strain of idealism in that position that it is hard not sympathize with. After all, the world would be an easier place to organize if nations weren't always selfishly putting their own aims and ambitions first. It would probably be better run as well.

And yet there was always something slightly odd about the way Germany refused to champion its own interests. It was born not just out of an enlightened sense of the global rather than the purely national interest, but rather out of a sense of shame. It was a way of atoning for a terrible past. And it would hardly be healthy or normal for that to last forever.

And in truth it wasn't going to make much difference whether it was a trend you welcomed or regretted. It was quite clearly happening. The only really relevant question was where it took you.

■ ■ ■

In Germany, debates about fiscal policy aren't really about accountancy or economics the way they are in most countries. They are fundamentally about character. And they are about moral choices.

"While U.S. policymakers like to focus on short-term corrective measures," wrote German Finance Minister Wolfgang Schäuble during the height of the Greek crisis, "we take the longer view and are therefore more preoccupied with the implications of excessive deficits and the dangers of high inflation. . . . This aversion, which has its roots in German history, may appear peculiar to our American friends, whose economic culture is in part shaped by deflationary episodes. Yet these fears are among the most potent factors influencing consumption and savings rates in our country."[9]

It was a good point, well made. By the close of the decade, when Greek profligacy was about to turn into a major crisis for the euro and the European Union, Germany had changed decisively.

For most of the postwar period, Germans had been happy to bury their national interests within the wider European project. The historical burden of two world wars, Nazism, and the Holocaust was too much for most ordinary Germans to bear. It is no coincidence that the word *angst* is a German one. Even at the best of times, they are a people wrapped up in introspection, often slightly gloomy, and with a culture that, however brilliant, is long on soul-searching and short on jokes. Europe was a way of escaping that, of disowning any form of German nationalism. French politicians stood up for France, and Italian ones stood up for Italy, but German politicians didn't ever stand up for Germany. It just wasn't the kind of thing they wanted to do. The language had been lost, and, even if they could find it again, the generation born during the war wouldn't feel comfortable with it.

Slowly, however, all that was fading into historical memory. There was, after all, no better behaved country than West Germany. If you were looking for an exemplar of the modern, liberal, prosperous nation-state, it was the best candidate you could find. As the decades passed, Germans were taking pride in their country again. The soccer World Cup, held in the country in 2006, was one example. Germans started flying the black, red, and gold flag again in a way their parents never would have done.

Angela Merkel, the Christian Democrat chancellor who came to power in 2005, personified that in her own life story. She was a product of the country's reunification, rather than the war and its division. The war was already over for nine years when she was born. Merkel had grown up in Eastern Germany and hadn't even had the chance to get involved in conservative politics until the Berlin Wall collapsed in 1989. Her own story emphasized a very different kind of narrative about Germany: a country that had overcome hardship and division, that had reinvented itself and stripped away the aggressive Prussian militarism that had so disfigured its past and replaced it with a far kinder, gentler version of itself. It had come out of 50 years of therapy and was starting to feel good about itself again. And why not? There was, after all, much to feel good about. German companies had conquered the world with their brilliant engineering, its filmmakers and designers were the equal of any in the world, and its scientists were among the most accomplished.

In short, Germany was just another country again, with its own interests and ambitions, just like all the other nations that make up the European Union and that had pooled their currencies into the euro.

It was, however, also a country with its own take on the world. As we have seen, in economics in particular, Germany had always stood outside the global consensus. When the rest of the world was embracing Keynesian demand management, Germany remained committed to sound money and free competition. In the 1980s, while the rest of the world swung toward deregulation and privatization, Germany again stood outside the consensus. It privatized and deregulated in some measure, but maintained its social market model, resisting the move toward financial market–led capitalism. The Germans are as keen on conspicuous, flashy consumption as the next country—the roads are full of great big Mercedes and BMWs—but they don't borrow money and they hardly even bother with credit cards. While the rest of the developed world went on a massive consumer-led, debt-fueled spending spree, Germany stood apart, nurturing its own science- and engineering-based export industries. And while the hedge funds, private equity houses, and investment banks started to dominate the Anglo-Saxon economies, they were dismissed in Germany as froth and trivia—nothing more than gamblers who were irrelevant to the serious business of making things that people actually wanted to buy.

That was clear in the statistics for debt—which stood in stark contrast to the Club Med countries. According to McKinsey, the combined growth of corporate, consumer, and government debt from 2000 to 2008 in Germany grew by 7 percent over the whole eight years, compared with 157 percent in the UK, 150 percent in Spain, and 70 percent in the United States.[10]

The result was a Germany that, while as hard hit by the collapse in trade that followed the credit crunch as any country in the world, still emerged with an economy that fundamentally was in pretty good shape. It was the second-largest exporter in the world, just behind China (and with the big difference that while China exports mainly cheap consumer goods made by armies of poorly paid, low-skilled workers, the Germans mostly export high-end, expensive capital goods made by highly paid workers). The industrial revolutions of Brazil, Russia, India, and China, the BRIC nations on which financial commentators dwell so much, are based on German machinery. As they grow, so do the armies of German engineering companies that sell them the equipment to build their factories.

Just as it had in the 1950s, Germany had taken its own path in the first decade of the twenty-first century and made it work brilliantly. So it should be no great surprise that the nation of 2010 was not just feeling okay about asserting its own national interest again. It was feeling self-confident about its own take on economics.

There was a problem with this new "normal, self-confident Germany," however. In a sense, the European Union had always been built around the idea of an "odd, self-effacing Germany." One take on the creation of the EU—and in fairness there are quite a few, so we have to tread cautiously here—is that the Union is a way of solving what many historians have described as "the German question." Ever since the unification of the German states into a single nation in the 1870s, Germany had always been the preponderant power in Europe. With 80 million people, it is bigger than France and Britain and Italy. And, as a result of its natural industriousness, it tends to be richer as well. Therefore, it has always been very hard to fit Germany into a peaceful system of European nations. Two world wars were the catastrophic consequence of that problem. The EU, fairly obviously, was a far better solution than constant warfare between the major states of Europe. In effect, the German state was dissolved within a larger European federal union. All of a sudden, the issue of an over-mighty Germany ceased to exist.

It is a reasonable analysis, and one with much to be said for it. It rested, though, on the Germans accepting that they had little right to assert their own self-interest and should be happy enough to dissolve their country into a wider political and economic bloc. For a time, for reasons we have already explored, they were happy enough to do that. The legacy of war made nationhood an uncomfortable idea for most Germans. And, for much of the 1990s, Germany was willing to accept compromises in exchange for the reunification of the country following the fall of the Berlin Wall. Indeed one take on the euro is that the Christian Democrat chancellor at the time, Helmut Kohl, only accepted French President Francois Mitterrand's plan for a single currency as a direct quid pro quo for the French accepting that East Germany be incorporated into a newly unified German state.

That may or may not be true. The important point is this: The European Union is critically dependent on Germany accepting what on the surface looks like a pretty unfair deal. For a small country such as Ireland and Belgium, the EU gives you a chance to immediately take a step up in the world. No one really cares what the Belgian foreign minister thinks about anything. The foreign affairs spokesman of the European Union is a different matter: If a Belgian politician can grab that post, they are taking a big step up in the world. Trading away your autonomy doesn't matter very much when you aren't very important anyway. But Germany by itself would be a major player in world affairs even if the EU didn't exist. The country loses as much as it gains from pooling its sovereignty—and arguably more.

Worse, it has to pay the bills as well. Of a total European Union budget of 105 billion euros, Germany contributes 21 percent of the money, a long way ahead of the next biggest contributor, France, which chips in 16 percent. But it is the net contribution figure that is really interesting. Fairly obviously, Germany has the biggest economy in the EU, so it is always going to have to pay more money in than anyone else. But it also gets much less money out. Only 11.4 percent of EU expenditure is devoted to Germany, according to Eurostat figures, significantly less than France and roughly the same as Italy, which is, of course, a much smaller country. The net result is that by far the largest net contributor to the EU's funds is Germany.

In short, it pays the bills for the EU. Insofar as money is redistributed around Europe by the bureaucracy in Brussels, it is transferred out of Germany and toward other places.

And the complacent assumption of much of the European economic and political elite was that Germany would always, in the end, pick up the tab. It might groan and mumble, but some more euros would always be found from somewhere to keep everything ticking over.

But a more "normal" Germany, one that didn't feel guilty about the war anymore, was always going to start asking questions about whether it needed to subsidize the rest of the European Union for all eternity. And those questions were always going to be very difficult to answer.

After all, Germany has always fundamentally believed in a very different set of values. And, as we have seen, it had always had its own very unique take on the way an economy should be organized.

As the Greek crisis started to unfold, all those factors were to come together to make the Germans pathologically opposed to the bailout of the Greek economy, even if it meant the collapse of the euro itself. The values of the Swabian housewife—frugality, thrift, responsibility, and self-reliance—had worked out pretty well for the Germans. They were pleased with the results: To Germans it seemed they were better economically and better morally as well. They weren't going to be shy anymore about suggesting the rest of the world might think about giving them a try.

Starting, as it happened, with the country that should never really have been in the euro in the first place.

Chapter 5

Fixing a Debt Crisis with Debt

On April 2, 2009, the leaders of the Group of 20 (G-20) industrial nations descended on London for a summit designed to discuss, debate, and, who knows, perhaps even fix the crisis that was engulfing the global economy in the early part of this year. British Prime Minister Gordon Brown had ensured that, despite the straightened financial circumstances in which his country suddenly found itself, no expense was spared. This was to be the first major foray that the exciting, dynamic new U.S. President Barack Obama had made into global summitry, and it was a coup for Brown to have made sure London was the venue.

The talks themselves were held at the Excel Centre in London's Docklands, a rather dull and soulless exhibition center. The kind of place you'd expect to find a trade conference on printer ink or building supplies, it was at least big enough to house the hundreds of politicians, advisers, officials, journalists, and security guards that would be attending the event.

The Queen welcomed the world leaders to the British capital with her usual good grace, and polite, if slightly reserved, small talk. President Obama and First Lady Michelle Obama visited Buckingham Palace for the first time. The Queen presented the First Couple with a silver-framed signed photograph of herself and the Duke of Edinburgh, her usual gift for heads of state, while they gave her an iPod: It is probably safe to say that both parties to that exchange were equally baffled by the choice of present. For the dinner, British celebrity chef Jamie Oliver had been drafted to prepare a menu that included organic salmon from the Shetland islands, followed by a slow-roasted shoulder of lamb from the Elwy Valley in North Wales, together with Jersey Royal roast potatoes and wild mushrooms, all followed by a traditional British favorite, Bakewell tart served with custard. J.K. Rowling, author of the Harry Potter stories, had been persuaded to come along as one of the celebrity guests, just in case some of the leaders in attendance wanted to talk about real wizardry rather than the political or financial sort.

But the meat of the summit wasn't the lamb served at the official dinner. Inside the conference center, Brown and Obama, together with sympathetic leaders such as France's President Nicolas Sarkozy, put together an agreement for a massive coordinated attempt to use the power of government spending to float the global economy off the financial rocks on which it appeared to be floundering.

The official communiqué took a couple of days to hammer out, but when it was finally published it was a hymn to the power of government to boost demand and stave off an economic depression. "It will get worse if people do not act," said Gordon Brown at a press conference in London opening the summit. "If people fail to take decisive action at the beginning you risk a longer recession. Governments are moving in where markets have failed and banks have collapsed."[1]

There was some resistance to the package being put together, most predictably from the Germans, but Obama was the crucial figure. Few world leaders wanted to stand up to the new U.S. president. He was a hugely popular figure globally, and he looked like he would be in power for a long time. There was little point in getting on the wrong side of him before he'd even got used to the job. And Obama, like Brown, believed that the government could spend its way out of this recession.

Outside, there were plenty of protestors. Thousands of demonstrators marched through the City of London toward the conference center. In total, 10,000 officers were put in place to cope with any violence, the biggest security operation London's Metropolitan Police had mounted since the coordinated al-Qaeda attack on the city in 2005. Inside, however, the mood was relaxed and peaceful despite the sometimes fierce debates. When an agreement was finally reached, the leaders of the G-20 agreed that they would boost their own economies with higher public spending, and that an extra $1 trillion would be made available to the International Monetary Fund to ride to the rescue of any country that might find itself in financial trouble.

"We are in the midst of the biggest fiscal boost that the world has ever had," Brown said at a joint press conference in London with President Obama. "The combination of all of this . . . is the most substantial fiscal stimulus, something on the order of $2 trillion. . . . It is remarkable this is happening."[2]

Everyone appeared to agree with that conclusion. "By any measure the London summit was historic," said Obama at the same news conference in London. "I have no doubt, though, that the steps that have been taken are critical to preventing us sliding into a depression."[3]

Well, maybe. The London summit, as it turned out, was to prove the high-water mark of fiscal activism. Leaders around the world had bought into the idea that a depression could be fought by massively boosting their own spending. The G-20 meeting in itself may not have achieved that—the G-20, itself, doesn't have any money to spend on anything. But it provided cover for leaders who were intent on spending their way out of the slump. They could go back home, explain that the whole world was following the same path, and hope to secure support for racking up public debts on a scale that had seldom been seen before.

But could it possibly work? There was little doubt that something needed to be done, and fast.

Six months earlier, the U.S. investment bank Lehman Brothers had collapsed. The credit crunch had in truth been building for more than a year. It started, strangely enough, not on Wall Street or in the City of London, but in Paris, in the summer of 2007. A hedge fund managed by the French bank BNP Paribas suddenly stopped redemptions by its investors. The problem? It couldn't get prices for many of the exotic, highly complex financial instruments the fund traded. Bits of paper that had been easy to trade one day no longer had any buyers, and if there weren't any buyers, you couldn't put a price on them. The European Central Bank stepped in to unfreeze the market, but, as 2007 turned into 2008, nothing seemed to work. In the financial markets, an atmosphere of mutual suspicion started to build up, as banks increasingly refused to trade with one another.

The markets contained the problem for the best part of 12 months, but by the autumn of 2008, the tensions were about to blow the whole system apart. First Bear Stearns went to the brink of bankruptcy. A rescue was mounted and, in March 2008, J.P. Morgan stepped in and rescued that troubled bank. That bought a bit more time. But when Lehman got into trouble at the end of a nervous summer, there were no rescuers left. U.S. Treasury Secretary Hank Paulson decided it was better to let the bank go under than rescue it with public money. After all, Lehman was not a retail bank, the deposits of ordinary savers were not at risk, and if the government stepped in to help a bunch of overpaid Wall Street traders every time they got into trouble, that was hardly going to look fair for everyone else.

That turned out in retrospect to be a huge mistake. The fall of Lehman provoked a catastrophic loss of confidence, creating what was in many ways the most dangerous moment for the developed economies since the Great Crash of 1929. An event that led to the worst depression in history and paved the way for World War II looked about to be repeated. As trust in the financial system evaporated, bank after bank went bust. It was like watching a wave of dominoes collapse, one falling after the other.

In America, nearly all the major banks needed some form of financial assistance from the government to stay afloat. Even the mighty Goldman Sachs, by far the most powerful of the Wall Street investment banks, had to transform itself into a deposit-taking institution to qualify for government backing if that proved necessary. Wall Street was suddenly dependent on Main Street to help it out.

In Britain, the Royal Bank of Scotland had expanded under its ambitious chief executive, Sir Fred Goodwin, to become one of the largest banks in the world. Even with the credit crunch underway, it had gone ahead with a crazily expensive deal to buy the Dutch bank ABN Amro. As the money ran out, it was effectively nationalized by the British government. So, too, was Lloyds, once the soundest of the British banks, but ruined by a calamitous merger with HBOS. Those were just the two biggest casualties. Plenty of smaller British banks were caught up in the crisis.

In Belgium, Fortis ran into trouble. In France, BNP Paribas needed help. In Germany, the government was forced to take stakes in Hypo Real Estate and Commerzbank. In Ireland, the government had to help out the Bank of Ireland and Allied Irish Bank. In Iceland, the government would have helped out its two main banks, Landsbanki and Kaupthing, if it could. Unfortunately, the money had already run out. In effect the whole country was already bust, forced into something close to national liquidation by the wild, reckless risk-taking of a small clique of well-connected speculators.

Around the world, governments were extending emergency credits to their financial sectors on an unprecedented scale. In the space of a few short months unprecedented sums of money were spent. A study by the Bank of England concluded that the cost of the rescue packages around the world came to a staggering £4,473 billion. It came to around 12 percent of the total global GDP, estimated at around $60,000 billion. Of that massive total, £395 billion was used to recapitalize banks and £397 billion was spent buying up their "toxic" assets. State guarantees to get the wholesale markets moving again cost another £2,927 billion, and another £754 billion had to be provided in loans and through bank nationalizations. It was without question the greatest coordinated government rescue effort ever mounted.

Nor was it to end there. If the credit crunch had merely been restricted to the banking industry, that would have been bad enough. But finance is more than just a profitable occupation for lots of sharp-suited young men in gleaming glass-and-steel skyscrapers. It is also the lifeblood of an economy. And the more globalized and interconnected an economy is, the more it needs lots of finance to keep it functioning successfully.

In the wake of the collapse of the banking system, global trade, and with it global manufacturing, suddenly fell off a cliff. In the final quarter of 2008, global trade dropped by 15 percent. It was the worst collapse in trade since the end of World War II. For a period, trade was collapsing as completely as it had during the Great Depression of the 1930s, and at a faster rate as well. Not just finance had evaporated; so, too, had confidence. No one wanted to sell anyone anything for fear of not getting paid, or indeed that the money would be worthless by the time it arrived. The financial system was starting to fall apart, and it was taking the global economy down with it.

Not surprisingly, by the start of 2009 that was starting to feed through to the GDP numbers. As trade collapsed, economies went into recession. The impact was sudden and brutal. For the first quarter of 2009, the annualized rate of decline in GDP was 14.4 percent in Germany, 15.2 percent in Japan, 7.4 percent in the UK, 9.8 percent in the euro-zone as a whole, and 6 percent for the United States. Again, those were the kind of numbers that economists hadn't seen since the start of the Great Depression. It was perfectly possible to believe that the world was on the brink of an unprecedented financial disaster.

The details of the credit crunch are already too well known to detain us for long here. Two points are important for our analysis: First, this was at heart a debt crisis. Second, and more importantly, governments chose to fix it with even more debt.

For years, all the developed economies had been surfing on a wave of debt-fueled expansion. The gradual relaxation of the financial markets of the course of the 1990s and 2000s had allowed banks and other intermediaries to find ever-more complex ways of lending more and more money to people, often with very little regard for whether they could ever pay it back.

There are lots of ways of illustrating that, but let's take just one example: the British credit card industry. It would be no exaggeration to describe the past two decades of relative prosperity in Britain as one long credit card splurge. Way back in 1992, according to Bank of England statistics, the British were borrowing around £2.8 billion a month on credit cards. By 2002, that had gone above £10 billion a month. It hit a peak in December 2008—one last Christmas splurge before the credit crunch hit, perhaps—when the British spent £12.1 billion of plastic money they didn't really have. Overall, the amount of debt owed on British credit cards had risen by 2010 to £54 billion.

Among Europeans, the British by 2010 had more credit cards in the average wallet than any other nation: 2.8 cards per adult, up from 2.4 in 2004. The Norwegians were second with 2.3, while the French, who still like cash, had just one. The cash for all those cards was provided by the international money markets. Millions of credit card debts were collected together, put into a great big bundle, and sold around the world. As of 2009, the six largest U.S. lenders, for example, had issued $375 billion of credit card bonds.

In the UK, two of the big ratings agencies, Moody's and Fitch, both track repayment rates on credit cards as part of the task of assigning ratings to all those bonds. The figures were, to put it mildly, the kind of thing to make Mr. MasterCard feel a bit queasy. In the United States, delinquency rates passed through the psychologically important 10 percent barrier early in 2009, and did the same in the UK. Moody's "charge-off index"—or what's known in plain English as not paying the money back—had "grown by 46.5 percent over the course of 2009, breaching the 10 percent mark for the first time since its inception in 2001," the agency concluded in an assessment published in 2009.

Even worse, Moody's forecast that with rising unemployment the index would pass 12.5 percent very soon and could well be "greater than 15 percent" before the recession ended. To put that in simple terms, 15 of every 100 pounds borrowed on credit cards wasn't going to be repaid. That's about £8 billion of the £54 outstanding.

It is worth dwelling on the details of that one example because the credit card industry was a microcosm of what was happening to a huge chunk of the global economy. Too much money was being borrowed by people who couldn't really afford it, and when there was a problem paying the money back, the money simply got written off.

Over many years, debt was seeping into every corner of the economy. Whether it was in credit cards, in mortgage lending to homeowners, by the private equity that loaded up companies with debts, or with listed companies that felt they had no choice but to "leverage" up their balance sheets so they could pay bigger dividends to their shareholders, by 2008 nearly all the main economies were drowning in debts. The economies had been turbocharged, using the power of debt to boost spending, increase their consumption, and, for a time, make everyone feel the economy was growing a lot faster than it really was. The financial system, allowed free rein to do pretty much whatever it wanted, had sliced and diced the debts, finding smarter and smarter ways to wrap up the borrowings that were being built up everywhere, put them inside new packages, and find new balance sheets to park them on. For a time, all the feverish motion disguised the grisly, unpleasant truth. Lots of money had been lent to people who couldn't really afford it and weren't ever likely to earn enough money to pay it back. It was a catastrophe in the making. The question was just how and when it would hit.

At root, that was what the credit crunch was all about: the realization that far more debt had been taken on than could ever realistically be repaid. And that someone somewhere—and you just had to hope it wasn't you—was going to lose a lot of money.

But when the crisis hit, governments felt they had no choice but to respond to it with even more debt.

There was a snag, however. Their balance sheets were not in any great shape to take the extra debt loads that were about to be placed on them.

■ ■ ■

In January 2009, President Obama kicked off his new presidency by tackling the economic crisis head-on. He announced a stimulus package worth an estimated $775 billion, one of the boldest attempts ever made by the U.S. government to kickstart an economy. It was a mix of tax cuts and big spending on infrastructure projects, including a plan to build high-speed trains, a novelty in a country where the automobile and the plane had long since taken over from the train as the preferred way of getting around.

In France, the government announced a stimulus package in February 2009 worth 26 billion euros. The plan was split into three parts: 11 billion euros to help businesses, 11 billion euros in direct state investment, and 4 billion euros of investment by state-owned firms, earmarked for modernizing the rail system, energy infrastructure, and the postal service. In Italy, a stimulus package worth 80 billion euros was announced, including 16.6 billion euros for infrastructure and 2.4 billion euros for low-income families. Measures to keep the banks afloat, speed up tax reimbursements, and help homeowners finance or refinance their mortgages were also thrown into the mix, along with a price freeze for utilities and motorways. In Spain, there was a 20 billion euro stimulus, including 2,000 euros from the government toward the cost of a new car for anyone who felt like buying one. In Greece, not very surprisingly, there was a 3 billion euro stimulus package for an economy that was already deeply in debt.

Even the Germans, abandoning their usual preference for fiscal caution, joined the global spending spree. In fact, Angela Merkel, despite all her protestations of responsibility, put in place the biggest spending program in Europe. An extra 82 billion euros was found to try and pump up an economy that had been particularly badly hit by the collapse in world trade. The government also made 100 billion euros available in credit and loan guarantees to German companies, including 25 billion euros in loans from KfW Group, the state-owned development bank.

It was a spending spree without precedent in peacetime. Government and central bank officials had been raised on textbooks that took the standard Keynesian line on the Great Depression of the 1930s. The slump that crucified both the European and U.S. economies had been blamed on a reigning fiscal and monetary orthodoxy that insisted governments should balance their books and rein in inflation, even in the face of collapsing demand and fast-rising unemployment. They were determined not to go down in the history books as the heirs of Herbert Hoover, the U.S. president widely blamed for creating the catastrophic slump of the 1930s, or indeed of Pierre Laval, the French prime minister of the 1930s who tried to cut wages in the face of an overwhelming economic downtown and wrecked the franc and the French economy in the process.

Whether there was really any comparison to be made between the fix the world economy found itself in during 2008 and 2009 and that of the 1930s was, to say the least, a debatable point. So much had changed in the way stuff got made, distributed, and financed in the intervening seven decades that there was good reason to suppose that there were in reality very few parallels. In early 2009, however, none of that mattered. The world's leaders and the economists and central bankers who advised them had bought into a narrative about the past, and the logic of that narrative told them to start spending, keep spending, and not stop spending until the global economy was safely through the recession.

No one had really stopped to ask what would happen if the money ran out.

■ ■ ■

The phrase *quantitative easing*, with which we all became so suddenly familiar by the end of 2008, was coined by the British economist

Richard Werner in 1995. He was working at the time as the chief economist of Jardine Fleming Securities in Tokyo, and came up with it to describe a novel policy being tried out by the Bank of Japan. Faced with the aftermath of a massive stock market and property bubble, the Bank had tried slashing interest rates but had already taken them about as low as they could go (for obvious reasons, you can't cut rates below zero). And it had tried conventional measures to increase the supply of money, but since the Japanese banking system was mostly bust, that didn't do much good either, because bankrupt banks won't lend money pretty much whatever the circumstances. So instead the Bank started intervening in the markets directly, buying up assets for which there would otherwise be no buyers.

Werner described that as "quantitative easing," and some-how or other the phrase took off. The Bank of Japan picked up on it and started using it in its own publications: It is known as *ryoteki kinyu kanwa* in Japanese. "There is a certain anodyne perfection to the phrase, quantitative easing, unlike anything else in the entire rather utilitarian financial or economic lexicon," recalled Werner much later, writing on "The Big Picture" website.

> It sounds wonderful, a functionally-useful tonic, though cer-tainly not dangerous or hazardous to our well-being. Yet it remains sufficiently innocuous so as to escape scrutiny and with it, the associated public examination that prying eyes bear. It is entirely Madison Avenue rather than inflated Goebbels-like propaganda.[4]

The point is well made. *Quantitative easing* sounds a lot better than *printing money*, or *creating inflation*, or some of the other ways that it might be described. It sounds even better in some other languages (although worse in others—the Swiss central bank, for example, trans-lated its version as "forceful relaxing," which is probably a contradic-tion in terms anywhere outside of the Bank's headquarters in Berne).

Whatever its origins, over 2008 and 2009, quantitative easing, or *QE* as it quickly became known to the news broadcasters, was all the rage among central bankers as the financial crisis unfolded. Interest rates were slashed to close to zero in all the major economies in a series of coordinated rate cuts after the collapse in global confidence started in the autumn of 2008. But it soon became clear that would not be enough to bring the global economy back to life. Just as in Japan, interest rates couldn't be cut any further, nor was the banking system in any shape to act as a transmission mechanism for increasing the supply of money. So instead central banks embarked on massive, direct interventions in the money markets, led most enthusiastically by the Federal Reserve in the United States and the Bank of England in the UK. The United States pumped $1 trillion into the U.S. economy through quantitative easing, and the Bank of England implemented a £200 billion program of asset purchases to kickstart its economy. But all the major central banks were embarked on the same course, even if some of them described it differently.

No doubt economics departments across all the main universities will be studying the experiment for years, debating whether it was effective. It will probably be years before we know for sure (and perhaps not even then—few debates in economics are ever definitively settled). In this story there are two important points about quantitative easing and the role it was to ultimately play in the sovereign debt crisis, and the near-collapse of the euro once Greece ran into difficulties.

The first was that it led governments into a false sense of security. Much of the money that was created by central banks in response to the crisis was spent on government bonds: In the UK, for example, the Bank of England spent virtually all the £200 billion it created on British government paper, known as *gilts*. In normal circumstances there are limits to what any government can borrow. It has to find investors to buy all the bonds it issues. If its finances get out of control, investors will start to get rattled. The prices of the debt will start to fall, and the rate of interest that has to be paid to find buyers for the paper will start to soar. In extreme cases, the bonds may quite literally become impossible to sell and the government in question will simply run out of money to pay its bills.

That is the disciplinary power of the bond market, and, over the years, governments have learned, usually through bitter experience, to treat it with respect. James Carville, President Bill Clinton's political guru, once said, "I used to think that if there was reincarnation, I wanted to come back as the president or the pope or as a .400 baseball hitter. But now I would like to come back as the bond market. You can intimidate everybody." That pretty much sums up the way bond investors were viewed by the political class. They were a scary force. Indeed, the economic policies of the Clinton administration had been reined in by the self-styled "bond vigilantes": hard-nosed money managers who took it upon themselves to save profligate governments from the consequences of their natural extravagance.

But once quantitative easing was underway, the bond vigilantes had lost their power. They were like tigers with their teeth extracted: They had no bite anymore. The central banks were buying all the government bonds. So who cared what those money managers thought?

In effect, the discipline on governments had been removed. They could spend just about whatever they wanted because the central banks were simply printing the money to finance their deficits.

Even more seriously, quantitative easing was to distort the financial markets, creating all kinds of perverse incentives. The way that finance ministers were fixing the credit crunch, was, ironically, paving the way for the next crisis, this time revolving around the euro and sovereign debt. To understand how and why, you have to get into some of the plumbing of how the global financial system works. This can at times be complex, even daunting to the non-specialist, but it is worth persevering because it illustrates how, in many ways, it was the fallout from the credit crunch that was to lead directly to the crisis in Greece, and may in time lead to the collapse of the euro.

In the wake of the credit crunch, the banks stopped lending to one another. They simply didn't trust each other anymore. They were well aware of how many crazy risks their own traders had taken on, and they suspected, almost certainly correctly, that the guys in the steel-and-glass skyscraper across the street had done deals that were just as bonkers as they had. It didn't make any sense to lend them money when they might well be bust by next Tuesday, taking your money down with them. The interbank market, the main source of liquidity in the financial system, ground to a halt.

In response, the central banks provided unlimited liquidity to the banks over which they had jurisdiction. They would, in extremis, lend them any amount of money they needed. In the United States and Britain, this moved on to the policy of quantitative easing: The

Federal Reserve and the Bank of England started buying financial assets from the banks directly in the market with money they had simply created on their computer screens. The European Central Bank, however, stopped short of that. It had too much of the old Bundesbank stamped into its DNA. Printing money was just not the kind of thing it did. German central bankers had tried that in the 1920s, and the results—World War II, the Holocaust—were scary enough to prevent them from repeating the experiment even several generations later.

Instead, the ECB printed money by the back door. It provided unlimited loans to the main European banks and allowed them to buy up assets instead. "With hindsight, the continuation and extension of passive QE postponed a solution of banks' solvency issues and even contributed to the sovereign debt crisis," argued Morgan Stanley in an analysis of the sovereign debt crisis published in June 2010.

> For the banks, virtually unlimited liquidity at 1 percent seemed like a panacea. Rather than raising capital more aggressively in the markets or through the various national TARP-like programmes that European governments had put in place, they were playing the carry game—borrow short from the central bank at near-zero interest rates and buy longer-dated, higher-yielding assets—hoping that this would restore profitability and thus allow them to generate capital internally over time.[5]

In effect what happened was this: A bank could borrow just about unlimited sums of money from the ECB, at a rate of around 1 percent. It could then use the money to, say, buy Greek government bonds, which paid interest at more than 4 percent. There was no risk to the trade, because the ECB at the time was prepared to accept the bonds of any euro-zone government as collateral for yet more loans. The difference between what the banks paid the ECB for the money and what the Greek government paid them for passing it on to them was in the region of 3 percent.

There is no activity that bankers are more skilled at than collecting a generous fee for acting as middlemen on an essentially risk-free trade. It is, to put it kindly, the purpose for which God put bankers on the planet. So long as the trade was there to be done, they would execute it. It was perfect. Free and easy money in unlimited quantities. Why should they resist?

The trouble was, it created a false sense of security. European banks were recovering, because all the easy money they were making on the trade of borrowing from the European Central Banks and passing the money onto governments was restoring balance sheets that had been ravaged by the credit crunch to something that looked like health. And, at the same time, governments were finding it very simple to finance their massive and ballooning deficits. "Financially, governments also benefitted from cheap and plentiful ECB liquidity," argued Morgan Stanley in the analysis referred to earlier.

> The artificially generated demand for higher-yielding government bonds kept bond yields for Greece and others lower than they would have otherwise been. This sent a message to governments that high fiscal deficits, which had swollen due to the recession and governments' responses to it, weren't a problem as the market (read: the banks) seemed willing and able to keep funding them.[6]

Precisely so. At one point, governments would have assumed, and quite rightly, that deficits in the region of 8 or 9 percent of GDP would have been simply unaffordable. The bond markets would have been in open revolt. There would be no buyers for the paper they were issuing. Currencies would have collapsed, and governments with them. But the "carry trade" meant all those issues were swept conveniently under the carpet. As deficits edged upward, the markets didn't murmur. The banks just kept on buying the bonds as if everything was okay. It was like drinking a fruit punch. You imagine you are just sipping fruit juice because you can't taste the vodka that has been mixed in with it. And then, at a certain point, you've drunk too much of the stuff and you are about to fall over.

Something similar was happening within the European monetary system. The problem was, what would happen if the ECB stopped injecting unlimited liquidity into the banking system? And what would happen if borrowing got so out of control, and the deficits so huge, that even markets lulled into a false sense of security started to take fright?

Those questions would be answered very soon. And the results were to prove far from comforting.

■ ■ ■

In the summer of 2010, the Bank for International Settlements published its annual report on the state of sovereign indebtedness. In stark detail it laid out the damage that had been done to the balance sheets of the major governments of the world in just a few short years. The cost of bailing out the financial system and then boosting demand in economies that were on the brink of depression had left all of them owing money on an unprecedented scale.

In 2007, before the credit crunch, the overall public debt of the advanced industrial economies stood at 76 percent of GDP. By 2011, it calculated, that would have risen past 100 percent. "And beyond 2011, many industrial countries face the large, rising pension and health costs associated with their ageing populations," the BIS report argued. "Unless tackled effectively and in a timely manner, such costs could lead to ever increasing deficits and debt levels."[7]

They certainly could. The last time public debt had exploded on anything like the same scale was during World War II, when public debt reached about 120 percent of GDP in the United States and 275 percent of GDP in the United Kingdom. There was a difference, however, and not just the rather obvious one that in World War II the British and U.S. governments had been engaged in the noble cause of defeating Nazism, and not just subsidizing bankers and making sure everyone could carry on buying flat-screen TVs on their credit card. The backdrop to the explosion of debt was a steady worsening in the state of public finances. Between 1970 and 2007, total public debt in the advanced economies had steadily risen from 40 to 76 percent of GDP. It had ratcheted upward relentlessly as political systems found it was far easier to spend money than go to the inconvenience of raising it. The harder a country was hit by the credit crunch, the worse its public debt was getting. So, for example, for the period from the end of 2007 to the end of 2011, the debt-to-GDP ratio is forecast by the BIS to rise by more than half in the United States and by four-fifths in Spain and to almost double in the United Kingdom and triple in Ireland. By any standards, those were scary numbers.

More troubling still, it came against a backdrop of a steadily worsening outlook for fiscal policy. In part that was related to the credit crunch itself. The tide of easy money that had been created in the 20 years leading up to the financial collapse had created a boom in financial services and construction. In many economies, and in the Club Med nations in particular, it often appeared as if the main form of economic activity was either building something or lending people money to build something. That had led to a big rise in tax revenues, since both financial services and property are fairly easy industries to tax (the bankers because they have so much money, and the property developer because you can't suddenly shift that new apartment block to the Cayman Islands at the flick of a few buttons). As those sectors collapsed, however, the tax revenues collapsed with them. With credit still in short supply, there was little reason to think that money would come back anytime soon. It was gone forever.

Not only were governments spending far more money than they had ever done before. They were also getting less in. It was not hard to see that as those two numbers moved in opposite directions the outlook for government deficits was hardly encouraging.

Even worse, the populations of all the major advanced economies were getting older. There is an old saying that economics is, in the end, just demographics, and there is considerable truth in that. The age profile of a nation has a huge impact on public finances. The more working-age people you have, obviously enough, the higher your tax revenues are going to be. And the fewer non-working-age people you have, the lower your expenditure will be. A huge proportion of government spending in modern democracies, which devote the bulk of state spending toward welfare systems, is taken up by babies and small children and old-age pensions. The children need support and education, and the old people need pensions and health care. More significantly still, in most European countries, pension systems aren't fully funded. The pensioners are not living off the income generated by investments they have made during their working lives. They are living off vague promises that they would be supported by the taxes of the younger generation in work, who would in turn be supported by the generation just below them. The maths of that system worked pretty well so long as populations were gradually expanding, as indeed they had been ever since the start of the industrial revolution. But if populations started to contract, or even just stagnate, the maths of that system didn't look so good after all. If that happened, suddenly there would be not so many young people supporting an ever-growing army of pensioners through higher and higher taxes. And that was going to be a terrible strain on the public finances.

And, as it happened, Europe was indeed getting much older, along with the rest of the advanced industrial economies. Two trends were coming together. One was that as traditional societies became more prosperous, and as women went out to work more, families kept getting smaller and smaller. Where once it had been common to have four or five children, now one or two was the norm. There was nothing very much anyone could do about that. The French, naturally horrified by the prospect of a world with fewer French people in it, had tried every kind of tax break and subsidy imaginable to get French mothers to produce more babies, but the rewards for their efforts had been marginal at best—the French birthrate was about the same as the British, whose government made no effort at all to encourage the birthrate. On top of that, of course, the second trend was that ever-improving health care meant people kept on living longer and longer. The net result was that there were fewer and fewer young people and a lot more pensioners.

The statistical outcome of those two trends was startling. According to a European Union report on the aging of the continent published in 2009, the population of the EU as a whole would be only slightly larger in 2060 than today, but much older. The population would increase from 495.4 million in 2008 by almost 5 percent by 2035, when it would peak at what on current trends would be an all-time high of 520 million. A steady decline would then start, with the population shrinking by nearly 3 percent, to 505.7 million by 2060.[8]

But while the numbers wouldn't change much, the age profile would shift dramatically. Half of the European Union's population today is 40 years old or more. In 2060, half of the population will be aged 48 years or above. The number of elderly people aged 65 or above already surpasses the number of children below 15, but their numbers are relatively close. In 2060, there will on current trends be more than twice as many elderly people than children. In 2008, there are about three-and-a-half times as many children as very old people (defined as above 80). In 2060, children would still outnumber very old people, but by a small margin: The number of very old people would amount to 80 percent of the number of children.

You could write a whole book about the aging of the global population. For our analysis here, however, two points are relevant, and both are of huge importance.

First, there is nothing you can really do about it. The age structure of a population reflects deep social trends, and the state of medical science, none of which government policy can impact no matter how hard they try.

And second, it is going to have a massive impact on the finances of governments. "Governments in advanced economies with a markedly growing ratio of the elderly to the working age population face yet another fiscal challenge—containing and funding the rising costs for health care and pensions in the medium to long term," argued the Bank for International Settlements report referred to earlier.[9]

Indeed they did. Governments for three decades had allowed their debts to steadily accumulate. They were too cowardly to spell out to voters the consequences of the expensive welfare programs they kept promising them, and found it easier to borrow more money than to do the hard work of raising more revenue through higher taxes. At the same time, the demographic trends meant that they were going to find it harder to raise taxes in the future, and the pressure on their spending was going to build and build.

At yet at precisely the moment when they should have been getting their spending under control and working out ways to make fiscal policy more sustainable over the next 30 years, governments had embarked on the greatest and costliest spending spree in history.

Was that going to prove sustainable? Almost certainly not. And over the next 12 months, finance ministers and the bond markets were about to find out why. It was going to be a very cruel lesson.

Chapter 6

Burying Your Head in the Greek Sand

George Papandreou's baptism into Greek politics was about as brutal as could be imagined. The scion of one of Greece's key political dynasties, he was threatened at gunpoint in 1967 when the Greek army seized power in a military coup and soldiers came to the family home searching for his father, Andreas.

While his maternal grandfather, a World War I veteran, locked the door on the soldiers, George armed himself with a shotgun and raced with his father up to the veranda on the roof. Glancing down to the street, he could tell they were surrounded and quickly concluded that one teenager with a single weapon wasn't going to be any match for the Greek Army. So he put away the weapon and hid his father. Then one soldier came through the veranda door and held a machine gun to the 14-year-old George's throat, demanding to know the whereabouts of his father. Rather than risk his son's life, Andreas Papandreou emerged from hiding and surrendered. He was promptly beaten to the ground with guns and rifle butts. "That was the moment that turned George from an extrovert to an introvert," his brother, Nick Papandreou, recalled in an interview with Bloomberg Business Week in June 2010. "It took George a long time to get over the trauma. He was more quiet after that. He seemed to think of the world differently."[1]

It was also a long time—perhaps understandably—before the junior Papandreou wanted to go anywhere near Greek politics. Which was why it was a surprise to most of the outside world—although probably not to the Greeks, who usually expect a Papandreou to be running the country on a fairly regular basis—when he eventually emerged as prime minister of the country in 2009.

The path to power was a long and sometimes confusing one. After the military coup, his father Andreas, an academic economist as well as a firebrand socialist politician, moved the family to America. Settling in California, Andreas would drive the family to New York and from there they would board a ship bound for Piraeus in Greece, a trip that took two weeks. He couldn't afford the plane fare to get back to the homeland in those days, and that was the cheapest way of staying in touch with the home country.

Instead of following his father into economics, however, Papandreou consciously chose to break with that tradition and studied sociology instead, earning degrees from Stockholm University and Amherst College in Massachusetts, and a master's degree from the London School of Economics. By 1981, as we have already seen, the military junta was part of Greece's past, and his father Andreas was back in Greece, running the country's first socialist government. Although in and out of power, both Andreas Papandreou and his socialist Pasok party were to dominate the next two decades of public life. And by the time Andreas died in 1996, his son George, despite his early misgivings about going into the family business, was already firmly established in the country's political life.

He was first elected to the Greek Parliament at the age of just 29, in 1981, and held two ministerial posts in his father's governments, first in education and culture and then as a junior foreign minister. By 1999, after his father had passed away, he had been promoted to foreign minister. Pasok was out of power for much of the first decade of the new century, and George didn't have his father's skills for creating a popular movement or stirring up a crowd. He is a gray, and often rather technocratic politician. As leader of the party between 2004 and 2009 he lost two general elections, scoring the lowest vote total for his party in a quarter-century in 2007 against Kostas Karamanlis, another scion of a political dynasty. He had to fend off an internal challenge for party leadership. When the party finally won back power in 2009 it was after five years out of office. His winning campaign in that year took many of its cues from American politics, perhaps reflecting its leader's youthful exile in that country. "Roll up our sleeves" was a motif of his campaign, filled with a very American can-do attitude toward the nation's problems, while one of his slogans was "Together, we can," a slightly over-obvious nod to Barack Obama's "Yes, we can."

When the results came through on October 4, 2009, it turned out to be a landslide. Papandreou had decisively turned around his earlier defeats. His Pasok party won 43 percent of the vote and 160 seats in the 300-seat legislature. The outgoing prime minister, Kostas Karamanlis, and the ruling New Democracy Party had 34.9 percent of the vote and 95 seats, losing more than a third of their current representation. Papandreou and his wife were mobbed by a crowd of thousands of supporters waving green-and-white Pasok flags as they arrived at the party's headquarters on Hippocrates Street in central Athens. Drivers raced through the city's streets honking their horns to celebrate the Socialist's return to power. It was a night for celebration. "Today we set off together to build the Greece we want and need," Papandreou declared in a triumphant victory speech. "We have no time to waste. We want it, we can do it, we will succeed. Nothing will be easy. I will always be honest and upfront with the Greeks."[2]

Like much political rhetoric, it was stronger on stirring phrases than it was on frankness. In reality, openness had not been the most obvious feature of Papandreou's election campaign. Kostas Karamanlis, the defeated prime minister, had called early elections in 2009, only two years into the life of the parliament, because he believed he needed a fresh mandate to cope with the economic crisis already starting to swirl around Greece and stave off labor unrest over the austerity measures that he already saw as inevitable now that the easy money had dried up. During the campaign, he argued for a freeze in public-sector wages to fight rising debt and unemployment, but had struggled to push through the important economic and structural reforms he felt were needed because he governed with a one-vote majority in Parliament. He needed a clear and decisive majority to do that. Papandreou had argued against that program during the election, insisting that Greece could spend its way through the crisis, and that this was not the time for cuts. The economy could not be "fixed with austerity," he told London's *The Guardian* newspaper in an interview as he strove for an election victory.

The Greeks, from the evidence of the election results, agreed with him, and overwhelmingly so. They had been offered tough choices, and, after examining them closely, had chosen to take the easy, painless option instead. They were, in short, choosing to bury their heads in the sand.

As he swept into power, Papandreou promised he had a hundred-day plan to stimulate the economy by creating jobs and cleaning up public finances. He had promised new laws to redistribute income to the poor, boost public investment, and clamp down on corruption. As part of a 3-billion-euro stimulus package, he promised salary and pension hikes above the rate of inflation next year.

Already, however, there were some dark warnings of trouble ahead. Standard & Poor's, the giant American credit ratings agency, which had cut Greece's debt rating in January 2009 to A-minus, the lowest of the 16 euro nations, welcomed Papandreou's pledge to focus on the deficit and debt reduction, but noted with a touch of acidity that plenty of similar promises had been made in the past without much evidence they would ever be made good on. "Given repeated budgetary slippages by consecutive Greek governments, it remains to be seen whether the new government will have the resolve to implement a credible budgetary strategy," noted Marko Mrsnik, an S&P credit analyst for Greece, in a note to investors that went out soon after the socialist party rode back into government.[3]

In October 2009, however, nobody was very interested in listening to the views of a few ratings agencies that advised on the arcane world of buying and selling government bonds. These analysts were not the sort of people governments had to pay very much attention to. Certainly, euro-zone governments didn't need to consider themselves subject to anything so vulgar as the discipline of the bond markets. Indeed, for Greece the main point of joining the euro had been to lift itself above such petty disciplines.

The irony of George Papandreou's premiership, however, was that it would fall to him to undo much of the work of his father. The legacy of first the rightwing, buffoonish Colonels and then the leftwing firebrands of Andreas Papandreou's generation was an economy that was among the most ruined in Europe.

And soon enough, burying its head in the sand wouldn't be an option for Greece anymore.

■ ■ ■

In many ways, the switch to the euro had worked out far better than many people in Greece, or indeed in the rest of the euro-zone, could ever have imagined. Since adopting the euro in 2001, the country had averaged an annual growth rate of 4.2 percent: That was the second-highest average growth rate in the euro-zone, and second only to Ireland. True, the trade deficit had soared to 14 percent of GDP, and the budget deficit was starting to spin wildly out of control. But with interest rates reduced dramatically, and with the country able to borrow money on the global capital markets on virtually the same terms as Germany, it was riding a tidal wave of exciting, if largely illusionary, prosperity.

And yet, in reality the country had embarked on an extravagant spending spree. There were two main factors behind the surge in Greek growth. The first was a big rise in consumer borrowing, as ordinary people took advantage of the big drop in real interest rates. The overall indebtedness of the country rose by the equivalent of 55 percent of GDP between 2002 and 2008, according to Eurostat figures, roughly the same amount as Ireland over the same period and only slightly less than Spain. (France, by contrast, became less indebted to the tune of 12 percent of GDP over the same timeframe.) At the same time, the government inflamed that boom by running a very expansionary fiscal policy, pumping up the consumer economy even further. The big decline in interest rates that came with euro membership should have enabled it to get its budget back into balance: Debt repayments were consuming 12 percent of government revenues in 1994, but by 2006 that had come down to just 4 percent of revenues. And yet, the official figures show that in eight out of the nine years between 2001 and 2008, the government budget deficit exceeded the 3 percent limit laid down in the Stability and Growth Pact, and averaged over 6 percent of GDP over the whole period. The bulk of that deficit was structural: That is, it reflected a permanent gap between taxes and revenues and not just a short-term smoothing out of the economic cycle. In short, the boom of the years between 2002–2008, just as in Ireland and Spain, was based on a reckless expansion of borrowing that was never likely to prove sustainable in the medium term.

As in the rest of the Club Med nations, that was reflected in a rapid widening of the trade deficit. Hitting 14 percent of GDP by 2009, and running at very high levels right through the decade, Greece's trade deficit was a reflection both of the very high levels of consumer demand, which far outstripped the productivity capacity of its own economy, as well as the steadily declining competitiveness of its industries. Greek labor costs rose in real terms by 35 percent over the course of the decade, one of the fastest rates in the whole of the euro-zone. But Greek productivity didn't rise by anywhere near as much. The result was that Greek workers were steadily pricing themselves out of the European market. Greek exports barely rose at all between 2000 and 2009. At a very simple level, the country just borrowed more money and imported more stuff. It was hardly the best model for national prosperity ever invented—nor, needless to say, the most stable, either.

The most telling symbol of Greek extravagance in the years immediately after the euro was introduced was the 2004 Olympic Games. It was understandable that Greece would want to host the Olympics at some stage. After all, this was the country that created the Olympics. It was part of its heritage. And there could be no better way, along with the euro, of announcing Greece's arrival on the world stage as a modern, dynamic country than hosting the world's greatest sporting tournament in Athens.

And yet the modern Olympics has also become a grotesque spectacle of extravagance and waste. The International Olympic Committee (IOC) demands that countries build vast new stadiums at massive expense, most of which will start to gather dust as soon as the month-long games have ended. It is not something that any sane government would go anywhere near. Greece was by far the smallest and poorest country to host the games (it has a population of 10.7 million people, compared, for example, with the 1.3 billion population of the 2008 host, China, or the 22 million population of 2000's Australia). There had always been nervousness at the IOC about whether the Greeks could really afford it. And those doubts, as it turned out, were pretty well founded.

The Pasok government that had won the games has estimated the cost at $5.9 billion. By the time the work was completed, which included a new airport for Athens as well as a new subway system, the total bill had almost tripled to close to $15 billion.

But it wasn't just the Olympics. It turned out that the entire Greek economy for the first decade of the euro's existence had, like the other Club Med countries, been surfing a wave of easy money. And much of the "improvement" in its economy had been based on lies and deception.

■ ■ ■

In September 2004, George Alogoskoufis stood before the Greek Parliament and made an extraordinary admission. A professor of Economics at Athens University, Alogoskoufis was a rarity among his country's finance ministers, both in knowing something about the how the economy actually worked and in having a commitment to reality as a good starting point for decision making. It was time, he conceded, for Greece to stop pretending it was obeying the rules laid down for members of the single currency. It wasn't, it never had, and, unless something changed radically, it never would. It had been lying since the start.

A day earlier, the European Commission had announced that it had gone back over the figures supplied by Greece when the decision was made to allow the country into the single currency in 2001 and found what is rather euphemistically described as "significant accounting errors."

"The problem would not be so serious if it had happened in only one year," Alogoskoufis told the Greek Parliament. "But the fiscal derailment is due to actions and omissions by the previous government, and we cannot hide behind our little finger anymore."[4]

The center-right government of Kostas Karamanlis that took power from the socialists in 2004 had decided to make a clean breast of it. If the figures had been fiddled, they needed to find out what the actual numbers were and get them out into the open if they were to get the Greek economy back on track again. The deception used to smuggle Greece into the euro had, as it turned out, been a significant one. The revised assessments of the figures in question, it emerged, had raised Greece's 2000 budget deficit to 4.1 percent of GDP, compared with the 2 percent the previous government had claimed it was. The total stock of outstanding debt, he said, had been revised from 102 percent of GDP to 114 percent of GDP. The deficit figures had been raised by at least two percentage points for each succeeding year, through to 2003. The figures hadn't been that hard to fiddle as it turned out. It transpired that defense spending, which at the time amounted to around 5 percent of Greek GDP, didn't need to be included in the statistics because it might endanger national security. Huge chunks of the welfare budget simply vanished from the books.

In the end, how the books were fiddled didn't matter very much. The important point was this: Greece had never qualified for the single currency after all.

Predictably, there was a furious reaction from Brussels. Eurostat, the official statistics agency of the EU, promptly began an enquiry into the manipulation of the Greek data. When it reported its findings in December 2005, it found that Greece had understated the size of its budget deficit by an average of 2.1 percentage points in every year since 1997. Greece's budget deficits during the three crucial years used to assess its preparedness for adopting the euro, 1997 to 1999, stood at 6.6 percent, 4.3 percent, and 3.4 percent, respectively, according to the Eurostat report. Greece had said that the deficits were 4 percent, 2.5 percent, and 1.8 percent during that period. There wasn't really any way of getting around the statistics. The Greeks had fiddled their way into the single currency.

The European Union threatened legal action against Greece. It was a clear breach of the terms of the Maastricht Treaty, to which the country was a signatory. But in the end, there was no meaningful penalty that could be imposed, so there wasn't much point in a trial. It was an embarrassing few weeks for the Greek government. But the EU didn't even contemplate doing the only thing that would have made sense in the circumstances, which was to tell the Greeks to start reminting the drachma, and come back once they were ready to play by the rules.

Worse, once they were inside the euro, the Greeks still didn't bother to stick to the demands of the Treaty. "We knew that Greece was cheating, it was clear as soon as they joined that there was something wrong [with their figures]," said European Union Commissioner for Trade Karel De Gucht, in an interview with the Spanish newspaper *El Pais*, published on May 5, 2010.[5] Why no one inside the EU establishment bothered to do anything about it remains one of the mysteries of the whole saga. As people often do, they probably believed it wasn't worth going to the trouble of making a fuss. Greece was a fairly small country, and with any luck no one would ever really notice that they weren't exactly sticking to the letter of the law. The trouble was, if you let them get away with it for a couple of years, the Greeks would conclude that there really wasn't any point in going to all the hard work of getting their budget deficit under control the way they were supposed to. And that was precisely what happened.

In the years after joining the single currency, Greece didn't once bother to stay within the limits laid down by the Treaty. It was not just that they misreported the deficit data, either. It subsequently transpired that the Greeks had been working with the investment banks to massage down even further deficit figures that were already blatantly dishonest.

As if all that were not enough, Goldman Sachs then popped up with a role in the unfolding drama. As the Greek crisis broke it turned out that the U.S. investment bank, which prides itself on being the smartest set of financiers on the planet, had helped out the Greeks with their deficit—and not in a way from which it emerged with any credit. It came out over the course of February and March 2010 that Goldman had used a series of elaborate swap arrangements that helped disguise the amount of money the Greek government was borrowing. Although there was nothing illegal about the deal, it seemed to have exacerbated the extent to which Greece was ignoring the restrictions on deficits. "They did produce a rather small, but nevertheless not insignificant reduction in Greece's debt-to-GDP ratio," Gerald Corrigan, chairman of Goldman Sachs's regulated bank subsidiary, told a panel of UK politicians when they questioned him on the issue in February 2010. The swaps were "in conformity with existing rules and procedures," he insisted in impeccable legalese.[6] That is no doubt true. And yet, in fact, the transactions reduced the country's deficit by 0.14 percentage points and lowered its debt as a proportion of gross domestic product to 103.7 percent from 105.3 percent, according to Goldman Sachs figures.

It certainly excited the politicians, particularly in Germany. "It's a scandal if it turned out that the same banks that brought us to the brink of the abyss helped fake the statistics," German Chancellor Angela Merkel said in a speech in February without naming Goldman Sachs directly.[7] Michael Meister, financial affairs spokesman for Merkel's Christian Democratic Union, said the Goldman swap arrangement "broke the spirit of the Maastricht Treaty."

There wasn't that much point in blaming Goldman, however. If you leave your sausages in the dog's kennel, there is not much point in shouting at the dog when you find out it has eaten them. What else were you expecting? Goldman exists to make money out of complex financial transactions. There is no point in expecting a New York investment bank to enforce the Maastricht Treaty when no one else can be bothered. In truth, no one was compelling the Greek government to massage its deficit figures. It wanted to, and Goldman was just helping out.

It was in reality just one more example among many of an economy in which deception had become a standard part of everyday life.

■ ■ ■

One illustration of how dishonesty was part of the fabric of the Greek economy, and one reason why the government budget was chronically in deficit, was that the Greek economy had become a massive exercise in tax evasion. Not paying your taxes had become a way of life for middle-class Greeks. Take the story of the swimming pools. Somewhere to splash about on a hot afternoon is an important asset in a country where temperatures nudge up toward 104°F for much of the summer. And yet, when tax inspectors looked at the returns for one prosperous suburb—Ekali—to the north of Athens, they found that only 324 people checked the box on their annual return owning up to having a pool. Suspicious of those numbers, the tax department looked at the satellite photos of the district, which are easily available to anyone who can load Google Maps onto their computer. They started counting the numbers of blue-colored rectangles in the back gardens of the big villas. The number? A staggering 16,974.

Switch those numbers around and it seems that 16,650 pools were left out of the count. The reason isn't hard to figure out. In Athens you need a permit to own a pool, and that can cost up to 5,000 euros a year. There is plenty of incentive to lie about it. And yet, it is the scale of the deception that is breathtaking. If those figures are accurate, then 98 percent of middle-class Greeks were in effect fibbing on their tax returns.

Alternatively, take doctors. A tax investigation in another suburb of Athens found numerous cases where doctors had never issued a single receipt or recorded a single patient's visit. Many were declaring an income of as little as 3,000 euros a year on their tax returns. It was hard to understand why many of them bothered to go to medical school if that was all they were capable of earning. Nor was it clear how they maintained practice rooms, or indeed managed to live. Except, of course, that wasn't their real income or anything close to it. Once again, tax avoidance was a normal, everyday part of Greek middle-class life.

Those anecdotes tell just one side of the story. The official figures paint much the same dismal picture. According to the Federation of Greek Industries, in 2009 the government was losing $30 billion a year though tax evasion. According to Transparency International, the pressure group that lobbies for higher standards of corporate disclosure, the black economy accounts for around 40 percent of Greece's GDP. Not only is corruption endemic, it is actually getting worse. Again according to Transparency International data, 13 percent of Greeks admitted to paying *fakelakia* (or little envelopes) in 2008. The bribes were mostly paid to doctors for preferential treatment via the public health system, for building permits, and, somewhat ironically, to tax inspectors, who would then turn a blind eye to fiddled returns. In total, 900 million euros was paid out in bribes in 2009, a 10 percent rise on the previous year—and probably the only part of the Greek economy that was managing to chalk up double-digit growth rates. Indeed, the average Greek family was paying almost 1,500 euros in bribes every year. It was in effect a kind of unofficial, off-the-books tax system. To get your car through a vehicle-emissions inspection, for example, would cost you about 300 euros and the cost to jump to the top of a waiting list for an operation in a state hospital was about 2,500 euros. The trouble was, none of it was actually being paid to the government and none of it was going to end up being used to pay off Greece's massive overseas debts.

The pension system was an even bigger problem. Under the way it worked before the IMF imposed changes on the country in 2010, some retirees were earning more than when they worked. With an aging population, Greece may spend 25 percent of its GDP on pension costs by 2050 unless policies are changed, according to official figures published by the Greek government. Greek pensioners on average live on 96 percent of the salary they had when they worked, more than twice the proportion of earnings as German pensioners, according to calculations made by the Organization for Economic Co-operation and Development. The retirement age was a mere 58, way below the average for the European Union, and again much lower than the German retirement age, which by 2010 had already been pushed up from 65 to 67 as that country tried to come to grips responsibly with the costs of both the financial crisis and its own aging population. There is now 1 pensioner in Greece for every 1.7 workers compared with 1 for every 4 in 1950, according to official Greek government figures. There are 637 occupations that the Greek state deems to be "arduous in nature": that is, so tough that the person has to stop work earlier than official retirement age. They include hairdressers, car washers, steam-bath attendants, and radio technicians; and yet none of those jobs would strike most people, in most other countries, as particularly stressful or difficult. Greeks get a pension calculated on the last five years of their working life, which are almost invariably the highest paid. By contrast, German, Italian, and Portuguese pensions are based on wages earned over a lifetime. Spain bases them on the best 15 years of work. Once again, the Greek system was far more generous than the norm elsewhere in the euro-zone. In the Greek civil service, the so-called replacement rate can be as much as 149 percent, according to a report by the European Commission in October. The rate is a measure of how effectively a pension system provides income during retirement. Indeed, until 1992, Greek civil servants didn't pay anything toward their pensions. Female civil servants with children under 18 can still get early retirement, although it isn't really clear why having a 16-year-old child means that you can't work anymore.

If the country kept all its generous benefits, Greek pension spending would rise to 24 percent of gross domestic product by 2060, double the proportion of 2007, according to European Commission estimates published in 2009. No serious economist would imagine that a country could spend 24 percent of its output on pensions without bankrupting itself. Add in the debt repayments that would fall due on the nation's massive borrowing, and just about the entire Greek economy would, on the path its politicians had mapped out for it over the middle of the past decade, be devoted to paying its pensioners and foreign creditors. There would be nothing left for the people doing the actual work—in the unlikely event there actually were any—to live on.

Examples of the extraordinary profligacy of the Greek state were everywhere. Take the example of unmarried women. The daughters of retired civil servants can carry on receiving their father's pension even after their parents have died, if they happen to remain unmarried. Bloomberg reported in June 2010 the story of Sophia Constantinidou, a 52-year-old single teacher at a private school in Athens. She was collecting 400 euros a month from the Greek government, part of her late mother's state pension, which was more than she earned from working as a teacher. The payment remains in place for the rest of her life, so long as she remains single. Even leaving aside the archaic sexism of the system—based as it appears to be on the assumption that a woman is incapable of looking after herself once her mother or father dies unless a husband has appeared to care for her—it is also grossly inefficient. A woman such as Constantinidou clearly has no incentive to get married even if Costas Right does finally show up on her doorstop. Maybe in an age when women didn't work and expected to be humbly married off by their fathers in their early twenties it might have made some kind of perverse sense. In a modern, twenty-first century economy, it was clearly crazy. And yet the system remained unreformed, paid for by borrowed money.[8]

Greek industry was not a great deal better. It remained stuck with the kind of obsolete, outdated systems that had been swept away in most of the rest of Europe at least two decades earlier. Take the railways. Greek railways lose more money than any other transport system in Europe. They have racked up huge debts: 11 billion euros in total or the equivalent of around 1,100 euros for every person in the country.

Germany's Deutsche Bahn, the biggest rail employer in the European Union, and France's SNCF both turned profits in 2008. Even Italy, hardly a country that has ever been famous for the efficiency of its rail network, managed to get the train operator into the black. But not the Greeks. It remained, as does so much of the country, riddled with restrictive practices and cushy sinecures. Total salaries on the network came to more than four times the annual ticket sales for the rail system in 2008. Only one line, the service linking Patras with Athens and Thessaloniki, has been consistently profitable. In total, the network was estimated by 2010 to be costing Greeks between 2 million and 2.5 million euros each day. According to one calculation, it would have been cheaper to shut the whole thing down and pay for the passengers to all get taxis than to keep it running the way it was. But then the railway is more about preserving jobs for its 6,500 workers, more than half of whom are over 50 and are looking forward to generous pensions, than it is about moving either stuff or people around the country. It was and remains a ridiculously overstaffed and expensive system that serves no one very well. But over decades, none of the successive Greek governments had had the willpower to reform the railway, despite their endless pledges of reform. They preferred to let it drift on, racking up ever-heavier debts, assuming that someone else would always pick up the bill.

In that sense, the railway system was an apt metaphor for the whole country. It remained stuck in the past and largely unable to compete in the modern world. Most of its foreign earnings came from tourism and shipping. There was practically no globally competitive industry to speak of. According to United Nations data, Greek exports came to more than $500 million annually in just three classifications of goods: light petroleum distillates, bulk medical supplies, and fish. In total, goods for export accounted for only 7 percent of Greek GDP, the lowest percentage in the entire euro-zone. Over the next year, learned economists were to produce endless papers explaining how the Greeks would have to export more for their economy to survive within the euro. But what exactly were they meant to export? There is only a certain amount of Greek fish the world wants to buy.

"Now we are paying the price for the fact that we lived above our means, with amazing profligacy, and failed to reduce the role of the state," admitted Yannos Papantoniou, the former Greek finance minister and the man who steered the country into the euro, in an interview with the *New York Times* after the currency crisis broke. "Some say we should have done more."[9]

Indeed they would. Over the next few months plenty of people would be working very hard to make up for that oversight. But for Greece and for the euro it was probably already too late.

It had cheated and lied its way into the single currency. It had gone on a massive borrowing spree to cover up the inefficiencies of its economy. When it was offered the chance to reform itself, it had rejected that option and chosen instead a socialist prime minister who peddled the easy line that the country could simply carry on spending other people's money to get itself out of trouble.

But you can't cover up reality forever. And for Greece, the debts were about to fall due.

Chapter 7

The Debts Fall Due

Outside of the arcane world of government bond dealing, the statement would have made little sense. On December 7, the credit ratings agency Standard & Poor's released a few terse lines on Greece. It was, it said, placing the A-minus long-term sovereign credit rating of the country on Credit Watch with negative implications. It may not sound that serious. "Negative implications" is a mealy-mouthed phrase, far too timid, you might imagine, to contain any real threat to anyone.

But, as it happened, it was the last thing the markets wanted to hear. And although it is impossible to pin the Greek financial crisis down as starting with one particular event on one particular day—rather like the origins of World War I it is far too complex a subject for that—the S&P downgrade was the moment when all the doubts and worries in the minds of investors about the solvency of the Greek state started to crystallize into a single word. And the word was *sell*.

The decision reflected "our view that the fiscal consolidation plans outlined by the new government are unlikely to secure a sustained reduction in fiscal deficits and the public debt burden," said the S&P statement accompanying the downgrade, put forth by a team of London-based analysts led by Marko Mrsnik.[1] The way things were going, it noted, Greek debt reach would reach 125 percent of GDP by the following year, the highest among the 16 countries using the euro, and that was more than the agency could feel comfortable with.

The downgrade had been some time in the making. S&P had already lowered its rating on Greece by one grade way back in January 2009. Its rival, Fitch Ratings, cut Greece to A-minus from A in October of that year after the new government increased its estimates for the budget deficit. Over the few days before the decision was announced, the price of Greek bonds had been sliding sharply. So, too, had the equities quoted on the Athens stock exchange. Slowly but surely investors were starting to lose faith in the Greek debt market—and every other kind of Greek financial market as well.

The most crucial number was the spread between the yield on a 10-year German government bond and a 10-year Greek government bond. Known as a *bund*, a German bond is the closest thing to absolute safety known to the European debt markets. The thought of the German government defaulting is unthinkable. All over the euro-zone, debt is priced in relation to the bund. The wider the difference in price—the spread—the riskier the market thinks it is to hold that country's debt.

On December 7, the yield on Greece's benchmark 10-year bond rose 10 basis points to 5.11 percent in trading in London, widening the difference with similar-maturity German bunds by 16 basis points to 194 basis points (a basis point is one-hundredth of 1 percent, so a 194-basis-point spread meant Greek debt yielded 1.94 percent more than German debt).

The second most crucial number was the price of *credit-default swaps*. These are instruments that allow you to insure against the possibility of default on any bond, in this case a Greek one. Just like any insurance policy, the higher the risk of something happening, the more it costs you to insure against it. On that day, credit-default swaps on Greece's debt rose by 6 basis points to 189. That meant it costs $189,000 a year to protect $10 million of the country's debt from default for five years. In other words, it was something that looked more like happening with every day that passed.

Already, there were signs that officials in Brussels and Frankfurt were starting to get worried about what was happening in the far south of the euro-zone. Greece was facing a "very difficult" situation and needed to take "courageous" decisions to bring its budget deficit under control, European Central Bank President Jean-Claude Trichet told the European Parliament when he was questioned on the issue the same day that S&P downgraded the country.[2]

The next day, December 8, 2009, was even worse. Fitch Ratings cut Greece one step to BBB–plus, the third–lowest investment grade the agency awarded. In response, the Athens stock market plunged more than 5 percent in a single day of trading, with the bank stocks leading the way down. The yield on the 10-year security climbed as much as 25 basis points to 5.39 percent, widening the spread with the German bund still further, and the cost of credit–default swaps was soaring as well.

Greek Finance Minister George Papaconstantinou tried to reassure the markets with a statement that his government was committed to reducing the budget deficit. "The government is proceeding with a plan," he told a press conference in Athens amid a mounting sense of crisis. "We will do all that's needed to bring the deficit down in the medium term. We will submit a supplementary budget if needed."[3]

The trouble was, the markets had taken a good hard look at the plan and decided they didn't think very much of it. The EU was stepping up the steady flow of reassuring words. Joaquin Almunia, the Economic and Monetary Affairs commissioner in Brussels, put out a statement on the ninth of that month stating that the European Commission stood ready to assist Greece "in setting out the comprehensive consolidation and reform program, in the framework of the treaty provisions for euro-area member states." The Commission would, he said, "continue to monitor the situation in Greece very closely." It was, he added, "a matter of common concern for the euro area as a whole."[4]

By the time the EU's leaders gathered in Bonn on Thursday, December 10, for the start of a routine summit, the Greek crisis was starting to push itself up to the top of the agenda. Stock markets were starting to tumble around the world, rattled by nervous talk about the stability and security of the euro. The price of Greek debt was still plunging, and the cost of insuring it was still rising fast. The Greek banks were starting to be downgraded by the ratings agencies on worries that the huge amounts of Greek government debt they held on their books might not be worth anything anymore. If the country's banking system went down, that would worsen the crisis a hundredfold: There was no way the Greek government could afford to bail out its banks. As the European Union's leaders gathered, the markets were looking for reassurance that the rest of Europe would stand behind Greece if necessary.

The words were starting to be found. "If something happens in one country, then all other countries are affected as well," Angela Merkel told reporters in Bonn as she welcomed her fellow leaders to the former German capital. "As we have a common currency, we also have a common responsibility."[5] That sounded good enough. European leaders slip easily into the rhetoric of solidarity. They've been mouthing the same sentiments for half a century, and, like old actors, they know the lines by heart and can even put some passion into them when the stage is big enough. But when it came to questions on specifics, on what that "common responsibility" might mean in practice, they turned out not to be nearly so well rehearsed. The chairman of the Bonn summit happened to be Swedish Prime Minister Fredrik Reinfeldt, and he seemed to think the crisis in the bond markets was just a Greek problem and something they would have to sort out for themselves. "What we now are seeing in Greece is of course problematic, but it is basically a domestic problem that has to be addressed by domestic decisions," he said as he arrived for the summit. "I'm not sure it will actually come up tonight."

To which the average bond trader would have said: "Hold on. That doesn't sound very decisive. Nor does this sound like a man who is in any great hurry to help the Greeks out."

In reality there had always been a confusion at the heart of the euro, and one that hadn't been tested in the decade since the currency was launched. The Maastricht Treaty was quite explicit on the point that there would be no bailouts permitted among the different member states that made up the single currency.

"A Member State shall not be liable for or assume the commitments of central governments, regional, local or other public authorities, other bodies governed by public law or public undertakings of another Member State," states Article 104b of the Treaty.[6] You wouldn't have thought there was much room for even the smartest lawyer to try to wriggle out of that. The words are simple enough. Bailouts are banned. Admittedly there was one get-out clause which allowed temporary transfers between states in the case of an exceptional shock to the system over which they had no control. But Greece's problems were quite clearly the result of decades of economic mismanagement, profligacy, and dishonesty. There were no exceptional circumstances that could be invoked. In stating that the Greeks were on their own, the Swedish prime minister was simply restating what had been agreed many years earlier.

The trouble was, the markets didn't really believe that. The investors in the bond market had always assumed that, in extremis, a bailout would be organized for any euro state that ran into trouble. That was why they had, rather complacently, been buying up Greek debt over the past few years without worrying too much about whether the Greeks would ever have the money to pay it back. They just assumed the rest of the European Union would help them out.

When EU leaders such as Fredrik Reinfeldt started suggesting there wouldn't be any bailouts, that this was a purely domestic problem, then that was very, very scary. They would have to take a look at the state of the Greek economy and decide whether it was really something they wanted to back—that is, without the treasuries of Germany and France standing behind it.

And yet somehow, with a rather queasy feeling, most investors already knew the answer to that: *certainly not.*

By the time the summit ended, the outlook had grown even worse. If supportive words from your neighbors paid off debtors, then Greece would have had no problems at all. In a world where cold hard cash is the only currency that counts, it was starting to look in serious trouble.

As the summit closed, it transpired that all the EU was really planning to do was wish Prime Minister George Papandreou well with his efforts to get the deficit under control, and leave it at that. "We're not asking for any gifts or favors," Papandreou told reporters at a news conference after the final session of the summit. "We will live up to our obligations. There is no possibility of a default for Greece."[7]

He promised that a new plan for stabilizing the Greek economy would be ready by the new year. Gone was the election campaign rhetoric of avoiding hard choices, preserving welfare systems, and fighting to keep wages rising. "We have such systemic corruption to the point that we often consider it normal," he said, somewhat ruefully. "It is not normal. Our economy can't progress, investments can't come to Greece, our economy won't stand on its own feet if we don't attack corruption mercilessly."[8]

That was all true enough. And yet, with the markets plunging, it was a bit late to start now. What the markets wanted was promises of help from his fellow euro states, preferably cast in iron. There was, crucially, absolutely no indication of that.

By the time he arrived back in Athens, Papandreou did at least appear to understand the urgency of the situation. With Greek bonds still falling, and with rising nervousness about whether the country would still be able to finance itself in the market, the prime minister tried to set out a bold, confident line. "In the next three months we will take those decisions which weren't taken for decades," he said in a speech in Athens on December 14, addressing union and employer-group representatives and politicians. Many of the choices would be "painful," he argued. But there was no longer any alternative. The debts for a decade of profligacy were falling due. And Greece would have no choice but to pay them.

The trouble was, he was running out of time. And so was the country.

In the wake of Papandreou's speech, Greek debt continued to fall in price. On December 16, Standard & Poor's delivered another blow, lowering the country's rating another notch to BBB-plus from A-minus. The spread with the German bund rose to 250 basis points and it was climbing all the time. "We're clearly disappointed by the downgrade," Finance Minister George Papaconstantinou said at a press conference in London, slipping into a script that was already starting to become dismally familiar. "We believe that it doesn't reflect the attempts being made by the new Greek government to stabilize public finances which have been derailed."[9]

Meanwhile, over in Germany, the country that would be crucial to any EU bailout, the mood was hardening. "With a view to some countries with very high deficits, let me say that each member state is responsible for healthy public finances," Angela Merkel told the German Parliament on the same date that S&P delivered its latest downgrade for the Greeks. "This is the precondition for long-term growth for all of Europe."[10]

A day later, European Central Bank Vice President Lucas Papademos was hammering home the same message. It was up to the Greeks to sort this mess out with cuts, cuts, and more cuts. The Greek government, he said, needs to take "substantial" and "courageous" decisions to cut Europe's largest budget deficit. It was probably no surprise to anyone that a week that had started with George Papandreou returning to Athens from the EU summit determined to grapple decisively with the nation's debt ended with one of the biggest falls in Greek bond prices on record, with the spread widening to 263 basis points between the Greek 10-year bond and the 10-year bund.

As Christmas 2009 approached, a pattern was staring to emerge. One of the big ratings agencies would downgrade Greek debts, the markets would panic, there would be a selloff in the bond markets, and finally the government would step in with another revamped austerity package.

But none of it was convincing investors that Greece was really able to get to grips with its problems. For all Papandreou's talk of tough decisions, the fact remained that he had been elected only a few weeks earlier on a platform of avoiding precisely those hard choices. There were yet to be any concrete plans for cutting spending, raising taxes, or bringing the budget back into balance. Even worse, there was no sign that the EU was willing to step in with any kind of a rescue package. Greece's plight had been met first with complacency and then with indifference. Neither was an adequate response to the scale of the crisis that was building up, nor to the threat it posed, not just to Greece but to the survival of the euro itself.

And as the new year started, the crisis was about to go from bad to worse.

■ ■ ■

On January 14, the Greek government announced its latest package of spending cuts. The plan pledged to "do whatever it takes" to rein in the budget shortfall and restore confidence in the country's finances. Presented for approval to the European Union, the plans called for about 10 billion euros of spending cuts and revenue increases in 2010 to bring the deficit down from 12.7 percent of GDP to 8.7 percent.

It was another attempt by Papandreou to calm the markets and to reassure investors that the deficit would be brought under control and that Greece would eventually pay off its debt. But while the prime minister was talking to the bond markets, he also had to talk to the Greek people. And they were proving just as reluctant to listen to him as the men and women in the dealing rooms in London, Frankfurt, or New York.

Greeks weren't used to the language of austerity, and certainly not from socialist leaders. And it was not clear that they liked what they were hearing.

On February 24, a general strike was called to protest about the latest package of cutbacks in spending. All flights were canceled out of the airports, along with trains, buses, and trucking services. Schools were closed and banks and hospitals were operating with only a skeleton staff as an estimated two million workers from the public and private sectors walked away from their jobs. On the streets of Athens there were violent clashes between the police and protestors marching through the capital. Banners were held aloft proclaiming "tax the rich" and "hands off our pension funds." Addressing the crowds, labor leader Yannis Panagopoulos stoked up the sense of popular injustice at the fate that was befalling the country. "We refuse to pay the price for a crisis that we didn't create," he proclaimed. Greece has become "a Ping-Pong ball in a game being played by global speculators. Today Greece is the guinea pig for EU stability and the euro's resilience. Today it is Greece, tomorrow it will be Spain, Portugal and Italy."[11]

A new actor had entered the narrative: the Street. Most dealing rooms are located in countries where militant trade unions are largely a thing of the past. There aren't many strikes of great significance anymore in London, Frankfurt, or Berlin, and certainly not in Singapore. Traders in government bonds may not have appreciated that Greece, like many of the Mediterranean countries, has a far more volatile and emotional political culture. Strikes and street protests are a far more normal part of everyday life than they are elsewhere, and the police are regularly getting out their helmets, truncheons, water cannons, and tear gas to deal with rioters. It doesn't necessarily mean that a revolution is imminent, no matter how lurid the pictures on television might be. Often it is just a way of letting off steam. But as they watched the riots and read about the strikes, it only undermined their faith in the Greek economy even further. It looked as if the government could announce all the austerity packages it wanted. If it couldn't make them stick, they didn't count for very much. A few might even have remembered Lenin's famous dictum after seizing power in the Russian revolution of 1917: "The debts of the Tsar died with the Tsar," he ruled. The Soviet Union never bothered to pay back the money owed by the old Tsarist regime. Might the same thing happen if the government was overthrown in Athens? It was surely one more thing to worry about. And one more reason to sell the bonds.

As February turned into March, there was still no sign of the crisis abating. The price of Greek bonds would rally from day to day and then start sliding again. Austerity measures were proposed and then met with fierce resistance on the streets of Athens. It was starting to be questionable whether the Greeks would be able to carry on borrowing the money they needed to stay afloat, or whether the whole country was about to slide under its weight of debts.

Across Europe, leaders were starting to raise the possibility of some kind of rescue package for the Greeks. The earlier line that it was a purely domestic matter couldn't hold any longer. Greece "won't be left alone," said Luxembourg's Prime Minister Jean-Claude Juncker on March 5, as the country was paralyzed by yet another general strike. "We're telling financial markets: Look out, we're not abandoning Greece. . . . The euro zone stands ready to guarantee financial stability in the euro region."

The trouble was, it was just words, and the markets had had plenty of those already. There were briefings and rumors that the European Union was putting together an emergency aid package for Greece. There was talk of bilateral loans directly to the Greek government, or else a new type of EU bond backed by all the euro members, which might prove more palatable to the bond markets than paper issued by the Greek government alone.

But even as the leaders of the bigger euro-zone countries were starting to realize they would have to come up with some kind of package to help out their smaller southern neighbor, something else was stirring that was to make any rescue almost impossible.

Just as the Greeks didn't think much of the proposals for years of austerity put forward by their government, so the rest of the euro area didn't appear to think very much of throwing the nation a lifeline, either. The governments might come round to the idea. But the people would take a lot more persuading.

■ ■ ■

With its bright-red masthead, its pictures of footballers and fast cars, and its overwhelming interest in girls in bikinis, *Bild* is instantly recognizable as a down-market tabloid newspaper, even though, in deference to the inherent seriousness of its home market, it is actually published in broadsheet form. Owned by the Axel Springer group, the paper boasts a circulation of almost four million a day, the largest of any newspaper in Europe and the fifth largest in the world.

The paper was founded in 1952 by Springer, a former journalist who spotted the market for a racy, down-market, populist paper for the emerging affluent working class of the new West Germany. Springer went on to take control of *Die Welt*, the most influential up-market paper in Germany, making the company a target for left-wing intellectuals and anarchists who objected to the strongly conservative views that are common to all the Springer publications. But *Bild* is important for this story, not because of its history but because of the role it played in the unfolding Greek crisis. Like all great popular newspapers, *Bild* had an instinctive feel for the prejudices and emotions of its readers. It knows precisely which buttons to press and how to capture a mood and ride with it. And it is not a paper that any politician, and certainly not one from the center-right Christian Democrats, can afford to ignore.

To put it mildly, the editors of *Bild* didn't quite understand why its hardworking German readers, who made lots of things that were exported around the world, should have to pay to bail out a lot of feckless Greeks who didn't really make very much of anything. And they weren't shy about saying so.

After the crisis erupted, the paper ran story after story and editorial after editorial, raging against the possibility of a bailout. "Who's to blame for the crisis?" asked its edition published on February 12, as the economic crisis swirling around the country started to edge the usual diet of footballers and models from the front page. "It's Greece!"[12] On March, 6, 2010, for example, ahead of George Papandreou's visit to

Berlin to meet with Angela Merkel, the paper's front page consisted of an open letter to the Greek prime minister. "You are in Germany, a country very different from yours," it opened, with a rare, and not entirely successful, attempt at German humor. "Here no one has to pay thousands of euros in 'special gratuities' to secure a bed in a hospital. Germany has high debt but pays it off as we wake in the morning and work all day. Our petrol stations have cash registers, taxi drivers give receipts and farmers don't swindle EU subsidies with millions of non-existent olive trees." The letter concluded: "We want to be friends of the Greeks, that's why we've given to your country 50 billion from the moment you enter the EU, but friendship also means that we remain honest."[13]

Ahead of the same visit, the paper published an interview with Josef Schlarmann, a senior member of Angela Merkel's Christian Democrats, and Frank Schaeffler, a finance policy expert in the Free Democrats, the free-market coalition partners in Merkel's government. "Sell your islands, you bankrupt Greeks! And sell the Acropolis too!" screamed the headline. Inside, the two financial experts suggested there was a lot of money to be raised by selling off the Acropolis or indeed the Parthenon. "The chancellor cannot promise Greece any help," Schaeffler told *Bild*. "The Greek government has to take radical steps to sell its property—for example its uninhabited islands."[14] The paper seemed very taken with the idea, perhaps because many of its readers take their summer holidays in Greece. "We give you cash, you give us Corfu," ran a subsequent headline, playing on the same theme that at the very least the Germans might expect a few sun-kissed islands for all the money they were expected to send to Greece. The paper kept up its attack with a withering, endless condescension. When some of the Greek media responded to the paper's campaign with calls for a boycott of German goods, *Bild* shot back with a forensic examination of how much a blow that might be to the mighty German export machine of which the paper is such a proud cheerleader. "How bad could the threatened boycott be?" it asked. "German companies should be able to cope with it. In 2009 they shipped €6.66 billion worth of goods to Greece, just 0.8 per cent of total German exports."

Bild led the way aggressively, but the German media market is as competitive as any other, and its rivals weren't going to let the paper have the field to itself. If Greek-bashing was what the readers wanted, then they would get in on the act as well. The German newsmagazine *Focus* in March 2010 ran with a cover story featuring the Venus de Milo statue, one arm restored to hold up a middle finger at the reader, with the headline, "Swindlers in the Euro Family."[15]

All of that had an impact. A poll of public opinion in *Bild* not very surprisingly showed four out of five Germans opposed to any bailout. The same poll found that 53 percent of Germans would prefer to expel the Greeks from the euro rather than pay anything toward a rescue. The mood was starting to seep across borders as well. "Not one cent for Greece," ran the front page of the Dutch paper *Trouw* in early March.

Bild's campaign mattered. It was the backdrop against which the political and economic decisions were being taken. And that backdrop very clearly showed that neither the Germans nor many other Europeans, either, were willing to tolerate a bailout of Greece. It was all very well for politicians to talk the language of European solidarity. But on the ground, where votes are won and lost and where the careers of politicians are ultimately made or broken, the rhetoric was meaningless. The voters weren't going to buy it. Any politician who meekly signed up to a Greek rescue package without any strings attached was likely to find himself or herself kicked out of office very quickly. Even if she wanted to, Angela Merkel was going to find it practically impossible to play softball with the Greeks.

It was the backdrop to the way the financial markets were reacting as well. They can read *Bild* on the trading floors as easily as anywhere else; indeed, most traders read popular newspapers voraciously, mainly because they share their interest in expensive cars and buxom blondes. For years, as we have seen, the markets had complacently assumed that if the worst came to the worst, Greek debts would ultimately be paid off by the Germans. As they looked at the lurid, inflammatory headlines and chortled over the suggestions about selling off the Acropolis, they could see that anyone holding a Greek bond shouldn't count on taxpayers in Hanover or Hamburg stepping forward to pay it off.

Bild was reflecting and reporting on the crisis. But the German popular press was also an actor in it, shaping the space in which politicians, central bankers, and market-makers could operate.

And in that space, a straightforward Greek rescue had become impossible.

■ ■ ■

In Athens, the mood wasn't much better. On February 24, 2010, Theodoros Pangalos, the Greek deputy prime minister, gave an interview to the BBC in which he tackled head-on the growing campaign in Germany against a bailout for the Greeks. The current crop of European leaders were all pygmies, he protested, of little consequence compared to the likes of Britain's Margaret Thatcher, Germany's Helmut Kohl, and France's Francois Mitterrand, who oversaw the creation of monetary union (even though Mrs. Thatcher, of course, fiercely opposed it). The burden of history especially weighed against German criticism, given the brutal way the Nazis occupied the country in World War II, he argued provocatively. "They took away the gold that was in the Bank of Greece, they took away Greek money, and they never gave it back," he said. "This is an issue that has to be faced sometime in the future."[16]

The idea that a bailout was a much-delayed war reparation was a novel one—and not one the Germans were about to take lying down. "A discussion about the past in the current situation is not at all helpful," a German Foreign Ministry spokesman told the press sharply. According to the Foreign Ministry, Germany paid 115 million deutschmarks in restitution for Greek victims of Nazi crimes under a 1960 treaty, in addition to funds paid out to victims of forced labor under the Third Reich.

And yet, it was a theme that was being picked up on and exploited in the Greek press. "Economic Nazism threatens Europe," proclaimed one newspaper headline, attacking German media jibes that the Greeks were being "cheats." "Racist frenzy and calumny against Greece," railed another.

The mood was getting worse and worse. The Germans were angry about the prospect of having to rescue Greece. The Greeks were resentful about having to go cap in hand to their richer northern neighbor, particularly when it was one that had treated the country brutally during World War II, and for which it had never had much affection. It was hardly an edifying spectacle, nor one in which there appeared to be much prospect of an amicable agreement.

The euro was meant to be a device for drawing the nations of Europe together, for uniting them economically so that in time they could be united politically as well. Instead, it was driving them further and further apart. Old wounds were being reopened. New resentments were being created. Just as the euro had failed to be a catalyst for the modernization of the southern European economies, now it was failing to be a catalyst for integration as well.

Even worse, one of the founding assumptions of this currency, as for any form of money, was that there was a sense of shared purpose between the people using it. In extremis, they would be willing to help one another. But the crisis had exposed that assumption as entirely bogus.

There was no unity between the Greeks and the Germans. And that would only make the crisis worse.

■ ■ ■

Greece's defenses lasted until April 11, 2010, but at that point the pressure had become too great. The country was ready to throw in the towel and ask for help. The markets kept testing and testing, and it eventually became clear that the crisis wouldn't be resolved until the European Union demonstrated its willingness to offer some assistance.

Two days earlier, Fitch Ratings had hammered another nail into the country's coffin, with yet another downgrade of its debts. It cut the rating on Greece to just BBB-minus, one level above what the markets call *non-investment grade*, and what the rest of the world refers to as a "junk bond." It was now on the same rating as those two paragons of financial responsibility, Bulgaria and Panama (neither of which had ever been, or were ever likely to be, asked to join a currency union with anyone other than themselves). Even worse, Fitch put a "negative" outlook on the rating, meaning that it was more likely to cut it again than it was to raise it. Greece faced an "intensification of fiscal challenges in response to more adverse prospects for economic growth and increased interest costs," Fitch analysts Chris Pryce and Paul Rawkins said in a statement.[17] In other words, as its debt became more and more expensive, the prospects for the Greek economy got worse and worse. It was trapped inside a classic vicious circle, and right now, no one could see a way out of it.

Greek bonds plunged once again, and the spread against the German bund rose to levels that hadn't been seen since before the euro was launched. A 10-year Greek bond now yielded 7.8 percent, and the price of the country's borrowing was getting more and more ruinously expensive all the time. The outlook for the country was moving from bad to worse. The EU was ready to help Greece "at any moment," French President Nicolas Sarkozy told reporters in Paris as the latest downgrade was announced. Herman Van Rompuy, the EU's newly installed and rather obscure president, was quoted by the French newspaper *Le Monde* as saying that officials are "ready to intervene."

No doubt that was true. But intervene *how*, exactly? And with what money? In the background there had been a fierce debate about what kind of rescue package should be organized for Greece should it become necessary. It was not just about how much money would be offered. It was about who would offer it and on what terms. Those were the issues on which the fate of the euro would ultimately depend.

The most crucial question was *who*. It had been assumed that the euro-zone would look after its own, that if a crisis broke in one country it would be up to the rest of the members to come to the rescue. There were, however, two problems with that. First, as we have already seen, the Germans just weren't going to stand for it. Nor, if it came to the crunch, did it look as if the Dutch or the French or indeed the Irish would, either (bear in mind that the Irish were going through a massive squeeze on public spending to get their deficit under control, so it was going to be hard to explain to them why they should come to the rescue of the Greeks, who were unwilling to put up with the same kind of pain they were enduring). And yet even in some parallel universe where the Germans were quite happy to subsidize the Greeks forever, it would still create perverse incentives within the euro-zone. After all, a straightforward bailout by the rest of the euro-zone would be effectively saying that it was okay to cheat your way into the club, run up massive debts you couldn't afford to pay back, and then pass the bill onto everyone else. Needless to say, the hardliners at the Bundesbank, with their framed deutschmarks on their office walls, didn't think much of that. But hardly anyone else did, either. If those were the rules, then it was hard to see how the euro could survive in the medium term. Everyone would have an incentive to do the wild-and-crazy spending, but no one would have any incentive to do the bailing out. It would be madness to try and proceed on that basis.[18]

"We have a Treaty under which there is no possibility of paying to bail-out states in difficulty," Angela Merkel had insisted on March 1. "The Treaties set out a 'no bail-out' clause, and the rules will be respected," the Bundesbank's Jürgen Stark had told the Italian daily *Il Sole 24 Ore* on January 6, 2010.

> This is crucial for guaranteeing the future of a monetary union among sovereign states with national budgets. Markets are deluding themselves if they think that the other member states will at a certain point dip their hands into their wallets to save Greece.[19]

"[The Greek Prime Minister] Papandreou has said that he didn't want one cent," German economy Minister Rainer Brüderle said on March 5, 2010. "The German government will not give one cent, anyway."[20]

The German member of the European Parliament, Markus Ferber, perhaps put it most succinctly of all, saying in a debate on April 3, "We'll be happy to give the Greeks anything, just not money."[21]

It was hard to see much room for doubt in those statements. If there was to be a bailout, it couldn't come just from the euro-zone.

The Greeks, meanwhile, had already noted there was very little sign of any concrete help from the rest of the European Union. They started casting around elsewhere. In early March, George Papandreou started making noises about looking for help, not from its neighbors in the euro, but from the Washington-based International Monetary Fund instead. "If markets don't respond as we would like them to, due to their speculative behavior, then the final resort would be the International Monetary Fund," he said on the third of that month.[22]

To the rest of the euro-zone, and to Brussels and the ECB in particular, that was an incendiary threat. The IMF was the pawnbroker of global finance: It was the place impoverished states went to raise some ready cash on desperate terms when all other options had failed. And, just like a pawnshop, it was not the kind of place where respectable people wanted to be seen. It was the refuge for failed African states, and rickety Latin American juntas. For a euro-zone country it was unthinkable. ECB officials would never live it down.

It was a clever if slightly humiliating way for Papandreou to turn up the pressure. It certainly was not the way the Greek establishment had viewed the single currency. As we have seen, it was meant to modernize and streamline the country, not turn it into the kind of place that needed rescuing by the IMF. But the situation was becoming critical and something had to be done. Surely, the prime minister must have reasoned, the European Union would step in and help rather than see the IMF descend on Athens?

Maybe, or maybe not. Naturally, there was dismay in some circles. The very next day, ECB President Jean-Claude Trichet made a point of ruling that out.

Calling on the IMF would not be "appropriate," he said at a press conference in Frankfurt. George Papaconstantinou, the Greek finance minister, upped the ante by calling the IMF a last resort if the European Union fails to "rise to the occasion." Jean-Claude Juncker, the Luxembourg prime minister who headed the euro-group that represented finance ministers for the euro-area, shot back: "This is a problem of the euro area and we have to deal with the problem as the euro area."[23]

In reality a game of chicken was being played out. All the talk of solidarity between euro nations turned out to be hot air. It didn't mean anything, and certainly not financial assistance for the Greeks to get them through the crisis. There was really only one weapon the country had in reserve: the power to humiliate the euro. For Greece either to default or to call in the IMF would ruin the pretentions of the euro to be a strong, world-leading currency. By the end of March it was about the only card the country had left to play.

Except, to some degree, the Greeks had miscalculated. Calling in the IMF might be humiliating, but for German Chancellor Angela Merkel it had some advantages as well.

First, it was the one body in the world with the expertise to deal with countries that had lost the confidence of the global capital markets. It had the people and the experience to handle that situation. Arguably, the European Central Banks or a new European Monetary Fund (which was already being proposed to help with the crisis) could develop those skills over time. But a crisis is no time to experiment or to learn new skills. If Greece was to be rescued, it needed to be done immediately.

Second, the medicine was going to be brutal. For any euro-area country that had to narrow its deficit on the scale that Greece needed to, there would have to be deep cuts in public spending. Wages would be reduced, jobs lost, and retirement ages raised—precisely the kind of measures that brought rioters out onto the streets of Athens. It was never going to be popular. The IMF was in many ways better suited to being the "bad cop." It could take all the criticism and divert public anger away from the European Union and the euro.

Finally, and perhaps most importantly, calling in the IMF would help preserve the *no-bailout rule* that was written into the treaties establishing the euro, even if it was in a rather roundabout way. The no-bailout rule was important, because, as we have seen, taxpayers in Germany didn't want to feel they were being forced to subsidize people in Greece or Spain or Portugal. In extremis, it might even force them out of the euro. Bringing in the IMF got around that obstacle. The world's main developed countries are the members and they contribute to its funding. If an emergency loan needed to be organized for Europe's high-deficit countries, it wouldn't be the euro members helping them out. It would be the whole world. The no-bailout rule between euro members would remain in place—just about, anyway. It would undoubtedly play better in Berlin than a straight euro-zone rescue package. And that might make the humiliation a price worth paying.

On April 11, the deal was struck, and Trichet, the ECB, and much of the Brussels establishment had been overruled. The agreement was announced on the Sunday evening, in the hope of calming the markets before they opened the next morning. The Greeks were offered an emergency assistance package worth 45 billon euros. Of that, roughly 30 billion euros would come from the euro-zone, while the rest would come from the IMF. The Germans had fought a running battle for the loans to be charged at market interest rates so that there wouldn't be any kind of subsidy for the Greeks. That, however, defeated the point of the package. Greece couldn't afford the market rate, which was why it was in this mess in the first place. In the end, Merkel compromised. The Greeks would be charged interest at 5 percent, significantly less than the 7 percent—plus the markets were demanding to lend the country money that week. It was a soft-ish loan: a subsidy of sorts, but not one that was so huge that it would necessarily stir up the resentment of voters in other countries. The decision "sends a clear message that nobody can play with our common currency and our common fate," George Papandreou told reporters at a press conference in Larnaca, Cyprus, as soon as the package was announced.

An important line had been crossed. The no-bailout clause had been, if not completely broken, then at least fudged. The euro had taken a decisive step from being a hard currency to being a soft one.

Not everyone was happy about that, and certainly not in Germany. "Germany buckled under the pressure—we shouldn't kid ourselves that such loans are anything but subsidies," said Frank Schaeffler, deputy finance spokesman for Merkel's Free Democrat coalition partners, in an interview. "The loans will hurt the euro, and help Greece only temporarily. We will be standing on very thin ice, legally, economically. The European treaties don't envisage member states plugging the deficits of their partners."[24]

True enough. The four professors who took the decision to join the euro to Germany's constitutional court were already threatening to do the same over the rescue package. They certainly had a case: The legal basis for the rescue was obscure, under both European law and the German constitution. Needless to say, the editorial writers at the head offices of *Bild* were not happy about it, either, to put it mildly. "Supposedly we have no money for tax cuts, no money for school upgrades, no money to maintain parks, no money to fix our streets," thundered German's biggest newspaper on April 28. "But suddenly our politicians have billions of euros for the Greeks who have deceived Europe."[25]

But the more immediate worry was not the legality of the rescue package, but its practicality. "The euro-group's decision today opens the door to contagion," said Hans Michelbach, deputy finance spokesman for Merkel's party, the Christian Democrats. "It's an invitation to speculators to make a killing on other euro-region bonds and a bailout spiral."

Would it work? Or would it just fuel more speculation against Greece and against the rest of the euro's high-deficit countries? Greece needed to raise 11.6 billion euros by the end of May to cover maturing bonds, and another 20 billion euros by the end of 2010 to pay debt coupons and finance that year's deficit. It still needed to maintain the confidence of the capital markets that it could pay its own way. The 45 billion of financial assistance would help, but Greece's total government debts came to more than 300 billion euros. It couldn't survive on that package alone.

The verdicts of the markets and the rating agencies were still what really mattered. But now it would be the credibility not just of Greece but of the EU and the euro that would be at stake.

■ ■ ■

It was perhaps inevitable that it would be a ratings agency that would deal the final blow. On April 27, Greece's rating with Standard & Poor's was lowered to BB-plus from BBB-plus, a drop of three grades in a single step. The country's debt had now, in the view of the agency, reached junk bond status. It was now on a par with Egypt and Azerbaijan. It was possible to go lower—Zimbabwe, for example—but not by much.

Just to add salt to the wound, S&P added that the holders of the Greek bonds faced losses of around 200 billion euros in the event of a Greek default, or between 50 and 70 percent of their entire holdings. If that didn't make you want to sell whatever Greek debt might remain in your portfolio, it was hard to know what would.

The selloff was immediate and brutal. On the day after the decision was announced, amid frantic trading, yields on 2-year Greek debt soared to 19 percent, up from just 4.6 percent a month earlier. The yield on the 10-year bond climbed 45 basis points to 10.05 percent. The stock market got hammered as the agency cut its ratings on the Greek banks to junk as well, restricting their ability to raise funds on the money markets. The National Bank of Greece slumped 10 percent on the day, and its share price had halved since the start of 2010. To make matters worse, S&P also cut its rating on Portugal. The Greek crisis was spreading out across the rest of the euro-zone like a virulent strain of flu that hops from country to country within a matter of days. Stocks and commodity prices were tumbling around the world. What had started as a small financing issue in a relatively small country was fast turning into the worst crisis the markets had seen since the collapse of Lehman Brothers two years earlier. It was, scarily enough, potentially even worse: After all, that only involved the collapse of banks, whereas this was about the bankruptcy of whole nations.

It wasn't hard to understand why S&P had made its move. A few days earlier, on April 23, George Papandreou had formally asked for help for the country under the EU-IMF package agreed earlier in the month. It was an unpopular move in Greece. A humiliation for the country, it would also bring in the IMF, and everyone knew its officials would impose austerity on a scale the Greeks weren't used to. "This is a premeditated crime against Greek society," Alexis Tsipras, the head of the opposition Syriza party, said as the move was announced. He immediately called for a referendum on the decision. "The majority of the Greek people are being tossed helplessly in the tempest of insecurity, unemployment and poverty," he proclaimed.[26]

Papandreou himself spoke with a certain dignity and honesty, addressing the country from Kastelorizo, a small island in the southeastern Mediterranean halfway between Rhodes and Antalya. A day earlier, Eurostat had revealed that Greece's budget deficit had hit 13.6 percent of GDP in 2009, higher than all previous estimates, and might turn out to be above 14 percent once what the statistical agency referred to as the "off-market swaps" were added into the calculations.

"Yesterday the data was announced on the real size of the 2009 deficit," the prime minister began.

> It reminded us all of the incomprehensible mistakes, omissions, criminal decisions and storm of problems we inherited from the previous government. We all inherited—today's government and the Greek people—a ship ready to sink; a country with no authority and credibility which had lost the respect of even its friends and partners; an economy exposed to the mercy of doubt and the appetite of speculators.[27]

Explaining that he given the go-ahead for aid to be requested, he argued that there was hope for the Greek people, but warned that the road ahead would be a hard one. "We are on a difficult course, on a new Odyssey for Greece. But we know the road to Ithaca (the home of Odysseus in Homer's *Odyssey*) and have charted the waters. We have ahead a journey with demands on all of us, but with a new collective conscience and common effort we will make it there safe, more sure, just and proud. Our final goal and destination is to free Greece from supervision and guardianship. I am absolutely certain we will make it."

Asking for the aid package to be activated was one thing. Getting the request accepted was another. It was without question unfortunate that the rescue package had been activated at the same time as regional elections had been called in Germany. The country still hadn't come to terms with the deal. "Greece has not just a liquidity problem, but also a fundamental growth and structural problem" and should "seriously consider leaving the euro area," Hans-Peter Friedrich, head of the Christian Social Union, the Bavarian sister party of the Christian Democrats, was quoted as saying in the newsmagazine *Der Spiegel*.

With the voters ready to cast their votes, Merkel found it impossible to ignore that kind of pressure. Speaking in the town of Soest in North Rhine–Westphalia, in the heart of the industrial Ruhr, where elections were due to be held on May 9, she upped the rhetorical pressure. "I've said for weeks that Greece must do its homework first," the chancellor thundered, drawing rapturous applause from an audience who was looking for a leader who would stand up for what they saw as German interests.[28] Merkel told the rally she wanted Greece to agree to several years of budget cuts before releasing any German aid. "Greece has put savings measures into effect this year, but one year won't be enough to restore confidence in the financial markets," she said. Whether in public, at a rally, or in private didn't make any difference. The message from Berlin was the same. The Greeks hadn't done enough yet to prove they had changed.

Greece had requested the aid package, but the Germans were not yet in the mood to allow the funds to be released. It was, therefore not much of a surprise that S&P downgraded the debt. It didn't really have any choice. Without the European Union and the IMF money it was very hard to see how the country was going to stay afloat.

The rescue package had fallen apart. Greece was bust. And it was hard to know what, if anything, the European Union might have left in its locker.

Chapter 8

The Trillion-Dollar Weekend

On Friday, May 7, 2010, the president of the European Central Bank, Jean-Claude Trichet, made the short journey from Frankfurt to Brussels. He armed himself with a single weapon. A graph, run up by his staff at Europe's most powerful financial institution, it showed plunging prices for bonds issued by the Spanish, Greek, Portuguese, and Irish governments. "My main message for the governments was: Some of you have behaved very improperly and have created an element of vulnerability for your own country, and by way of consequence for Europe," Trichet recalled in an interview for Bloomberg published in June 2010. "Now the situation calls for taking up responsibilities."[1]

When European heads of state gathered in Brussels over the weekend of May 7, 2010, the mood was tense and nervous. Everyone present knew precisely the stakes they were playing for. For a few brief days, the survival of the single currency was in question—and with the euro, the survival of the European Union itself, a political dream that three generations of politicians had dedicated their careers to making a reality. A game of poker doesn't get any tougher than that.

All around them the markets were clamoring for action. In the wake of the collapse of the EU-IMF rescue package for Greece, the markets were turning choppier and choppier. Over the course of a nervous day's trading, equity markets on all the major European bourses had started to skid, recording some of the worst falls seen since the collapse of Lehman Brothers and the financial panic that came in its wake. The CAC-40 in Paris was down 4.6 percent on May 7, while the German DAX dropped by more than 3 percent. Currency and bond markets were swinging wildly. The extra yield investors demanded to hold 10-year Greek, Spanish, or Irish debt instead of bunds surged to the highest since before the euro's debut in 1999. U.S. Treasuries, the traditional safe haven for investors in moments of panic and turmoil, soared in price as bankers and fund managers started to switch their investments out of a beleaguered euro that looked close to collapse.

"Greek Crisis Becomes Global," read the title of an analysis by the German bank Commerzbank, which argued that the European Central Bank had failed to calm investors worried about contagion from the Greek mess. That pretty accurately summed up the mood. On Wall Street, late on the Thursday, there was a sudden drop of nearly 1,000 points, or more than 9 percent, on the benchmark Dow Jones Index. It was later ascribed to a computer error, but in the heat of the moment there were wild stories of another major banking collapse, with losses on Greek debt the most likely source of the crisis. President Barack Obama said at a press conference that he'd spoken with Germany's Angela Merkel on the phone and the two of them had agreed on the need for a strong response to a crisis that appeared to be rapidly spinning out of control.

Rumors started to emerge that the euro-zone's finance ministers would gather over the next two days and try, for one final time, to shore up confidence in the single currency. If they failed, then all bets were off. The euro might not have been around in a few days' time. It was the start of the trillion-dollar weekend—a last-ditch rescue effort to salvage a currency that appeared to be not just on the edge of an abyss, but walking straight toward it.

■ ■ ■

On the same day that Jean-Claude Trichet was preparing his charts for delivery to Brussels, the German Parliament, the Bundestag, was still debating the provisional bailout deal for the Greeks that had been agreed the previous month. The politicians took their seats in the historic parliament building in the heart of Berlin: Built to house the old Reichstag in 1894, it was abandoned after World War II but had been magnificently restored by the British architect Sir Norman Foster, and reinstated as the meeting place of German democracy after the reunification of the country. The Parliament still needed to vote on the German funds to be contributed toward the rescue package, which would be released as soon as the government was convinced that George Papandreou and his colleagues had done enough to get the deficit under control.

No one was under much doubt that the funds would be approved. But the collapse in world markets was making officials nervous. The yield on Greek debt was soaring again. So, too, and rather more worryingly, was LIBOR, the London Interbank Offered Rate, which measured the interest rates at which banks were willing to lend to one other. At the height of the credit crunch it was the refusal of the banks to lend money to one another, fearing there were huge losses tucked inside their rivals' balance sheets, that had led to the collapse of so many financial institutions. Now the banks were nervous of losses on sovereign debt and refusing to lend to each other once again—a mood captured in the alarming and sudden rise in the LIBOR rate.

Jens Weidmann, the German chancellor's senior economic adviser, and the man she listens to most closely on market movements, penned Angela Merkel a short memo that morning on the deteriorating situation. Merkel was due to address an election rally in Düsseldorf that afternoon, and her attention was inevitably distracted by the tough challenge her government would inevitably face when the voters went to the polls in a few days' time. Whipped up by *Bild* and the rest of the press, there was plenty of hostility to the prospect of a Greek bailout. Even so, the markets couldn't be ignored. This required her attention.

When the debate started, the arguments were clear enough. Plenty of German politicians, both in the governing party and in the opposition, were instinctively opposed to the rescue package. It went against the principles around which the German state had been reconstructed and it was hard not to feel nervous about what it predicted for the future. An endless round of Club Med bailouts was not something any of them could look forward to. "We must defend the common European currency in its entirety," said German Finance Minister

Wolfgang Schäuble, speaking for the government. "In doing so, we are also defending the European project."[2]

Under current rules, a Greek default would be "devastating," Schäuble insisted. The aid package was essential for the euro's stability and the future of the whole European Union. "We have no better alternative. Any other way would be more expensive and more dangerous."

Not everyone was convinced by the logic of that argument. "I cannot support a bill that tosses the euro's no-bailout rules overboard in favor of creating a massive financial transfer union within the eurogroup," argued Frank Schaeffler (whom as we have already seen was leading the opposition to the bailout) to the Parliament. "We've put the Greek patient on a drip and we've let his creditors off the hook."[3]

When it came to a vote, the legislation to help the Greeks passed by 380 votes to 72. But that hid the extent of the opposition. There were 139 abstentions in the 622-seat Bundestag, as most of Germany's Social Democrats, the main opposition party, abstained. The opposition Green Party backed the bill, but the anti-capitalist Left Party voted against, as did some rebels in Merkel's own coalition.

Still, the legislation had been passed in the country that mattered most. If the Germans could be persuaded to help the Greeks, there was still a possibility that a full-scale collapse could be avoided.

The trouble was, the rescue package they had just voted on was already largely irrelevant to the scale of the crisis now engulfing the markets.

That same morning, over at the Frankfurt headquarters of the Bundesbank, the steady erosion of confidence in the single currency was being noted with mounting concern. Most mornings, a document entitled "Current Market Developments" is prepared by the bank's staffers and circulated to senior officials: Designed to alert them to any important news from the bond, currency, or equity markets, it is a useful way of keeping abreast with the news from the trading floors. Ever since the Greek crisis had started, the briefings had been produced daily: This was a drama in which events were being decided in dealing rooms, and if you didn't know what was happening there minute-by-minute you wouldn't have much of a clue what was really going on. On this particular morning, the market developments note drew attention to the rapid decline of confidence in the single currency in the past 48 hours alone. "Substantial gains in federal bonds due to ongoing flight into safe investments," it pointed out to the few officials with access to the briefing, in terse note form. "Losses in European stock markets due to growing concerns about the periphery of the euro."

Over in Brussels, the same trend had already been noted. It wasn't exactly a secret. Anyone who felt like checking the prices on any one of a dozen different financial news websites could have figured it out for themselves. Before the morning was finished, it was worrying enough for European Commission President José Manuel Barroso to put a call through to Angela Merkel. When he got hold of the German chancellor on the phone, he said he needed to discuss a "worrisome development in the markets."

Merkel was already well aware of the slides on all the main European bourses. The issue was what they could do about them. They agreed that the rescue package already put in place, and just ratified by the German Parliament, was not in itself going to bring calm to the markets. After all, it had all been agreed, the money was in place ready to be transferred to Athens, and yet the prices of Greek bonds were still tumbling, and the threat of the crisis spreading to another of the high-debt euro nations was growing worse by the hour. They would, they decided, have to discuss it again at the European Union summit scheduled to start in Brussels that very evening. So far, there were no concrete proposals on the table. But one thing was clear. Something would have to be done.

Meanwhile, in Washington, both at the White House and at the headquarters of the International Monetary Fund, officials were watching with growing horror as the European Union failed to come up with anything that looked like a coherent response to the crisis. Indeed, the lackadaisical response of the European Union to what was quite clearly a problem within its own backyard had been causing rising exasperation in Washington over several months. U.S. policymakers tend to be suspicious of the ability of their counterparts in Brussels to move quickly or decisively on anything. But this, even by tardy EU standards, was, in the opinion of many of them, turning into a joke—although unfortunately one with the ability to wreak terrible damage on the whole global economy.

According to a report in the *Washington Post*, as early as February officials from the IMF started warning their EU counterparts about the way the markets were turning against Greece. But those warnings were largely discounted. "Don't worry," was the message from Paris, Berlin, and Brussels. "This is our territory, we can handle it."

Rather like the credit crunch, there were plenty of alarm bells ringing all around the capital markets, but the officials at the top chose to ignore them even though they were obvious to staffers lower down the chain and indeed to anyone who had day-to-day dealings with the markets for euro-zone government bonds. "What the IMF said from the beginning is that you need a much more comprehensive program," said a top IMF official quoted in a *Washington Post* analysis of the Greek debacle. "The economics of it got worse and worse because market sentiment was essentially in a free fall. What could be seen as a small, manageable problem six months ago transformed into a huge, over-sized problem."

On that analysis, Europe's leaders were initially daunted by the cost of shoring up the European financial system. In February 2010, the IMF was already estimating that it would cost in the region of $35 billion to restore confidence in the Greek economy. That appeared far too much at the time, although of course the delay meant that final figure for the rescue was multiplied many times over. It was very reminiscent of the collapse of the investment bank Lehman Brothers two years earlier. While the bank could have been saved at the cost of a few billion to the U.S Treasury, the cost seemed too great. Yet after it went bust, it cost many more billions to rescue banks all around the world that started to collapse in the wake of the Lehman bankruptcy. Political leaders, and particularly European leaders, didn't appear to have memories that stretched back even 18 months. The world's financial system has become so complex and so interdependent that it is always better to fix problems early and decisively. There is no time or space left for dallying and delay. But as February stretched into March, that appeared to be all that Europe could offer.

By late February, U.S. Treasury Secretary Timothy F. Geithner began pushing his European counterparts to get on top of the situation in Greece. But both he and his main officials were met with shrugs and a languid indifference that they found infuriating. In early

February, finance ministers from the Group of Seven economies gathered in Iqaluit, in Canada's North-West Territories. They were taken dog-sledding and offered seal meat for dinner. As they talked, Geithner pressed the Greek issue with an increasing sense of urgency, even as his European counterparts insisted they remained in complete control. European leaders "will make sure it is managed," France's Finance Minister Christine Lagarde said as she left the meeting. Asked how he felt about Greece's situation, European Central Bank President Jean-Claude Trichet summed up the feeling on the European side: They were "confident," according to a *Washington Post* report. The American attempts to find an early solution to the crisis were being comprehensively ignored.

There were, of course, reasons for that. The euro was not an explicitly anti-American currency. But underlying the entire European project there had always been a sense of building a genuine rival to the overwhelming power of the United States. No European currency on its own could ever hope to match the power of the dollar—not even the deutschmark, and certainly not the French franc or the Italian lira. Their economies were simply too small compared with the scale of the United States. But the euro was right from the start a natural rival for the dollar. It allowed European leaders to finally escape from U.S. financial dominance. In that context, the last thing they wanted to do was take lessons from Washington in how to fix the Greek crisis. One of the points of the euro had been to escape from American cajoling, not to encourage it. Not surprisingly, therefore, they were in no mood to listen to Geithner even while they might have had plenty of worries of their own.

But as the sense of crisis grew that Friday, and with the Dow in freefall the night before, Geithner tried again to knock what he saw as some sense into his counterparts on the other side of the Atlantic. By 2:00 P.M., Central European Time, and early morning over in Washington, the U.S. Treasury secretary had persuaded the finance ministers of the seven largest industrial nations to hold a teleconference that very day. When he got them all on the phone, he made his point forcefully and clearly. The markets were getting more and more nervous, he repeated. The leaders of the European Union had to make it clear to the markets that they were willing to do whatever it took to make sure the euro survived. The time for dallying was over.

It was a sobering experience—and a reminder that for all the grandstanding as it celebrated its tenth anniversary, when it came to calling the shots in the world economy, it was the dollar that had the real clout and not the euro. When the teleconference finished, Germany's finance minister, Schäuble, called Chancellor Merkel immediately to brief her on what had been discussed. She had just been on the phone with Italian Prime Minister Silvio Berlusconi and President of the European Council Herman Van Rompuy. "Things are coming to a head," she confided in her trusted finance minister, as she concluded the call. Her flight to Brussels had just been rescheduled so she could get to the Belgian capital an hour earlier. It was clear that the markets were moving too quickly for any delay to be tolerated.

In Brussels, French President Nicolas Sarkozy was the first major European politician to arrive for the summit. He'd just attended a memorial service in the small French town of Neuilly-sur-Seine for police officers killed in the line of duty. Changing his suit, he rushed straight to the French summit office to prepare for the hours that lay ahead. The hyper-energetic Frenchman had been a relatively low-key player in the Greek crisis so far, and he was perhaps feeling slightly aggrieved at his inability to seize the moment so far. The euro had, insofar as it could be pinned down to any one nationality, been a French idea, pushed as part of the French elite's ideal of an ever-closer union among the nations of Europe. The French, too, had always viewed the euro as a stepping stone to an economic government for Europe, with harmonized tax rates, a coordinated fiscal policy, and single trade and industrial strategy and in time a single welfare system as well. It was a long-term ambition of the French, who have long railed against harmful tax competition within the EU, which inevitably makes it a lot harder to maintain their own high-tax, big government, generous welfare version of modern capitalism. If ever there was a moment both to defend the euro and yet also to seize the opportunity for a decisive step toward that single economic government, then this was surely it. Sarkozy, who like all short French leaders is never a man to lack grand visions of himself, must have known this was an occasion for him to steal the limelight.

A "French Plan" for resolving the crisis had already been sketched out. It would involve a decisive step toward that single economic government outlined above. It would, as was usually the way, proceed by stealth. The instrument this time would not be the euro itself but a new type of bond issued jointly by all the euro-zone governments. The *Eurobond*, as it would inevitably be known, would be a seemingly innocuous-sounding innovation, designed to help ride through the worst of the crisis. But it was a reform that would fundamentally change the way the euro, and indeed the EU, worked.

A Eurobond would allow the countries that made up the single currency to issue debt jointly in the name of all the members. The way the euro worked in its first decade, the Germans still issued bonds for which they alone were liable, and so did the French, the Italians, the Spanish, and so on. Countries shared the same currency but not the same liabilities. The new bond would be issued by everyone. If the Greeks couldn't pay off their debts, then the rest of the euro-zone would be liable for them. The same applied for the Italians, Spanish, and Portuguese. At a single stroke, the Greek crisis would be brought to an end. The markets were reluctant to lend any more money to Greece because they were worried it wouldn't be paid back. But if the bonds were backed by the whole euro-zone, those doubts would disappear. There would no longer be any differences in price between the debts of any of the euro-zone countries because they would all be the same.

It would fix the crisis, of that there could be little doubt. But it would also be a huge step forward toward closer integration. After all, if the Germans and the French were to take on responsibility for all the debts of the Club Med countries, then they would expect to have a say in how their economies were run as well. After all, one country can't take on another's debts without demanding some say in how its economy is run in return. That would be plainly unreasonable. The Eurobond effectively meant common fiscal policies, tax policies, and trade policies. It was the step toward a single economic government that many people had quite rightly predicted was the inevitable result of the euro.

The issue was whether, in the heat of the crisis, and with the risk of a full-scale collapse of the euro when the markets opened again on Monday morning concentrating everyone's mind, the French would be able to ram through the kind of centralizing reforms they had always wanted.

There were still a couple of hours left until Angela Merkel's plane would touch down in Brussels. Sarkozy took advantage of the time to prepare the ground. He met privately with Portuguese Prime Minister José Sócrates, Italian Prime Minister Silvio Berlusconi, and Spanish Prime Minister José Luis Rodríguez Zapatero, spending a few minutes with each man one after the other. None of them were natural allies of the French: The Spanish have more often sided with the British in European Union negotiations in recent years, and the Italians have never been reliable allies for anyone within the EU. But there was a purpose in singling out those three men for special attention. They were all the leaders of countries with crushing debts. They all knew that the markets might turn on them at any moment, and then they would find themselves in the same desperate position as George Papandreou. If any countries were going to be receptive to the French plan, then Portugal, Spain, and Italy would be. A condemned man, particularly one who can see the gallows being built outside his cell, is always open to proposals for a jailbreak, even if it comes with a heavy price tag attached.

At six that evening, the leaders began to arrive for the start of the official summit. The location was the Justus Lipsius building, a functional office building that had been the home of the European Council since 1995. It was named after the Belgian philosopher, Justus Lipsius, a Reformation thinker who had blended stoicism and Christianity to create what historians of philosophy refer to as *neostoicism*. Stoicism, at least in its colloquial rather than its strictly philosophical sense, would certainly be required of the leaders over the next 48 hours. They faced challenges to their monetary system that none of them could have foreseen, and the consequences of failure would be unthinkable. They would need to steel themselves for a tough few hours during which their resilience and fortitude would be tested to the limit.

The agenda for the summit was familiar enough to all the participants. Usually, very little is decided at these occasions. The hard work is done in advance between officials from the different countries taking part. The leaders gather, talk, have a fine meal, and then ratify a communiqué that has been agreed on already. That was the way the evening was arranged: The plan was simply to finalize the financial assistance package for Greece that had been hammered out weeks earlier, and then head back to their respective capitals.

Before joining the rest of the leaders, Merkel arranged a short one-on-one session with Sarkozy. The Franco–German axis has always been the core of the European Union. The two nations dominate its decisions. Other countries such as Italy or Britain might be of a similar size to France, but their government is too chaotic in the case of Italy, or too instinctively suspicious of European integration in the case of Britain, to wield the same kind of influence. Some of the new nations of Eastern Europe, such as Poland and the Czech Republic, were starting to bring their own vision of how the continent should manage its affairs to EU summits, but they weren't yet rich enough or senior enough to have the same kind of influence. Sarkozy and Merkel hadn't struck up the kind of intimate working relationship that had characterized past pairings of French presidents and German chancellors: They had never replicated the closeness of Francois Mitterrand and Helmut Kohl in the 1980s or Valery Giscard D'Estaing and Helmut Schmidt in the 1970s. Still, when there was a crisis, they were still the two leaders who would have to call the shots. History showed that a united Franco–German front could usually impose its will on the rest of the European Union. The question was whether they could find enough agreement between themselves to make a deal stick.

Sarkozy told Merkel that he wanted to establish a separate bailout fund. The issue had gone beyond just Greece. They had to show they stood behind all the high-deficit countries. If they didn't, they could rescue the Greeks but the markets would just move on to the next victim. Both leaders by now probably recognized they had been too slow in their initial response to the sovereign debt crisis. If they had acted earlier and more decisively, as the Americans had been urging them, they would have probably prevented it turning into the catastrophe it became. They knew they had to make sure they didn't repeat that mistake again.

The funds should be taken from the EU budget, Sarkozy told Merkel. They kicked around some numbers, but there were no specific figures penciled into the French plan yet. Somewhere between 35 billion and 70 billion euros was under discussion. The French president kept stressing that time was of the essence. They had to create the impression of decisiveness to convince the markets that *they* were in charge of events, not the bond dealers of the City of London, nor the hedge funds of Mayfair, Grand Cayman, or Geneva. In part, that reflected Sarkozy's personality: Without much in the way of firm principles, he is one of those politicians for whom the impression of decisiveness is everything, without much apparent thought being given to what the decisions actually are. Merkel is different: A more naturally cautious leader, with little in the way of rhetorical gifts, she has little personality and is charismatic only insofar that being in charge of Europe's largest country lends a person a certain weight. By nature she prefers to prepare each policy carefully rather than sign up to one of Sarkozy's back-of-an-envelope wheezes. Even so, this time around she was forced to concede that decisiveness was what was needed.

She had some questions on the plan. Who would distribute the money from the bailout fund? How would they account for it? Merkel was only too aware that European Union funds had a tendency to disappear into the black hole of extravagance, and that standards of bureaucratic honesty in Portugal and Greece were not what the Germans were used to. She knew as well that reporters from *Bild* would be out scouring the Club Med countries for examples of bailout funds—or what they would inevitably refer to as honest German taxpayers' money— being squandered by corrupt local officials. Those headlines, if they ever emerged, would make for some very uncomfortable election rallies for the politicians who signed off on the funds. They should be avoided at all costs. The bailout money should be distributed with complete transparency, rigor, and honesty.

By the end of the meeting, there was still no clear agreement between the Germans and the French. They had, however, both signed up to the idea that something needed to be done, and that in itself was progress. They sat down with the other leaders to a dinner of asparagus followed by turbot. On a screen that everyone could see, Jean-Claude Trichet flashed up the graphs that his staff had prepared for him earlier that day showing the plunging prices of Greek, Spanish, and Portuguese bonds. There were some surprised faces around the table. They thought they were here to talk about Greece. They hadn't realized that *all* the high-deficit countries were on the agenda.

The message from the ECB president, a man they all respected, was uncompromising and stark. He told them that interbank lending between the main European financial institutions had ground to a virtual halt over the previous 24 hours. Panic was spreading through the markets. There was risk of an even worse financial calamity than the disaster that followed the fall of Lehman Brothers. Central bankers are usually measured and cautious in their tone. They are as hostile to hyperbole as they are to printing money. So when Trichet said they were staring into a disaster, everyone assembled at the dinner that evening was inclined to believe them.

When he had finished, Sarkozy addressed the room. "The euro zone is experiencing the worst crisis since its establishment," he said. "We must find a systemic response," agreed Angela Merkel in her remarks to the summit.

The German chancellor proposed using the weekend to find a solution. A meeting of finance ministers had been scheduled for Sunday. With the markets closed until Monday, they had a narrow window of time to find a deal before trading kicked off again. They would, she warned her colleagues, get only one more shot at this, so they'd better get it right.

By the time the dinner broke up, an exhausted Angela Merkel said just a few brief words for the German press, and then left to get some much-needed rest. A smiling, tanned Silvio Berlusconi told the assembled press room that a rescue was underway. "When a house is burning, it doesn't matter where the water comes from," said the Italian premier. "I am very pleased with this evening. France and Italy have prevailed."

As so often, Berlusconi was exaggerating. It was in fact France that had prevailed while the Italians had done little more than cheer from the sidelines. It was the energetic Sarkozy, often at his best late at night, who was determined to grab the media narrative and shape it toward his own ends. The European Union would have an "intervention unit" in place when financial markets reopened on Monday, May 10, to fend off speculative attacks against euro members, Sarkozy announced.

As was so often the case with the French president, the grand statement came first and the details could be sketched in by someone else later. The "intervention unit" had no money, no staff, no offices, and no plan of action. It was being summoned into life out of nothing late at night in Brussels.

But one thing was clear enough. It would now have to be ready by the time the markets opened on Monday, or there really would be chaos. The trillion-dollar weekend had begun.

■ ■ ■

Christine Lagarde usually spends the weekends at her country home in Normandy. A slim, elegant woman, Lagarde is a rarity in the senior ranks of French political life. Not only is she a woman, but she is someone who made her career in America and in the law and before joining the government, and she has brought a rare directness to the sometimes inward-looking world of European financial politics.

Born Christine Lallouette in 1956, in Paris, she grew up mostly in the rather dismal port town of Le Havre, where her father was an English professor, which perhaps helps explain her excellent command of the language, and her ease—untypical for senior French politicians—with the Anglo-Saxon world. She studied law at the University of Paris and later earned master's degrees in English and labor law. In 1981, at the age of 25, she joined Baker & McKenzie's Paris office, launching a legal career focused on employment law and mergers and acquisitions. Her rise was meteoric. In 1987, she became a partner and, eight years later, was elected as one of two European representatives on the firm's seven-member executive committee. In 1999, at the age of just 43, she was elected by the law firm's partners as chairperson. It was rare for a woman to run one of the largest law firms in the world, and even rarer for a French woman. Along the way, Lagarde had two children, but divorced her husband. On taking the chair of Baker & McKenzie she moved to the firm's Chicago headquarters.

In 2005, Lagarde got a call from then–Prime Minister Dominique de Villepin asking her to join the French government. She joined his administration as Trade Minister. After Sarkozy succeeded Jacques Chirac as president, and appointed his own prime minister and cabinet, Lagarde was made finance minister. There has not in the years since then been a huge amount of evidence of the free-market revolution that Sarkozy promised for France when he was running for election. Policy has been run along traditional, state-directed, interventionist lines. Even so, Lagarde has made some changes, argued the case for business and markets, and impressed her colleagues across Europe with her charm and intelligence.

Over the course of the trillion-dollar weekend she was to be a crucial figure in turning the French plan from words and bluster into concrete action. At her Normandy weekend retreat Lagarde spent the Saturday morning juggling phone calls from Sarkozy, Germany's Wolfgang Schäuble, and Dominique Strauss-Kahn, the Frenchman who runs the International Monetary Fund. As she switched from one conversation to the next, Lagarde was perfectly well aware of the challenge that lay ahead over the next 36 hours. "The only thing the markets understand is money," she said in an interview with Bloomberg published later in May 2010. "We had to get real, which meant get big. If you don't have a big number on the board, they'll think you are really just a bunch of amateurs."[4]

The night before, in Brussels, Sarkozy and Merkel had been talking of a fund of around 35 billion to 70 billion euros, but it soon became clear, not least to Lagarde, that a much bigger sum would be needed. The EU had made timid responses already and they hadn't worked. What they needed was something that would blow the markets out of the water—the financial equivalent of the "shock-and-awe" strike on Baghdad with which the U.S. Army had kicked off the first night of the Second Gulf War. A hammer-blow that would leave the enemy reeling and confused.

But agreement on what it should be was still a long way away.

In Paris, Sarkozy was already briefing the media to expect something spectacular. "This crisis is systemic, the response must be systemic," he said after the Brussels summit had ended. "It is the whole euro-zone that needs to defend itself" through a "general mobilization," he argued, slipping into the military language he enjoys. "On Monday when markets open, Europe will be ready to defend the euro. We can't let the euro fall. The euro is Europe and Europe is peace."[5]

Sarkozy may well have been exaggerating by describing the weekend as preserving peace across Europe—exaggeration and hyperbole are second nature to the man—but by a strange coincidence, the weekend was also dominated by memories of World War II. In Moscow, the anniversary of Russia's victory over Germany was being celebrated in Red Square. Most of the main European leaders were meant to be there. Amid the chaos in the markets, both Berlusconi and Sarkozy canceled their visits, citing the threat to the future of the euro as a more pressing call on their time. It was more important to win this war against the markets than commemorate an old one against the Nazis. Angela Merkel, understandably, felt it would be an unforgivable slight not to attend the sixty-fifth anniversary of her country's defeat. The German chancellery had repeatedly assured the Russians that she would be there. It was the first time that foreign troops had been invited to take part in the annual Victory Day parade and march through the Russian capital, and world leaders such as Hu Jintao of China would also be watching the spectacular display of fighting hardware. German leaders may have their faults, and they may sometimes be as arrogant as the country they represent. But they are always willing to sit through the endless round of World War II memorials, even though it would sometimes be understandable if they would prefer to be somewhere else.

The trouble was, it took her away from the negotiations for most of the Saturday. While the package to rescue the euro was being put together, the German chancellor, the most important actor in the drama, was watching soldiers march up and down Red Square. Although she had a brief conversation with China's Hu Jintao about the euro, assuring him that a solution to the debt crisis would soon be found, she was out of the loop for the crucial hours. It was going to be hard to regain control of the negotiations from the French.

At 12:00 noon the next day, Bundesbank President Axel Weber asked his driver to take him straight to his office in Frankfurt. The German central bank's staff don't usually work on Sundays, but this weekend was exceptional, and Weber is not a man who would ever be likely to take the weekend off while the future of the euro was in the balance. Weber was to emerge as a crucial figure in the rescue package, and, as one of the two main candidates to succeed Trichet as president of the ECB when his term expires in 2011, may well prove to be the man who either saves or finally breaks up the euro.

Weber became Bundesbank president in 2004, after a long and distinguished career specializing in applied monetary and international economics. Although married to an Englishwoman, and fluent in English, he is a stern protector of the traditions of the Bundesbank and well aware of its crucial, sometimes almost mystical, role in German national life. He grew up in Glan-Muenchweiler, a village of 1,200 people surrounded by tree-covered hills in southwestern Germany less than 30 miles from the French border. It is not far from the lush countryside of Verdun, the site of the bloodiest fighting between the French and German armies during World War I, with more than 700,000 casualties on both sides in 1916 alone. No one growing up in that part of the world could fail to be aware of the shadow that the carnage of Verdun cast over the years that followed, or fail to appreciate that preventing another European war was always the paramount duty of every generation, a consideration beside which any other interest could be simply set aside. His father, Hans, taught at the local primary school, and from there Weber went on the University of Konstanz. Afterward, Weber taught and did research from 1982 to 2004 at the universities of Siegen, Bonn, Frankfurt, and Cologne. As an academic, Weber developed ties to the inner circle of Berlin politics. He was a member of the so-called Five Wise Men, the government's panel of economic advisers, from 2002 to 2004. His former students include Germany's Deputy Finance Minister Joerg Asmussen, and Jens Weidmann, the chancellor's chief economic adviser. Indeed, Merkel has increasingly enlisted Weber to help sell unpopular financial bailouts at home and abroad. He holds a position right at the center of the country's economic and political establishment, and as Germany's debate over the euro progressed, his voice was always going to be one of the most influential.

That Sunday lunchtime, most of the Bundesbank's executive board was, as you might expect, at home. Weber briefed them on the phone, updating the board on the state of the negotiations. There was not a huge amount that he could say, except that rather alarmingly there was a lot more money at stake than anyone had thought at first. The German government had asked the bank to come up with an estimate of the total liquidity requirements of the high-deficit countries over the next two years: that is, not the total amount they owed, but what they would have to raise over the next 24 months, both to roll over existing debts that were falling due and to finance their planned deficits. The Bundesbank's staffers had crunched all the numbers and come up with a scarily enormous figure. In total, it would come to 500 billion euros.

The questions from the board were straightforward. Would the funds be provided in the form of straight loans from the rest of the euro-zone? Or would they be in the form of loan guarantees to those countries? Weber didn't really know. Those decisions were still being made. But they were being decided, not here in Frankfurt, but in Paris and Brussels.

For Weber, it must surely have been a sobering moment. The Bundesbank had lost control of the money that ordinary Germans used, that they kept in their wallets and savings accounts, and of which it was meant to be the ultimate guardian. It could fight that if it wanted to, but the price, if it chose to, would be a high one. There was much for the Bundesbank president to think about that afternoon, but he would have to do so alone, a long way away from the real action.

That was all centered on Brussels. Even before the finance ministers of the euro nations had gathered for their special meeting, the tone had in effect been set by a statement released by the European Commission. Under its draft proposals for the rescue package, the involvement of the International Monetary Fund would be ruled out in the future, there would be a time limit on aid offered to the high-deficit countries, the consent of all member states would not be required for approval, the loans would be financially backed by all the member states of the euro-zone, and a European bond would be created to raise the money. "The document read as if it had been written at the Elysée Palace," commented the usually well-sourced German news magazine *Der Spiegel* in its summary of events. "For the German representatives at the meeting," it was clear that the goal of the French delegation was to "force them up against a wall."[6]

It was about to get even worse for the German delegation. Just before three that afternoon, their finance minister, Wolfgang Schäuble, arrived at the underground car park of the Justus Lipsius Building. On the drive in from the airport, he had already started to feel ill. Inside, he was taken to an emergency medical room, where a paramedic took care of him. His condition showed no sign of improvement and was beyond the expertise of the paramedics on site. In 1990, Schäuble had been shot three times in an attempted assassination, and had been confined to a wheelchair ever since. With great bravery, he had overcome those horrific injuries and risen close to the top of his party, becoming a key member of Merkel's government. But he was still on constant medication and had reacted badly to it that day. An ambulance was called, and the minister quietly left the building and was driven to the nearby Cliniques Universitaires Saint-Lu, where he was immediately admitted to the intensive-care unit.

The timing could hardly have been worse. As the finance ministers gathered for the most important meeting since the launch of the euro, Germany didn't even have a representative at the table. As the rest of the ministers took their place in the large conference room, the seat reserved for Germany had to be taken by a relatively inexperienced state secretary in the Ministry of Finance, Joerg Asmussen (ironically, as we saw earlier, a former student of Bundesbank President Axel Weber). As proceedings started, Olli Rehn, the Finnish Economic and Monetary Affairs commissioner for the EU, stood up to present the Commission's plan. Speaking nervously, he argued that Europe must deliver a "decisive response before the markets open again." But the plan he was presenting was, to all intents and purposes, the French blueprint cooked up by Sarkozy and fleshed out by Christine Lagarde. If the Germans were to force any changes now, they were leaving it for very late in the day.

At four that afternoon, German Interior Minister Thomas de Maizière was walking in the woods near his home close to Dresden when one of his bodyguards handed him a mobile phone. The chancellor was on the line. Wolfgang Schäuble has been admitted to the hospital, Angela Merkel told the minister. They needed someone to take his place in the negotiations, and although de Maizière was not an economist or a financial expert, he was close to the chancellor and she trusted him to fight in the country's corner. As he hurried back from the woods, a plane was already being rerouted to collect him and get him to Brussels as fast as possible. By 6:15, he was already in the air.

In Berlin, nothing was really going right for Merkel. Elections were being held in North Rhine Westphalia that very day, and by midafternoon private exit polling was available for the chancellor. Her Christian Democratic Union and the center-left Social Democratic Party were running virtually neck-and-neck, but the Greens were doing almost twice as well as the liberal Free Democratic Party, the key partners in Merkel's center-right coalition. From the look of the polls, the coalition was finished in that region and would lose power to the left. In itself that might not matter too much, but Merkel's federal government coalition would now lose its majority in the Bundesrat, Germany's upper legislative chamber that represents the interests of states.

Whether the Social Democrats would have handled the negotiations over the Greek bailout was a moot point. After all, they had been just as committed to the creation of the euro, and to Germany's central place in the European Union, as the Christian Democrats had been.

But it was a reminder for Merkel that ordinary Germans were furious about the rescue package, didn't want to help the Greeks or any of the other high-deficit countries, and would punish at the ballot box whoever happened to be in power when a deal was agreed. Her determination to make the rescue as tough as possible for the Greeks can only have increased.

On the phone, Merkel spoke again with President Obama. Over the course of that afternoon, he'd phoned both the French president and the German chancellor to stress how seriously the Americans took the crisis. According to White House Press Secretary Robert Gibbs, he told both leaders to take "resolute steps to build confidence in the markets."[7] *Der Spiegel* reported some days later that Merkel promised the president that the Europeans would make a "decisive response" to the crisis by later that day. By "decisive," she assured him, she meant that a number would be attached to the package that was big enough to convince the markets the issue had been settled once and for all. In return, she wanted Obama to make sure that the International Monetary Fund would agree to play a role in the rescue: The IMF is based in Washington, and although usually run by a European is generally regarded as, to put it mildly, susceptible to pressure from the White House.

Soon afterward, her office in Berlin contacted Sarkozy's office in Paris to assure them that the German government was willing to increase the euro countries' portion of the bailout fund to €440 billion.

The number was getting bigger all the time. But was it big enough? That was still to be decided.

A press conference to announce the results of the finance ministers' meeting had been due to be held by 6:00 P.M., but as the hours ticked by it became clear that that deadline had no hope of being met. Germany's de Maizière finally arrived at the Justus Lipsius building at 8:30 P.M.: At least now there was someone at the table who was able to negotiate with Merkel's full authority. But agreement was still a long way away. Asmussen had filled up the time addressing issues of protocol, so no real progress had been made. He was just playing for time until the heavyweight politicians arrived. Now there were only a few hours left before trading opened in Sydney. If they didn't have a deal in place by then, despite the promises of Friday night, they could expect the response of the markets to be swift, brutal, and quite possibly fatal. "That's the deadline we have to make," Christine Lagarde told her colleagues. If we don't make it, the speculators will be back in charge.

A question was left unspoken. Surely, no one wants that? But de Maizière, speaking with Angela Merkel's full authority, made it clear that he could not accept the Commission's proposals for a common European bond. Even leaving aside the fact his government didn't like it very much, he argued that it would be unconstitutional in Germany. If it simply got ruled out by the constitutional court, that wouldn't help anyone. "This solution is completely out of the question," he insisted.

Over the next hour there was a heated discussion of the issue. The Eurobond was central to the French plan, and they had signed up plenty of other countries. But the German interior minister was adamant. He wouldn't accept it. Now there were just two-and-a-half hours until the Sydney markets opened. And still there was no plan.

Hundred of miles away, in the Chancellery building in Berlin, Angela Merkel had gathered her most-senior colleagues. Opened in 2001, the Chancellery is one of the largest government headquarters buildings in the world. Covering 12,000 square meters, it is almost eight times the size of the White House. A glass, steel, and concrete postmodern building, it was designed by Charlotte Frank and Axel Schultes and includes a small apartment for the chancellor, although Merkel prefers to live in her own apartment in Berlin, and uses it just as an office. That evening, she was joined by her economics minister, Rainer Bruderle, her foreign minister, Guido Westerwelle, the leader of her coalition partners the Free Democrats, and her justice minister, Sabine Leutheusser-Schnarrenberger.

All of them were following the negotiations in Brussels with intense interest, aware that the future of the government could well hang on what was agreed over the next few hours. They were mainly worried about whether the bailout package would be constitutional. Everything, they decided, would depend on the precise wording of the eventual bill that would have to be presented to the German Parliament.

Over in Frankfurt, Axel Weber and his colleagues at the Bundesbank were following events just as closely. At 10:30 P.M., Weber updated his executive board by phone for the second time that day. The news hadn't got any better, at least not for the men who regarded themselves as custodians of Germany's postwar monetary orthodoxy. The European Central Bank, he told them, had decided to start buying up the bonds of the countries that needed credit, and might start doing so as early as Monday morning. Even on a conference call, the moment of shocked silence was telling. It was, in the view of more than one member of the board, a direct breach of the Maastricht Treaty, not to mention the guiding principles the Bundesbank had used to steer the postwar German economy toward prosperity and stability. If the ECB was buying bonds directly in the market, then the euro-zone was now jointly liable for the debts of all of its members. And the European Central Bank had effectively compromised its independence, buckling to political pressure at its first real test, and directly financing the profligacy of a few nations on the periphery of the euro-zone. It wasn't hard to imagine the likes of Wilhelm Vocke, and the rest of the stern bankers who had created the mighty deutschmark, spinning in their graves.

One of the board members asked Weber if the chancellor had been made aware of the consequences of the decision. It wasn't hard to work out the significance of the question. Surely a German chancellor wouldn't sign up to this if she understood what it actually meant. No economist herself, maybe she'd been bullied into it by the French and the Italians? Surely, once she understood that this meant Germany was abandoning everything that had made its postwar society so much more successful than the catastrophic state that had preceded it, then she would change her mind? Weber chose his words carefully when he replied. He said he had voted against the decision when it was put before the governing council of the European Central Bank. In addition to Weber, the ECB's chief economist, Jürgen Stark, another German, and Nout Wellink, president of the Dutch central bank, had also voiced their doubts about the proposal. But those were the only three voices raised in opposition. All the others were in favor.

There was still a card to play. According to the plan as it was being drafted in Brussels, the Bundesbank would have to buy government bonds from the high-deficit countries worth eight billion euros. That was its contribution to the rescue package. But that couldn't happen without the consent of the central bank's executive board. The politicians had assumed that was just a formality. The central bank's board would do what their elected masters required of them. And yet, late on the Sunday night, according to a *Der Spiegel* report, the board discussed withholding that consent. It would be a nuclear option, risking a huge showdown with the government. To many it would appear a coup d'état by a group of unelected central bankers that would provoke a constitutional crisis. To others, however, it would be stating plainly and simply that a stable currency was the bedrock of a stable Germany, and far from challenging the constitution the Bundesbank would be defending its most basic principles by refusing to go along with the ECB's decision. Those were weighty issues to discuss late on a Sunday night.

After a debate, the board agreed it was a step too far. They weren't willing to oppose an ECB decision that by now had already been approved by all the other central banks that make up the euro-zone. It was significant, however, that the Bundesbank, or at least some members of the board, didn't have any qualms about briefing the German press later on that the issue had been debated. The warning to their political masters in Berlin was quite clear: We accepted the decision this time, but you shouldn't always assume the Bundesbank will go along with what it sees as the debasement of the currency. In most countries, a threat from the central bank would mean nothing. They are not institutions that have any public support. But Germany was always different in that respect. In a showdown between the revered Bundesbank and the government, it would take a brave gambler to place any bets on which way public opinion would swing.

Even once the Bundesbank had voted, there was still no deal in place. Back in the heated conference room of the Justus Lipsius building, a new compromise proposal had been drafted by the EU's increasingly tired and exhausted officials. It ran to 10 paragraphs printed out on one-and-a-half pages. But the deal was still deadlocked on the issue of the Eurobond, the line that Angela Merkel had drawn in the sand. The Germans were still pushing for what it called bilateral assistance: that one nation would help another with emergency loans when it ran into trouble, rather than all the euro-zone countries issuing bonds jointly. It might seem a minor point, but the distinction was crucial. Emergency loans were temporary and could be unwound. The Eurobond was a permanent, irreversible step toward a single economic government.

The Italians were objecting that emergency loans would require special legislation to be passed by the Italian Parliament. It would take months. Several of the smaller countries agreed with that point. "This is not a strong signal," Christine Lagarde told the meeting sharply. "We need guarantees for the markets."

Only a few more minutes remained before the Sydney markets opened. A deal clearly wasn't going to be reached by then. Lagarde, who had already emerged as the unofficial moderator, argued they should forget about Sydney and focus instead on getting a statement ready for the opening of the Tokyo market at 2:00 A.M., Central European time. That gave them another hour and a half. Break up into small groups and see if we can hammer out a compromise, suggested the French finance minister.

The trouble was, the more they talked, the more objections emerged. The Spanish economics and finance minister, Elena Salgado, teamed up with her Portuguese counterpart, Fernando Teixeira dos Santos, to squabble over whether they should both be mentioned in the statement as highly indebted countries. They both were, of course, but it is not the sort of confession from a government that plays well with the markets. In the end they won that one; the finance ministers simply agreed on a "pledge" in the closing statement, "to pursue substantial additional consolidation measures." They were watering down the commitment to get their deficits under control, which was precisely the kind of behavior that had got them into this mess in the first place. But it was past midnight. And although at least some of the ministers present realized that was a mistake, it was too late to fight that battle now.

The British, rather cheekily for a country that was not even a member of the euro, created some last-minute trouble. The ruling Labour Party had lost an election a few days earlier, but was still hanging onto power while the opposition Conservative and Liberal Democrat parties negotiated a coalition that would install Tory leader David Cameron as the new prime minister. The outgoing Labour chancellor, Alistair Darling, on his last official trip to Brussels, demanded guarantees that the British would not be held liable for the defaults of euro countries, either now or in the future. He may not have had much authority left, but as it happened it was a point the fiercely anti-EU Conservatives would have agreed with completely had they already been in office.

"[That is] completely unrealistic," Swedish Finance Minister Anders Borg said angrily. The City of London would be the first to suffer from the collapse of the euro. The British economy would be hit as hard as any. Why shouldn't they pay their share? The French joined in with some quips about how the British didn't understand the single currency, and never had. To the British, however, it seemed they had understood it well enough from the start. They'd stayed out of the mess and wanted to keep out of it in the future. In the end, however, there was no time to debate the issue. Whether the nations that are members of the European Union but not of the euro are responsible for the debts of the euro countries remains undecided—and will no doubt only be resolved by another crisis.

By 1:45, just 15 minutes before the Tokyo market opened, another draft statement was ready. The Eurobond was dropped, and so was the idea of bilateral assistance, but there would be a new institution backed by the member states, charged with rescuing the high-debt nations. De Maizière insisted on imposing a three-year time limit on the bailout package, and by then everyone else was too exhausted and too aware of the looming deadline to fight the proposal. Finnish Finance Minister Jyrki Katainen objected that he wanted a tax on financial transactions to fight the speculators. The rescue package wouldn't work politically without tighter controls on the financial markets, he insisted. In fact, there was no evidence to suggest that the crisis had been created by the financial markets. They were just pointing out that the Greeks had borrowed far more money than they could afford to pay back, which was obvious to anyone who cared to look at the numbers. But it remained an article of faith to many European politicians that it was the markets that were the problem, not the euro itself. A tax on financial transactions would make the package an easier sell, or so they believed.

At this time of night, however, Germany was in no mood to deal with last-minute grandstanding objections from the Finns. The Free Democrats, their pro-business coalition partners in Berlin, were firmly opposed to a tax of that sort. In the end, the document included a nebulous statement that the European Union would "examine the possibility of a global transaction tax."

It was the last change to the text. Everything else had been agreed. It was time to breathe a sigh of relief.

With only minutes to spare before the Tokyo markets opened, the deal was done. A text message from the Elysèe Palace to one of the French delegation read simply: "Bravo." Back in Berlin, Angela Merkel held one last telephone conference with her key advisers and her team in Brussels. "Well done, everyone," she concluded. Their main demands had been met.

The text was ready to be released. The trillion-dollar weekend was coming to an end. But had the euro been saved? And if it had been, what sort of currency was about to emerge?

■ ■ ■

The impact of the statement was certainly decisive. When the package was finally unleashed on the markets, it included all the "shock and awe" that had originally been promised. In total, 750 billion euros or $1 trillion was to be made available to stabilize the euro and to make sure the high-deficit countries could finance themselves through the next few years regardless of whether the markets were willing to support them. The money would come from the euro-zone itself, as well as the International Monetary Fund if necessary. At the same time, the European Central Bank was stepping into the markets to buy the bonds of the Club Med nations directly, a move it had previously refused to contemplate. For the traders and speculators, a juggernaut of money was heading their way, and few would want to stand in its way. "This is Shock and Awe, Part II and in 3-D," wrote Marco Annunziata, chief economist at UniCredit Group London's office, in an e-mailed note to his clients released just hours after the package was announced. "This truly is overwhelming force, and should be more than sufficient to stabilize markets in the near term, prevent panic and contain the risk of contagion."[8]

"The message has gotten through: The euro zone will defend its money," Christine Lagarde told reporters in Brussels after the marathon 14-hour meeting she had mainly chaired finally broke up.[9]

The details of the package showed how much work had gone into it. The euro-zone governments would offer guarantees of 440 billion euros to a special fund, which would sell debt directly to the markets and use that cash to buy the bonds of the high-deficit countries. Another 60 billion euros would come straight out of the European Union's budget and 250 billion euros would come from the International Monetary Fund, the concession that Angela Merkel had demanded from President Obama on Sunday afternoon. As the markets digested the scale of the package, the dealers quickly realized that it had for the moment fixed the crisis. The price of bonds for the high-deficit countries started to rise, helped along no doubt by the intervention of the European Central Bank into the market. Yields started to fall. There was less talk of contagion. Even the euro, which had taken a hammering on the foreign exchange markets over the past few weeks, started to recover in value.

Not everyone was happy, however, and certainly not back in Germany. Although Merkel's cabinet backed the package on Monday, the press was immediately hostile. The chancellor had turned the Germans into "Europe's jerks," roared the editors at *Bild*. European leaders "robbed the euro of its best preventive shield, the ban on aid and an independent central bank, with a vague promise of coming up soon with a tougher mechanism to enforce fiscal good sense," the normally sober *Frankfurter Allgemeine* newspaper argued in an editorial.[10] "What was carved in stone the day before no longer has any validity," argued *Die Welt* in its edition of May 11, 2010. "And nothing symbolizes this more than the ECB's loss of independence. The separation of powers between monetary and fiscal policy in Europe now belongs to the past."[11]

But for Jean-Claude Trichet, and for the ECB, securing agreement on the rescue package for the euro was to prove far harder than anyone would have imagined. One key element of the rescue package, as already noted, was that the ECB would for the first time start buying government bonds directly in the market. If no one else would buy Greek, or Portuguese, or Spanish government bonds, then as a last resort the central bank would intervene in the market and buy them itself. It was probably a necessary move to prevent a complete rout in the bond markets when they opened for business again after a frantic weekend of horse-trading among European leaders. It was only that kind of total, unqualified support for the single currency that would convince investors that governments were willing to support the euro no matter what the cost might be.

But, as we have already seen, Bundesbank President Axel Weber opposed the deal. Then, on Monday May 10, just as the rescue package was being announced, Weber broke ranks with the rest of the governing council, giving an interview to the Frankfurt-based newspaper *Boersen-Zeitung* that was later posted on the Bundesbank's own website. "The purchase of government bonds poses significant stability risks, and that's why I'm critical of this part of the ECB council's decision."[12]

The cat was, at least, out of the bag. The ECB had taken a decisive step, one that would change the character of the central bank, and indeed the euro as well, forever. It was not something the Bundesbank would support, and it wasn't holding back on broadcasting its views. Nor, in time, did it seem very likely that the German people would support it, either. Certainly Weber and his Bundesbank colleagues didn't appear in any mood to go out and sell it to them. On May 19, Weber spoke in a cramped meeting room in Berlin's Bundestag building. His task: selling the euro bailout program to lawmakers. As he spoke, he clearly wasn't enjoying himself. "I'm personally dismayed about the fact that following the bank rescue program and help for Greece, I am now appearing before the German parliament for the third time," he said. "It creates the impression that one is being driven by markets and is not in control of markets."[13] The Bundesbank president's tone was counterproductive, commented Steffen Bockhahn, a legislator for the opposition Left Party who attended the hearing, according to a Bloomberg report. That was putting it mildly. It would be just as reasonable to conclude that Weber no longer felt a rescue package for the Greeks was the right thing for the euro-area countries to be doing. And, if he did become ECB president, it wasn't going to happen again.

In reality, as Weber and his colleagues had already realized, the euro was no longer the same currency the country had signed up to a decade earlier. "The foundation of the euro has fundamentally changed as a result of the decision by euro-zone governments to transform themselves into a transfer union," wrote former Bundesbank President Karl Otto Pöhl in an article for *Der Spiegel* that no doubt reflected the view of many of his former colleagues at the bank. "This is a violation of every rule. In the Treaties governing the functioning of the European Union, it explicitly stated that no country is liable for the debts of any other. But what we are doing right now is exactly that."[14]

No one could really disagree with that. "The 400 billion euros mechanism is nothing less than the importation of Nato's Article 5 mutual defense clause applied to the euro-zone," French Europe Minister Pierre Lellouche conceded in an interview with the *Financial Times* published on May 28, 2010, a few weeks after the deal had been struck. "When one member is under attack the others are obliged to come to its defence. It is an enormous change. It explains some of the reticence. It is expressly forbidden in the treaties by the famous no bailout clause. De facto, we have changed the treaty."[15]

The treaty had indeed been changed, and so had the euro. No one was more aware of the enormity of the challenge, or indeed of its importance, than Jean-Claude Trichet himself, the man who in the view of his German critics had surrendered the independence of the central bank he had been put in charge of. "You must be inflexible on your long-term compass. My long-term compass as a central banker is price stability," he told Bloomberg in June. "My life compass has been the deepening of European unity based upon reconciliation and a profound friendship to the service of prosperity and peace. This historical endeavor, which started 60 years ago and was reinforced by the fall of the Soviet Union, goes on."[16]

"In the last few weeks I understood one thing: In Germany, some things are interpreted differently," Trichet said in an interview with Germany's weekly *Welt am Sonntag*. "The no-bailout clause means that there is no duty to offer subsidies or transfer. But it does not mean that in exceptional circumstances, one country should not be allowed to offer support to another."[17]

The trillion-dollar weekend had certainly changed the euro fundamentally, on that no one seemed to disagree. It is worth dwelling on how it had been transformed. Some of the detail is complex, but it illustrates how the euro has been changed overnight from one kind of currency to another.

There were three main elements to the rescue package. The first was the "European Stabilization Mechanism." Under this scheme, designed for any high-deficit country in trouble, the European Commission is allowed to raise up to 60 billion euros on the money markets at low interest rates by issuing bonds, using the EU's 140 billion euro annual budget as collateral. It can then lend that money to euro-area states that are struggling to pay their debts. The effect is that the Commission can lend at much lower rates than those struggling euro-zone countries could have done by themselves. The decision on who will qualify for the loans will be made by Qualified Majority Voting, on a proposal by the Commission, which means that no individual member state will have a veto. Since the EU budget is used as collateral, every member state in the EU contributes to the scheme, including countries that don't belong to the euro, such as Britain. Of course, no country is required to provide money upfront. However, should a country that has received loans default on them, every European Union state is required to cover that default by contributing extra money to the EU, depending on its share of the total contributions to the EU budget. So, rather unfairly, British taxpayers are potentially liable for some eight billion euros in euro-zone loans (corresponding to the UK's 13.6 percent share of the EU budget), which would prove controversial should it ever actually happen.

Is that actually a Eurobond? Well, since it involves the EU borrowing collectively using its budget as collateral, it is very close to it. The difference, if there is one, is more semantic than financial.

If that 60 billion euros runs out, and it might well do so, the rescue package sets up a backstop with an extra 440 billion euros in loans and guarantees called the "European Financial Stability Facility." Under this mechanism, the euro-zone countries will establish a so-called Special Purpose Vehicle that can issue bonds, and then forward those on as loans to struggling euro-zone member states. The IMF committed an additional 250 billion euros to the total package. The SPV was set up on June 7, 2010, and is registered in Luxembourg and backed by individual guarantees provided by all 16 members of the euro-zone, based on their shares in the ECB. Member states also committed to guarantee an extra 20 percent beyond their ECB share, in case some countries are unable to provide financial guarantees due to running into financial difficulties themselves. After all, it wasn't really clear that countries such as Portugal or Ireland would be in any kind of shape to contribute to the bailout, and indeed the Slovaks later refused to pay up their share, on the quite reasonable grounds that they were a poorer country than Greece.

The plan was for the Facility to go live once 90 percent of countries participating in it had ratified the package in their respective parliaments. The interest rates would be modeled on the markup charged by the International Monetary Fund and similar to the one that Greece was charged (around 5 percent). Although the agreement in May mentioned that the SPV would "expire after three years," a concession to the Germans, only a couple of weeks later its life was extended to five or six years, after it was decided that recipient countries would need longer to get themselves back in shape. As with the 60-billion-euro stabilization fund, no money will be spent upfront by member states, but if a country that receives the assistance defaults, the other euro-zone members will have to provide cash to cover the losses. So in effect European taxpayers are potentially liable for an enormous amount of money, with the Germans leading the league table with potential liabilities for a massive 120 billion euros.

The third leg of the package, and the part the Bundesbank objected to most vociferously, was the decision by the ECB to start buying government bonds directly in the markets. "The EU Treaties explicitly prohibit the ECB from buying government debt directly, but the Bank circumvented this ban by buying bonds from banks on the secondary market," argued the London-based think-tank Open Europe in a report on the rescue package called "The Rise of the EU's Economic Government." "This was widely seen as a blow to the ECB's political independence, and a step towards a French-style monetary policy in which the central bank plays an active role in underwriting and financing a government's economic policies."[18]

Indeed it was. Initially, and outrageously, the ECB at first refused to publish details about its bond purchases, but subsequently revealed that as of June 4, 2010, it had bought 40.5 billion euros' worth of bonds, mainly issued by the Greek, Irish, and Portuguese governments. It tries to pretend that this is not really printing money, because the operations, in the jargon of central banks, are "sterilized"; that is, when it injects money into the system in one place, it takes it out somewhere else. Not everyone is convinced that really works. It is a lot better at the putting the money in than the taking it out. Anyway, it might not make much difference. If Greece, Ireland, and Portugal default on their debts, the ECB will take a huge loss on the bonds it has bought, which will have to be financed through increases in the financial contributions to the ECB by member states, mostly from the long-suffering Germans, or through printing more money. Either way, that would feed through to more instability, and more inflation—and would be yet another violation of the no-bailout rule in the Maastricht Treaty.

In effect, the rescue package had finally tossed the no-bailout clause into the dustbin. The euro had been transformed, as Pohl put it, from a monetary union into a debt union. It was hard to see how a single economic government could be very far behind.

Later on, even senior European ministers would admit they had got to grips with the issue far too late. "If we had been able to address it right from the start, say in February, I think we would have been able to prevent it from snowballing the way that it did," French Finance Minister Christine Lagarde said in an interview with the *Washington Post* in June.[19]

That was certainly true. The euro-zone's leaders had ignored the crisis brewing in Greece for year after year. When it broke into the open, they tried to pretend it wasn't their problem, then blamed everyone else, and, once it threatened to overwhelm them, allowed themselves to be rushed into a solution that, while it may have fixed the immediate crisis, was only storing up even worse problems a little further down the road.

The trillion-dollar weekend was not just a violation of the existing EU treaties and a flagrant rewriting of the ECB's mandate. It wasn't even that likely to work. The new stability package suffered from the same problem as all the other ones the European Union had come up with in the months since the Greek crisis started rattling the markets at the start of 2009. It tried to fix the symptoms, not the causes.

Greece had exposed deep structural problems within the euro. There are no mechanisms to stop governments breaking the rules. There is no popular support for massive fiscal transfers between countries. The rules for the euro area have turned out to be unreliable. And there is no way to start stimulating economic growth again in the heavily indebted nations. Those are the hard questions. And even $1 trillion didn't get close to answering any of them.

First, where were the incentives for governments to stick to rules? The crisis arose because the euro-zone didn't enforce the Stability and Growth Pact, which limited budget deficits to 3 percent of gross domestic product in all but exceptional circumstances. If the Pact had been rigorously enforced, Greece would never have been allowed into the euro. Once in, it would have been disciplined for allowing its deficits to balloon even when the economy was booming. If it got bailed out for behaving badly, why should any other government behave itself? The bailout package talked about tougher disciplinary measures, but nobody said what they might be. Were tanks going to be sent into Dublin if Ireland didn't stick to its austerity program? Would the Portuguese get kicked out of the euro if they didn't control their deficit? Of course not. The only credible deterrent was letting Greece default. By wimping out of that, the EU had no ammunition left. Enforcement of the rules, for all the bluster from Brussels, had been turned into a joke.

Next, there was no popular support for the massive fiscal transfers between countries that were now proposed. That much was clear the same day the deal was put together, when Angela Merkel's coalition suffered a heavy regional defeat. Where is the 750 billion euros supposed to come from, if not ultimately from taxpayers? If they didn't want to pay it, what happened next? In reality, no one knew.

Third, the rules of the euro-zone area turned out to be about as solid as a slice of brie left out in the midday sun. Everyone was told there wouldn't be any bailouts between member states. They were told the European Central Bank wouldn't buy government bonds in the market. They were told the Stability Pact would be enforced. None of those promises turned out to be true. If the rules of the euro can be rewritten on a Sunday night in Brussels once, they can be rewritten next time there is a crisis. Investors will remember that. And they won't believe what they are told about how the euro operates from now on.

Perhaps most significantly, the rescue package didn't address the issue of how you get the heavily indebted countries growing again. The problem in Greece, Portugal, Spain, Ireland, Italy, and potentially France as well wasn't just that governments would have to push through huge and painful austerity programs. It was that they couldn't devalue their currencies at the same time to provide some relief to their economies—and to provide some hope of future growth. You can't run an economy with just sticks, not in a democracy, anyway. You need some carrots as well. The euro-zone not only has to fix the debt problem, it has to provide the money to stimulate growth as well. But, for all the reasons explained above, that isn't going to happen. The money isn't available.

In truth, the trillion-dollar weekend had bought some time, at huge cost. Everything had been thrown at trying to restore some confidence in the single currency. But as we are about to see, it hadn't begun to fix the real problems.

Chapter 9

Contagion

It was the news officials at the European Commission in Brussels and at the European Central Bank in Frankfurt least wanted to hear. On May 28, 2010, only slightly more than two weeks after assembling the "shock and awe" rescue package designed to save the euro and put a decisive end to the sovereign debt crisis, the ratings agency Fitch downgraded Spanish debt. It wasn't a catastrophic markdown. The rating on Spanish debt had been triple A, but Fitch took it down a notch to AA-plus, citing worries about the size of its budget deficit and about the credibility of the government's plan to get its spending under control.

But it was enough to send stocks skidding, bonds into turmoil, and commodity prices into a sharp downward spiral. There were certainly a few dealers, and probably some officials at central banks, thinking to themselves: *Oh, no, here we go. It's Greece all over again.*

Whether that turned out to be true or not, one thing was perfectly clear. This wasn't really a Greek problem. It was an issue of the euro. And it was part of a global sovereign debt crisis. Europe might be caught up in the vortex of the storm, but that didn't mean the winds weren't blowing elsewhere. And if it was going to be put right, the timeframe would be measured in years, and possibly decades, and certainly not weeks.

In reality, it was a crisis that was hitting most of the countries in the euro-zone, and indeed most of the developed world. They had all been borrowing far more than they could really afford. And, like a new, virulent virus, the crisis was about to hop from one nation to the next.

Let's start with Spain, because in many ways that was the country that was always going to be central to this crisis. The European Union could always afford to bail out Greece if it had to. It is a relatively small country. So are Portugal and Ireland. Spain is a different matter. With a population of 40 million people, it is slightly smaller than Britain or France or Italy, but of a similar scale. As we saw earlier, the extraordinary expansion of its economy over the past decade had made it a crucial component of the whole euro-zone economy. Its banks had risen to be some of the largest in the world: Santander, by 2010, vied with BNP Paribas to be the largest bank in Europe. And its boom was so focused on property development and bank lending that it was always going to be hugely vulnerable to any fluctuations in the credit markets. So not only was Spain acutely vulnerable to the sovereign debt crisis that was sweeping across the European markets in the spring of 2010, it was also likely to be the nation with the greatest potential to turn that crisis into a full-scale catastrophe.

If any country was going to break the euro into pieces, it was always going to be Spain.

The pressure in the Spanish markets had been building for days before Fitch delivered its ratings downgrade. Much of the property lending had been through the *cajas*, small regional banks, and many of them had become badly overexposed as the Spanish property market started to implode. The government had been promoting mergers between the cajas as a way of strengthening their balance sheets but it hadn't always gone according to plan. One example, and in many ways typical of the problem, was CajaSur. Based in the southern city of Cordoba, the 146-year-old lender was controlled by the Catholic church, and, indeed, run by a Catholic priest, Santiago Gomez Sierra. The Catholic church is famous for many things, and justly so, but financial wizardry isn't really among them. The bank had run into difficulties, losing 596 million euros on 426 million euros in revenue in 2009 as property deals turned sour. Sierra began his last board meeting with a prayer and the directors crossed themselves as they met for the last time, but their entreaties to the Lord remained unanswered. Perhaps not very surprisingly, God has better things to do with His time than restructure the balance sheets of small, regional Spanish banks. The Bank of Spain felt compelled to seize control of the bank on May 22, 2001, to prevent it going under.

It was, unfortunately, only the tip of the iceberg. The cajas had boosted lending fivefold during the long boom and accounted for half the country's outstanding debt. The seizure was the first under a state-financed rescue plan that Standard & Poor's estimated might cost as much as 35 billion euros, a huge burden on a country that was already struggling to get its finances under control.

Spain's deficit for 2010 was already projected to rise to 9.3 percent of GDP, according to EU calculations, and in 2009 had run at more than 11 percent. It was the third highest in the EU, after Greece and Ireland, and way over the 3 percent limit that was meant to apply to members of the single currency. Prime Minister Jose Luis Rodriguez Zapatero had pledged to get the deficit back to 3 percent of GDP by 2013, and had made a start with a budget presented to the country in May 2010 that certainly sounded tough. Civil servants' wages would be cut by 5 percent in 2010, then frozen in 2011, and then pensions would be frozen as well. A 2,500 euro subsidy for new parents was scrapped and plans were announced to put up value-added tax. Members of the government accepted a 15 percent cut in their own wages. It was a sudden and dramatic reversal for a socialist government, which, like the administration of George Papandreou in Greece, had been elected on a platform of fighting cuts in public spending, not implementing them. But after the latest rescue package cobbled together in Brussels, there was no longer much choice. Spain would have to cut its spending or Madrid would soon find itself in precisely the same predicament as Athens, inviting the International Monetary Fund and the European Union into the country to make the cuts it found too painful to make itself.

It was at the very least questionable whether Spain would be able to live with the kind of austerity being imposed on it: There were worries over the state of the banking system, over the decline in the economy, and over an unemployment rate that was already running at a staggering 20 percent of the workforce. By late May 2010, all the same red lights that had been flashing in the run-up to the Greek crisis were warning of precisely the same trouble ahead in Spain. The spread between the price of Spanish debt and the German bund was widening all the time. The cost of insuring yourself against the risk of a Spanish default was heading up by the day. The Spanish banks were becoming more and more reliant on funding from the European Central Bank, suggesting that the global capital markets were increasingly reluctant to advance any further funds to the country's financial institutions.

By the middle of 2010, fiscal pain was starting to become entrenched in Spain. The 17 regional governments, which spend almost twice as much as the government in Madrid, had been on a decade-long spending boom, subsidizing orchestras and arts festivals and building subways and roads, the results of which could be seen all over the country. But by 2010, they were carrying combined debts of 95 billion euros. For 2010, they agreed to slice 12.5 billion euros from their budgets, impose 5 percent wage cuts, and replace only 1 in 10 retiring employees. But local government still needed to borrow vast sums of money, more than 44 billion euros in 2010, the most of any regional government in Europe apart from Germany (which is, of course, a far larger country). The price of that debt was rising all the time: It cost a lot more for the regional governments to borrow than the national government. Public projects were being scaled back right across the country. By August, Catalonia, which accounts for a fifth of Spanish GDP, had been frozen out of the credit markets. Galicia had asked to suspend payments to the central government amid a cash crisis, and Madrid had canceled bond sales as buyers vanished. For Spain, the days of easy money, and the growth and jobs that came with it, were well and truly over.

"The process of adjustment to a lower level of private sector and external indebtedness will materially reduce the rate of growth of the Spanish economy over the medium-term," Brian Coulton, Fitch's head of Europe, Middle East, and Africa sovereign ratings in London, said in a statement that accompanied the agency's downgrade of Spanish debt.[1] Other analysts agreed. The London forecasting firm Capital Economics calculated that the Spanish deficit would still be running at more than 11 percent of GDP in 2011 unless the government was willing to push through even more painful cuts. Even if it did, there was a risk that the damage inflicted on the economy would be so great, and the impact on tax revenues so severe, that the date for finally getting the deficit under control would disappear into the far-distant future.

It was a more than reasonable point. Spain was not a disaster area—not yet, anyway. But it was stuck in a debt crisis from which it was far from clear there would ever be any escape. And the rescue package agreed a few weeks earlier in Brussels, while it might mean Spain was not about to go bust, was not going to do anything about that.

■ ■ ■

Spain's smaller southern neighbor, Portugal, doesn't usually loom large in discussions of the European economy. The country had always been one of the relatively poor members of the European Union, with an economy that was backward and underdeveloped in almost every respect. Portugal was highly dependent on low-paying industries such as tourism and agriculture, and while it was gradually catching up with the rest of Europe after joining the euro, it wasn't doing so at anything like the same rate as Greece and Spain, and was a long, long way behind Ireland. So when the acronym PIIGS—covering Portugal, Ireland, Italy, Greece, and Spain—was coined by the financial markets to cover the countries most at risk of being caught up in the sovereign debt crisis, it was no great surprise that Portugal was right at the head of the list.

"You are the next victims," Greece's deputy prime minister, Theodoros Pangalos, told the Portuguese newspaper *Jornal de Negocios* rather undiplomatically in an interview published in April 2010. "I hope it doesn't happen and the solidarity prevails and we find an exit from this escalation of [borrowing costs]. But if this does not happen, the next probable victim will be Portugal."[2]

It was a blunt assessment, but not one that many people would disagree with too vehemently. By 2009, the Portuguese budget deficit had jumped to more than 9 percent of GDP, and even though it was not quite as high as Greece's, and the country did not have the same track record of fiddling its books, the financial projections did not make happy reading. Overall national debt was creeping up toward 90 percent of GDP by 2010. The economy was stagnant. Ever since it joined the euro, Portugal hadn't really developed any competitive advantage in anything. Its major industries are tourism and the export of paper and pulp and cork (38 percent of the country is forest), but neither has been booming, and growth has been running at an annual rate of 1 percent over the past 10 years. It wasn't in great shape going into the downturn, and there was nothing to suggest the global recession would make things better. And by late summer, the ratings agencies once again were starting to get concerned.

On July 13, 2010, Portugal had its ratings cut two levels to A1 by Moody's. "The Portuguese government's financial strength will continue to weaken over the medium term," the agency said, in the kind of statement that was now becoming dismally familiar to governments and central bankers right across the euro-zone. "The Portuguese economy's growth prospects are likely to remain relatively weak unless recent structural reforms bear fruit over the medium-to-longer term."[3]

The amount that Portugal has to pay to the bond markets to keep itself afloat had been rising all the time. By the summer of 2010, the yield on a 10-year Portuguese bond was more than 5.55 percent, compared with 2.6 percent on a German bond of the same duration. Ridiculously, the Portuguese government would have to borrow money at 5.5 percent to fund its share of the European Union rescue package, which it would then have to lend on to the Greeks at 5 percent, making a loss on each euro that got transferred. It was a classic example of how the euro forced the relatively responsible to subsidize the completely profligate. But that was the way the economics of the euro-zone debt market now worked.

The government of José Sócrates announced plans in March to slash the budget deficit from 9.3 percent of GDP to under 3 percent by 2011, using the measures that were now the standard textbook for all the Club Med countries: freezing government salaries, cutting social programs, and a blitz of privatization of public companies.

But, just as in Greece and in Spain, it was by no means clear the public would tolerate it. When the package was announced, the opposition conservatives refused to say whether they will support the austerity package while the Left Bloc and Communist Party, upon whose votes the government depended, denounced the measures as "violent" and "anti-worker" and said they planned to vote against them. The government in turn warned that a vote against the bill would effectively turn Portugal into another Greece. They might as well phone the International Monetary Fund and ask them to fly straight to Lisbon. "Under the current situation of nervousness and volatility in the international financial markets . . . it is essential for Portugal to show a firm political commitment to implement its growth and stability programme," the finance ministry said in a statement on the cutbacks.

It was by now a drearily familiar story. The euro, for most of the peripheral countries, was becoming a currency that was associated with debt, deflation, and crisis. How long people would tolerate that was, to put it mildly, open to question.

■ ■ ■

There is no country in the euro-zone with a greater capacity to turn expectations on their head than Ireland. Just as the country had amazed everyone with its sudden rise to the top of the global prosperity leagues, so it caught people unawares again with the sober, responsible way it responded to the downturn in its fortunes in the wake of the credit crunch.

No major nation was harder hit by the collapse of the banking system in 2008. A joke was swapped among dealers in the City of London during much of 2009: What's the difference between Iceland and Ireland? The answer: one letter and about six months.

There certainly seemed to be much truth in that. The economy shrank by a terrifying 7.5 percent in 2009, and was expected to contract by another 1.25 percent in 2010. House prices by 2010 had fallen by 45 percent from their 2007 peak and were still going down throughout that year. Unemployment was rising fast. Most of the major banks have had to be bailed out by the government. It was a train-wreck of an economy.

But the Irish also came up with one of the toughest austerity packages in the world, and crucially, they did so in 2009, before the Greek crisis forced every government in the world to face up to the task of controlling their deficits. The 2009 budget set out plans to reduce the deficit from more than 11 percent of GDP to less than 3 percent of GDP by 2014. Public-sector pay was to be cut by 10 percent, and cabinet ministers saw their salaries reduced by at least 15 percent. Welfare payments for the unemployed were reduced, along with child benefit. Just as importantly, the government took the pain on the spending side of the balance sheet, refusing to raise taxes overall. Crucially, the 12.5 percent corporation tax rate that had made Ireland a magnet for foreign investment remained in place. Workers appeared to accept that the only way the county could pull through the crisis was to cut their living standards and reduce wages, and so make their industries more competitive in world markets. Irish labor costs will drop 10 percent between 2009 to 2011, compared with an increase of 3 to 4 percent across Europe, according to estimates from the European Commission. It would be hard to imagine a more sober response to the crisis—and it was a world away from anything the Greeks had managed.

Why the Irish managed to respond quicker, and more courageously, than the rest of the euro-zone was an interesting debate. Some commentators put it down to the suddenness of the country's wealth. Because the Irish were so surprised to be suddenly one of the richest countries in the world, they didn't see it as that unusual when it all collapsed. Easy come, easy go, summed up the attitude. Others ascribed it to the country's agricultural roots. Ireland remained basically a farming society, they argued, and farmers accept that their income varies with the seasons, the weather, and the state of the harvest. There had been some good years, and now there were some bad years, and that, too, was, for many Irish people, part of the natural order of things. Alternatively, it might have been part of the national character to meet adversity with stoicism. "The scale of cuts in pay and spending here are unprecedented across Europe," said Garret FitzGerald, Irish prime minister during the 1980s, in an interview with Bloomberg published in July 2010. "We're Northern European, less emotional, and more accepting of what needs to be done in a crisis."[4]

Whatever the reasons, the more pressing issue was whether it would do the Irish any good. It certainly helped them to escape the worst of the sovereign debt crisis. While Greek bonds were collapsing in price, the Irish bond markets held up. They fell, but not catastrophically. The Irish government still had access to the global capital markets.

That didn't mean it was out of trouble. Far from it. In July 2010, the ratings agency Moody's cut its credit rating on the country to Aa2 from Aa1, following on from an earlier cut back in July 2009, when the country was stripped of its triple-A status. "It's a gradual, significant deterioration, but not a sudden, dramatic shift," said Dietmar Hornung, Moody's lead analyst for Ireland, commenting on the day the decision was announced.[5] Rather like Greece, all the numbers coming out of the economy just kept on getting worse and worse. Although it had planned on a budget deficit of 11 percent of GDP for 2009, the actual number tuned out to be 14.3 percent (the highest in the developed world, and even worse than Greece's) for 2009. The recession and the slump in the property market had taken a brutal toll on tax revenues.

Worse might be on the way. The Irish, as they had always done in past economic downturns, were heading out into the world once again, seeking better opportunities elsewhere. According to a 2010 study by Ireland's Economic and Social Research Institute, around 70,000 people would leave the country in that year and another 50,000 in 2011. The total could rise to 200,000 by 2015 the way unemployment trends were looking. While those numbers include immigrants, mostly from Poland and other Eastern European states, returning home, Ireland last year became a net emigration country for the first time in 13 years, with 18,000 Irish-born people leaving. Becoming an importer rather than an exporter of people had been a major boost for the Irish economy, but if that goes into reverse, it will make it even harder for the country to start growing again at anything like its Celtic Tiger rates. The evidence was starting to mount up that that financial collapse and the sovereign debt crisis had done significant structural harm to the Irish economy.

"The damage done to the Irish economy by the loss of competitiveness, consequent on the property market bubble, has been greatly aggravated by the related collapse in the financial sector," concluded a report on the long-term prospects for the Irish economy published in 2010 by the country's Economic and Social Research Institute. "The ensuing collapse of the Irish financial sector has had much wider economic implications. While the loss of competitiveness may, in time, be reversible, this wider damage will continue to affect the level of potential output for the next decade."[6] Indeed the Institute forecast in July 2010 that the deficit may climb to 19.8 percent of GDP for that year, in part because of government pledges to inject 13 billion euros into two banks. If anything like that number turned out to be the final result, it would be no surprise to anyone if the markets were rattled and started selling off Irish debt.

The Irish had played the crisis straight out of the central banker's textbook. They had faced up to their problems, cut spending, and started pushing down their wages. It was austerity-max—precisely what the European Central Bank kept telling everyone was the only way out of the crisis for the peripheral nations.

But would it work? There were some signs of light at the end of the tunnel for the Irish. "Ireland is emerging from a deep slump into a modestly paced recovery," the International Monetary Fund concluded in a report on its economy published in July 2010. "The challenge is to wean the banking sector from public support and stabilize public debt in a testing environment."[7] It predicted that after suffering what turned into the deepest slump of any developed nation since the Great Depression of the 1930s, the Irish economy would start to grow modestly again in 2011 and 2012. But there were still risks to that outlook. There were signs that prices were falling, which would vastly increase indebtedness, both personal and corporate, and could easily kick off another round of bankruptcies. The banking system was still a long way from any kind of normality. And it would be a long time before the economy would grow strongly enough to get tax revenues back up again and do anything to close that budget deficit.

From the evidence of the whole decade, and looking forward to the next one, it was very hard to conclude that the euro had been good for Ireland. The economy had, as we have seen, been doing brilliantly by itself. After joining the single currency, however, the reduction in interest rates that followed created a massive asset bubble. When that collapsed, enormous damage was inflicted upon the Irish economy, from which it may take a generation or more to recover. Now it faces years of grinding austerity and wage cuts. And for what? No one could argue that, like Greece of Spain, Ireland needed the euro to modernize itself. It was doing that fine on its own. Nor did it need to share a currency with France and Germany to build export industries: It was already a hub for global manufacturers. In reality, all it got from monetary union was a monetary policy that was completely unsuitable for its own situation. It was a rotten deal.

Even worse, it may never get any better. In reality, the Irish economy posed a scary question for the rest of the euro-zone. What if even the huge cuts in wages and public spending that the Irish had accepted were not enough to rescue it? What if all the single currency had done was suck economies into a debt trap from which there was no possibility of escape?

If the Irish couldn't make it through the crisis with austerity and discipline, there wasn't much point in any other nation even bothering.

■ ■ ■

In Sir Arthur Conan Doyle's story, "Silver Blaze," Sherlock Holmes solves a mystery by concentrating on "the dog that didn't bark in the night." As Holmes quite correctly understood, sometimes it is something that is *not* happening that is more important than what is.

As the markets turned their fire onto the likes of Spain and Portugal, one country had remained so far under the radar. And yet, if you had asked people a decade earlier which of the countries joining the single currency posed its greatest risk, there would have been little debate about the answer: Italy.

And yet, in truth, although it had not yet attracted so much attention, by 2010, the Italian economy was in a terrible state. It was hard to see how it could remain in the euro much longer, and whether the Italians were any longer willing to pay the grim price that euro membership was demanding of them.

Of course, no country had been a more enthusiastic supporter of the single currency than Italy. Its postwar experience with the lira had hardly been a happy one. The currency had been devalued so many times it had turned into a joke on the foreign exchange markets. While the postwar Italian economy had rapidly industrialized (*Il boom*, as those years were known to the Italians), growing wealthier hadn't been translated into currency stability. Weak governments and perpetually high deficits meant Italy was always an inflationary country, and the lira was always losing value. Trying to stabilize the lira was like trying to balance a glass of water on a life raft in the middle of the Atlantic. It was an impossible task.

The analysis of Italy's financial and industrial elite in the 1990s was that their country had a fundamentally sound economy bedeviled by a catastrophically weak currency. If they could simply swap the lira for something more like the deutschmark, then Italy would go from strength to strength. Shorn of the weak lira, its companies could forge ahead. Inflation would be conquered and debt tamed. It would be a new Italy. It would still have all the flamboyant design brilliance for which it was known, but now it would have strong finances as well. It would be a formidable combination.

Not everyone saw it that way, of course. In Germany in particular, the thought of sharing a currency with the Italians was enough to make Bundesbank officials shudder nervously. "I believe it was a mistake to let Italy in," said Karl-Otto Pohl, former president of the Bundesbank, quoted in David Marsh's book, *The Euro*.[8] He admitted that he'd agreed with the view of the Banca d'Italia at the time that euro membership would be a useful discipline for the country, but pointed out that it very quickly became clear that the country was squandering its chance to reform itself, and in the long term that was going to make it very hard for it to stay within the single currency.

A decade into its existence, it was becoming painfully clear that euro membership had not proved any kind of a panacea for the Italians—and that Pohl's analysis had much to be said for it.

The performance of the Italian economy has been dismal. Since joining the euro-zone in 1999, Italy has plunged into recession on no less than four occasions. Over this period, the economy has expanded at an average annual rate of 0.6 percent a year. Look at the figures in per-capita terms—that is, the increase in output per person, which measures how much richer the average Italian is—and they appear even worse: a rise of just 0.1 percent in output annually. Statistically, that is about the same as zero growth. And this, remember, was a decade when the global economy was booming and just about everyone else in the world was getting a lot richer. There was a party going on somewhere, but the Italians very definitely hadn't been invited.

Why was it so bad? The discipline of euro membership meant that Italy could no longer regularly devalue its way out of trouble. The impact on the competitiveness of its factories and workplaces was catastrophic. While productivity growth was weak in much of the euro-zone, Italy's record was truly terrible. Since 1999, output per worker has actually fallen. And yet compensation per employee has continued to rise much faster than in Germany and almost as fast as in France. So people were getting paid more for producing less, and in a harder currency as well. As a result, unit labor costs soared by over 30 percent, five times faster than those of Germany, during its first decade of euro membership.

Italian workers inside the euro were rapidly pricing themselves out of the market. One measure of that was the volume of exports. While German exports climbed by around 80 percent over the first decade of monetary union, and French and Spanish exports climbed by 30 and 40 percent, respectively, over the same decade, Italian exports were completely static. Italy wasn't managing to sell any more stuff at the end of the decade than it had at the start, even though the world economy was of course a lot larger.

In the past, the result would have been a currency crisis, a sharp devaluation of the lira, and suddenly Italian factories would have been back in business. Now that that was no longer possible, the only other option was for Italian companies to steadily drive down the wages of their workers until they were competitive with the Germans once again. But that was going to take a very long time and be very hard and painful work. "Italy might have to suffer more than two decades of stagnant wages to restore full competitiveness," concluded the London-based consultancy Capital Economics in a study of the Italian economy published in 2010.[9]

Inevitably, that was going to impact its budget position. Going into the sovereign debt crisis, the Italian budget deficit was not in too bad shape. At the height of the crisis, it was only a little over 5 percent of GDP, fairly modest by Greek or Spanish standards. The problem was not so much the debts that it was running up right now, but the outstanding stock of Italian government debt. Italy is still paying a heavy price for its past profligacy. Between 1970 and 1989, Italian budget deficits averaged 9 percent a year, far higher than any other major developed economy. Over those years, it built up huge debts. Overall public debt climbed from 55 percent of GDP in 1970 to 116 percent of GDP in 2009, the highest levels in the European Union. Greece and Spain were catching up fast, but Italy was still way out in front. When it came to running up irresponsible debts, the Italians had been playing the game far longer than anyone else.

When Italy joined the euro, there was a huge reduction in the cost of servicing all those past debts. As we have seen, interest rates in the euro-zone were far lower than they had been for the old currencies of the Club Med countries. That was in effect a one-off windfall. The money could have been freed up to reform Italian government and industry, making it more efficient, and better able to compete with Germany. Or it could have been used to pay down old debts. Instead, the money was largely squandered.

By 2010, Italy faced unpalatable choices. "Weak productivity growth means that Italy will need to accept years of wage and cost deflation and economic stagnation if it is to restore competitiveness within the euro-zone," concluded the Capital Economics study. "With the economy having barely expanded over the past decade, Italy could be staring at a total of more than twenty years of stagnation!"[10]

Whether any country can stand that kind of pain is a debatable point. It will mean in effect that an entire generation of Italians will have lived with zero economic growth. It would hardly be surprising if some of them, perhaps even a majority, started to conclude that they were better off without the euro.

Even worse, there was the persistent threat that the markets would start getting nervous about Italian debt. If bondholders started to worry that Italy was not going to be able to pay back all the money it owed, then they would start to push up yields on Italian government debt the same way they had Greek and Spanish debt. The cost of servicing those massive borrowings would start to soar. And then, very quickly the country would find itself insolvent. It would have no choice but to go cap in hand to ask for a bailout from the European Union.

Would it be forthcoming? Possibly not. If you remember that the Italian economy is more than seven times the size of the Greek, and bear in mind how little the Italians had done to reform their industrial base in the past decade, then a bailout might be more than the rest of the European Union is prepared to contemplate.

Italy remained, by late 2010, on a knife edge. But it could turn into the next domino to fall at any moment.

■ ■ ■

Contagion didn't just impact the countries caught up in the panic that was sweeping across the government debt markets. It was sending shockwaves through the financial markets for another reason as well. Greece was always a relatively minor problem for the euro-zone. It could be contained. If necessary, the whole country could be put on life-support just about indefinitely. But if the collapse in confidence in sovereign debt spread to other, larger European nations, the implications of that would be far more worrying.

Perhaps most importantly, the European banking system could be easily tipped into a fresh crisis. One consequence of monetary union was that banks had become a lot more relaxed about holding debt across borders. French banks bought a lot of Spanish debt, German banks bought Italian debt, and so on. On one level, that was a mark of the single currency's success in its first decade. The continent's financial markets had become far more integrated. Money moved more easily across borders. But what was a strength while everything was going well could quickly turn into a weakness once a crisis struck.

"Foreign holdings accounted for about one-third of government debt in Germany, Italy and Spain at the inception of the euro area," noted Morgan Stanley in a study published in July 2010. "The equivalent figures for 2009 show that foreign holdings are more important across the board, with a share of the total ranging from 95 percent for Finland and three-quarters for Portugal, to a little over half for Germany and Spain, and 45 percent for Italy."[11]

Once you started digging into the statistics, there were some frightening numbers. For example, France, Germany, and the UK between them had a combined exposure to Spain, Greece, Portugal, and Ireland amounting to $1.2 trillion in 2010, again according to Morgan Stanley calculations. If you added Italy to the "at-risk" list, and there was no reason not to, the amount approached $2 trillion.

Relative to the size of their respective economies, these were big numbers. For Ireland, cross-border bank lending to Italy, Spain, Greece, and Portugal exceeded 40 percent of GDP. For France and the Netherlands it amounted to 33 and 31 percent of GDP, respectively. Those were potentially huge losses to be borne by countries that were already grappling with recessions in their own economies and with the aftermath of the banking crisis. Nor did it end there. Exports to the peripheral euro countries—a significant source of growth during the first decade of monetary union—were likely to be hit as those nations tipped back into recession. More broadly, there was likely to be a big impact on sentiment. Most countries were struggling to get credit flowing through their financial systems again. Another big round of losses for the financial system would hit confidence at precisely the wrong moment.

The implication was clear. A default by the any one of the highly indebted euro-zone countries was going to put the whole banking system at risk. And it would put paid any hopes of a quick recovery for the euro-area economy as a whole. They were, in short, all in this together.

The euro-zone countries had discovered that their financial systems had become so interconnected that it was impossible to let one or two members of the system collapse—or at least not without paying a very high price for your own economy.

This was not a Spanish or a Portuguese or an Italian problem. It was a problem for the whole of Europe—and indeed the whole world.

■ ■ ■

The sovereign debt crisis may have focused on a few countries— Greece, most obviously, and soon afterward Spain and Portugal—but it was by no means restricted to those nations. It was like World War I: Most of the heavy fighting might have been in Flanders, but that didn't mean it wasn't a global conflict. Greece was in that respect simply target practice. Investors were getting more and more worried about the buildup of sovereign debt, and they happened to pick on that country as the place to bring those issues to a head. But they could have picked on any one of a number of countries. Greece just happened to be first.

According to Bank for International Settlements data, in July 2010, Greece's total sovereign debt stood at 133 percent of GDP. Japan was worse, with debts totaling a staggering 227 percent of GDP, the legacy of two decades of trying to fix an economy through Keynesian public spending. But lots of other countries were not much better. Italian public debt stood at 120 percent of GDP, and Belgian at 100 percent. The United States was at 93 percent, and France, Portugal, and the UK were only slightly behind. More significantly, all those countries were still running huge deficits year over year. The debt mountain was getting bigger all the time—and there certainly wasn't any sign of it getting repaid.

Many of those deficits were structural, the result of a permanent imbalance between spending and tax revenues. Again according to BIS data, the UK in 2009 had a structural deficit of around 10 percent of GDP (the legacy of 13 years of Gordon Brown as chancellor and then prime minister spending lavishly but lacking the political courage to put up taxes to pay for it). In the United States, the structural deficit was 9 percent of GDP, in Ireland it was also 9 percent, and in Japan it was 7 percent.

Even those scary-looking numbers assumed each country was being honest about the figures. And, of course, they weren't. Even leaving aside the kind of statistical sleight-of-hand the Greeks indulged in, there were plenty of liabilities that governments in the developed economies were not owning up to. A paper by the London-based think-tank Policy Exchange calculated that unfunded British pension liabilities totaled another 73 percent of GDP. One calculation reckons that the health-care commitments of the U.S. government are now equal to seven times the nation's entire annual output. The Organisation for Economic Co-Operation and Development estimates that unfunded government liabilities amount to 330 percent of GDP in France, 190 percent in Germany, 150 percent in Japan, and 130 percent in Italy.

If those figures are right, then public debts are just going to rise and rise, even if governments do manage to get their current spending and revenues back into balance. The BIS has forecast that debt ratios will rise inexorably, climbing to 300 percent of GDP in Japan at its peak, to more than 200 percent in the UK, and to more than 150 percent in Belgium, Greece, France, Ireland, Italy, and the United States.

That is the context in which the Greek crisis needs to be understood. It was not that one smallish and not historically very significant country had run into a debt crisis. The global financial markets could take that in their stride fairly easily, just as they did the Argentinean currency crisis of the late 1990s. The problem was that it looked to many people like a harbinger of far greater problems to come. Rather like the collapse of the investment bank Bear Stearns right at the start of the credit crunch, it was the first stiff breeze that told you a hurricane was on the way.

True, Greece was always the most vulnerable, partly because of its very high debts, and partly because of the inefficiency and corruption that were woven into its economy. The Dutch-based Rabobank produced a league table in 2010 it called the "Sovereign Vulnerability Index," which ranked the countries most likely to default on their debts using factors such as the stock of debt, the interest that had to be paid on it, and how much of the debt was held by overseas investors to generate each score. Greece, not very surprisingly, came right at the very top of the list. But Italy, Portugal, Japan, and the United States were all in the top five. It was calculations such as these that were making investors nervous. Portugal didn't bother anyone very much, and they had always sort of suspected Italy might be bust. But if Japan and the United States were to default on their debts, even if only partially, then that really would be a cataclysmic event.

Is there a serious danger of a wider sovereign debt crisis? True, investors have been worrying about sovereign debt for a long time. Adam Smith, the founding genius of economics, complained about the state of English public debt in *The Wealth of Nations*. Debt, he noted, "has gradually enfeebled every state which has adopted it." Investors, in his view, were right to be nervous. "When national debts have once been accumulated to a certain degree, there is scarce, I believe, a single instance of their having been fairly and completely paid."[12]

As usual, Smith was right on the money. Countries have repeatedly defaulted on their debts. Nearly every major country has reneged on some of its debts at some stage of its history, and many minor ones have done so repeatedly. There was no reason to suppose that countries wouldn't start defaulting again.

After all, as we have already seen, Greece was not that exceptional either in the scale of its debt or in the rate at which it was running even further into the red. Nor was it unique in the way its debt was structured. The average maturity for Greek national debt was eight years, while for the United States it was four years. So if the Greeks could run out of money, then so could the U.S. government as well.

There were reasons why Portugal, Ireland, Italy, Greece, and Spain were at the epicenter of the storm. They all had poor credit records, very high and rising debts, and they had all been critically dependent on artificial lending booms, the collapse of which meant their economies could well be weak for years to come. Most significantly, they were locked into the single currency and couldn't devalue their way out of trouble. Neither could they inflate their way out.

Countries that have control of their own central banks and their own currencies can default on their debt by stealth. If a currency depreciates by say 30 percent, then foreign holders of that country's debt will face a 30 percent loss on their holdings (a *haircut*, as it is known in the terminology of the financial markets). If most of the debt is held by domestic investors, then so long as the central bank prints enough money to create inflation, you can achieve much the same result. Inflation of 7 or 8 percent a year, hardly catastrophic by historical standards, will erode even a mountain of debt pretty fast when measured in real terms.

True, there are limits to how often either trick can be pulled. If a country devalues too often, then foreign investors will build that into their expectations and demand a big premium to buy any more of that country's debt. In extreme cases, they won't buy it all (ask the Zimbabweans, for example). Likewise, if inflation is endemic, domestic investors will get wise to that as well. They will demand that the government issue bonds linked to the inflation rate to compensate them from the potential losses (and once you do that there isn't any point in creating inflation anymore). In extremis, they won't lend any money to the government, or indeed to anyone: In an economy with endemic, rampant inflation, the only rational thing to do is to spend all your money as soon as you get your hands on it because pretty soon it won't be worth anything anymore.

Neither devaluation nor inflation is a free lunch: Economics famously rules those out in all circumstances, and sovereign debt is not an exception. But in extreme circumstances both are an important safety valve. If they are used sparingly, they can help a country get through a crisis.

So the markets were right in judging the highly indebted euro nations the most acutely vulnerable. But that didn't mean that other countries weren't vulnerable as well.

No one could say for certain whether the sovereign debt crisis was going to explode outside of the euro-zone. Nor where. It wasn't as if there was any shortage of candidates. Britain was clearly one target.

The UK had built up catastrophic debts during the decade up to 2010. Unrestrained increases in public spending meant that just like Greece the country had been running big and rising deficits even during the boom years of 2006 and 2007. When the credit crunch struck, the recession, and the horrendous cost of bailing out the banking system, sent the deficit up past 11 percent of GDP. A coalition Conservative and Liberal Democrat government elected in May 2010 brought a greater sense of realism to the task of tackling that deficit and pledged itself to driving it down, but the rating agencies were still keeping a close eye on the country and it was by no means certain that it would escape a downgrade. The UK had benefited to some degree from the turmoil in the euro-zone. It had distracted attention from its own deficits and made the pound something of a safe haven for investors getting out of the euro. None of that meant it was in the clear, however. An attack on the British debt markets could start at any time.

The United States was no better. By 2012, according to official government figures, the total of outstanding U.S. government debt will rise to more than 100 percent of GDP. With deficits running at more than 10 percent of GDP in 2010 and 2011, there was no sign of that coming down any time soon. Indeed, by 2020, the total debt load is predicted to reach 130 percent of GDP, around the same level that Greece is at now. The U.S. government has huge liabilities in health-care and Social Security payments that don't show up in the official figures. Indeed, in February 2010, Federal Reserve Chairman Ben Bernanke felt compelled to warn the U.S. Congress of the consequences of its irresponsible spending: "It's not something that is 10 years away," he said, speaking about a likely backlash from the markets over U.S. debt levels. "It affects the markets currently. It is possible that bond markets will become worried about the sustainability [of yearly deficits over $1 trillion], and we may find ourselves facing higher interest rates even today."[13]

Of course, the United States has many strengths. It has a fundamentally strong economy and a growing population. The government is still relatively small as percentage of GDP, although it has been expanding fast. And in the dollar it has the world's reserve currency. But it also runs huge trade deficits and is critically dependent on foreigners needing to buy dollar assets to finance itself. If the dollar ever lost its preeminence in the global economy, and the United States had to finance itself on the same terms that every other country does, then there is little doubt that it would be facing an epic financial crisis.

And Japan, of course, was the worst offender of all. After the stock market and property crash of 1989 to 1991, the government had embarked on two decades of red-blooded Keynesian economics. It had pumped and pumped the economy, running ever larger deficits, and printed money like crazy. It had tried to fix a debt crisis with debt, the same way the rest of the world had in 2008. The result had been an economy that remained stagnant, and a ton of debt. Outstanding long-term government debt is set to reach 862 trillion yen or $9.72 trillion at the end of March 2011, or 181 percent of the country's gross domestic product, according to figures published by the Japanese Ministry of Finance in May 2010. If short-term debt is added, Japan's liabilities will hit 197 percent of GDP in 2010 and 204 percent in 2011, the highest among advanced economies and far worse than Greece's debt load, according to statistics from the Organisation for Economic Co-operation and Development. True, there were ways in which Japan's position was better than that of other countries. Nearly all Japanese debt is owned by domestic investors, while in Greece, for example, 70 percent of the borrowing comes from foreigners. While foreign investors often flee a country, domestic investors usually stay put. And, of course, it maintains control of its own currency, and has a powerful manufacturing base and one of the most formidable export machines in the world (just take a look at all the stuff made by Toyota, Sony, and Nintendo you can see around you). And yet, the fact remained that with a debt burden on that scale, Japan was living on a knife edge. If confidence cracked, the country could easily find itself facing a crisis on a massive scale.

"It began in Athens. It is spreading to Lisbon and Madrid. But it would be a grave mistake to assume that the sovereign debt crisis that is unfolding will remain confined to the weaker euro-zone economies," argued economic historian Niall Ferguson in an article for the *Financial Times* published in February 2010. "For this is more than just a Mediterranean problem with a farmyard acronym. It is a fiscal crisis of the western world. Its ramifications are far more profound than most investors currently appreciate."[14]

The developed world had in truth been borrowing too much for too long. The International Monetary Fund had forecast in a report published in May 2010 that debt in developed economies will expand to about 110 percent of GDP by 2015, up from 73 percent in 2007. For the Group of Seven countries, the ratio is the highest since World War II, it said. To bring debt back below 60 percent of GDP by 2030, the level before the financial crisis of 2008, advanced economies would need to bring their budget balances excluding debt payments to a surplus of 3.8 percent of GDP by 2020, from a deficit of 4.9 percent of GDP this year, the IMF estimated. That was going to represent a huge challenge in the way societies were run. For two generations, governments had broadly been able to spend more than they raised in tax revenues. Now, for a generation and perhaps two, they would have to spend less. And they would have to do so at a time of aging populations, sluggish birthrates, and rising pension and health-care costs.

In reality, the sovereign debt crisis was a verdict—and a damning one—on three decades during which governments across most of the developed world had pushed up spending without paying any serious attention to whether their economies, and an often-dwindling, over-taxed workforce, could pay for it all.

Whole economies had been irresponsibly living beyond their means. And now the debts were coming due.

Chapter 10

The Debt–Deflation
Death Spiral

n the late 1990s, when the euro was first being created, one of the things the new currency needed was a symbol. The dollar had one, and so did the yen and the pound. They were a universally recognizable shorthand, and you could find them on the top row of every computer keyboard. The euro could no more go out into the world without a symbol of its own than a baby could go out into the world without a name.

But what should it be? The other currencies' symbols were created out of centuries of tradition. No one really knows precisely where the dollar-sign came from, although it dates back to the 1770s. Some historians believe it was a corruption of the Spanish and Mexican abbreviation for *pesos*, with an *S* gradually being written over the *P* to create something that looked like an *S* with a line through it. Other explanations are that it derives from the symbol for pieces of eight (a slash through the numeral eight); from the sign for Hermes, the Greek God of bankers, thieves, messengers, and tricksters; or indeed from the Spanish coat of arms. It's so old, its origins have been lost sight of. The pound-sign derives from the capital *L*, for *libra*, the basic Roman unit of weight, which is in turn derived from the Latin word for *scales* or a balance. And the pound was originally based on the value of a pound of metal, which is the source of the word. The origin of those symbols and words, however, does not matter very much. They are instantly identifiable and grounded in the countries in which they circulate.

The euro was different. It would be created out of nothing and yet have to have a potency and simplicity that would allow it to gain acceptance very quickly. The task was entrusted to Jean-Pierre Malivoir, a French EU official, who, at the time the euro was being created, held the post of "chef d'mission Euro" in Brussels (the euro mission chief, that is). The consensus was that a panel of the continent's leading design consultancies should be appointed. It was the kind of work they did all the time for multinational companies, creating new logos or designing symbols and packages that could make products that had been dreamt up by the marketing department a few days ago look like the kind of thing your grandmother used to know and trust. Malivoir, however, was a rarity among the French officials based in Brussels: a man who believed in economy and thrift, and in doing things for yourself if at all possible. He could almost have been German he was so reluctant to spend money unnecessarily.

Rather than spend a few tens of millions on teams of design experts, Malivoir decided to have a go himself. He noticed that the dollar, yen, and pound symbols all featured parallel straight lines. That gave him a starting point. Then he decided to take the Greek letter epsilon, on the simple grounds that an epsilon is an *E*, and *E* stands for *euro*. How about an epsilon with two parallel lines running through it? What could be simpler? It was sent out to focus groups across Europe to gauge the reaction of the people who would actually be scribbling the new symbol onto invoices, or tapping it into their computers, and everyone liked it. The symbol for the euro was born. Within a few months, Microsoft had even built it into its Word program, the ultimate in twenty-first-century status and recognition. And it was all based on a simple Greek letter and a couple of squiggles.

That a Greek letter was chosen as the basis for the symbol of the euro was proof, if it were needed, that irony really is the great driving force in human affairs. Because, of course, it was to be Greece that not only lent the new currency its symbol but also broke it asunder.

As we have seen, Greece had fiddled its way into the single currency. It had sparked a sovereign debt crisis across the euro-zone. Then it had to be bailed out at massive cost to the other nations sharing the single currency, and the rescue had meant ripping up all the rules that had been established for the management of the euro.

But that wasn't the worst of it. Far from it. The real problem was that for all the hard work that had gone into salvaging the Greek economy, the country was trapped inside a debt-driven deflationary trap, from which there was no escape so long as it remained locked into a monetary union with its far-richer neighbors to the north.

The real challenge to the euro was still to come.

■ ■ ■

The news was released late on a Monday evening. As it flashed up onto Bloomberg and Reuters screens in banks and trading rooms on June 14, it was clear to many people that Europe's single currency was now more than ever in serious danger. Moody's, the most respected of the big-three credit ratings agencies, had just released its latest assessment of the Greek economy, the progress toward cutting its budget deficit, and the chances that investors would ever get back the more than 300 billion euros they had lent to the Greek government.

The verdict was savage, and could be summed up in a single word: *Junk*. In a single step, Moody's reduced its grading by four steps, from A3 to Ba1. The terminology was obscure to people outside the slightly arcane world of debt rating, but the message was clear enough. Greece had been expelled from the ranks of creditworthy nations. It could no longer count itself alongside Germany, Britain, Switzerland, or the United States as a safe and reliable home for investors' money. Instead, it had to take its place among nations such as Colombia, Morocco, and Azerbaijan, places where you might invest some money if you felt brave, but where you'd have to not mind too much if you didn't get it back again. For an economic area that was meant to be built on the most solid of financial foundations, it was the most humiliating moment possible.

The guts of the Moody's report didn't make for comfortable reading, either in the government buildings in Athens or at the headquarters of the European Central Bank in Frankfurt. While the firm acknowledged that the country had laid out a serious and in places radical plan for cutting a budget deficit that had, over the course of the spring of 2010, reached 14 percent of GDP, and while it accepted that the emergency bailout package put in place by the European Union and the International Monetary Fund meant the country was in no immediate danger of running out of cash, it also pointed out that their medium-term risk of default was still a serious one. "We've got a lot of uncertainty around the growth outlook for Greece," Sarah Carlson, vice president—senior analyst in Moody's sovereign-risk group, commented in an interview at the time the news of the downgrade was released.[1]

In some ways, the Moody's downgrade wasn't a complete surprise. On April 27, its rival, Standard & Poor's, had already downgraded the status of Greek debt to junk, the first time that any euro-area country had been downgraded that low by any of the major agencies. But that was two months earlier. What was then a single opinion was now a consensus.

Naturally enough, the Greek finance ministry disputed the verdict. In a statement rush-released within minutes of the Moody's downgrade, the finance ministry argued that the ratings cut "does not reflect in any way Greece's progress over the past months." There was much support for that view from the most senior voices within the European Union. Jean-Claude Juncker, head of the euro-zone finance ministers' group, called the move "irrational," notably in light of substantial support for Greece from the European Union and the International Monetary Fund. "I am totally convinced that . . . a few months from now, the financial markets will see that they were wrong. They're misinterpreting the decisions which have been taken," he protested soon after the Moody's decision was announced. In the well-rehearsed response of any EU politician grappling with bad news, Olli Rehn, the European Union's main economic commissioner, chose to whack the messenger on the head. In his speech he paid as little attention as possible to what was actually being said. He told the European parliament that Moody's decision was "surprising and highly unfortunate" and said it raised questions about the role of ratings agencies in the financial system.[2] Actually it had raised questions about the viability of the European Union's rescue package, but Rehn had conveniently decided to ignore those.

Plenty of people in Greece were willing to see dark forces at play. "New Suspicious Quadruple Blow from Moody's—Sudden

Downgrading of Greek Economy," ran the headline in the daily *Imerissia* newspaper the next day.[3] "Moody's Plays Dirty," declared the front page of *To Vima*, somewhat aggressively.[4] The pro-government paper *Ta Nea* accused Moody's of "sabotage"[5] while the liberal *Kathimerini* described the move as "a blow below the belt."[6] Others were at least slightly more reflective, willing to blame the Greek people as much as the Anglo-American-German capital markets for the agony the country was being put through. "A generation leaves ruins behind it. It has spent more than it has produced," said the daily *Estia* on its front page.[7]

Yet whether it was part of a sinister foreign-directed conspiracy, or whether, rather more plausibly, it was the inevitable result of years of wild profligacy, the Moody's decision couldn't really have come as much of a surprise. As we have seen, Standard & Poor's had already downgraded the status of Greek debt to junk. The numbers hadn't added up for a long time. The markets had already priced in a significant risk of default. Junk was in fact a fair description of a Greek government bond. If anything, it was too kind. By now, most investors would rather have put the contents of a garbage bin into their portfolio than any promissory notes from the Greek government.

While the Greek government may have tried to put the best spin it could on the figures, the markets knew exactly what it meant. The giant American investment bank Citigroup said Greek debt would be removed from its World Government Bond Index, the EMU Government Bond Index, and the World Broad Investment-Grade Bond Index by the end of June. It also transpired that Greek bonds could be removed from Barclays Global Aggregate and Global Treasury indexes. Membership of the indexes may be an arcane subject to most people, but it matters hugely to the capital markets. Most bond investors are big pension funds, central banks, or sovereign wealth funds. Their managers have strict mandates governing what they can and can't invest in. They are meant to stick rigidly to the safest of assets, ones where there is a zero possibility of ever losing any money. Junk bonds most definitely are not on the list. In effect the ratings cut was a way of shutting the door. Greece was slowly but surgically being removed from the global capital markets. It already looked to be a long time before it would be allowed back in again.

The euro had been designed as a catalyst of modernization. It was meant to be a tool for dragging nations out of the past, polishing them up, and transporting them into the twenty-first century. But it was fast turning into precisely the reverse of that. As some of the analysts noted immediately following the Citicorp decision to remove Greece from the main global bond indices, it would instead qualify for the emerging markets index. The country hadn't been in that category since 1999, and even then the Greek government protested loudly at what it saw at the time as a slight to its national pride. Now it was back to where it was two years before it even signed up for the euro. Instead of being an agent of modernization, the single currency was serving as an agent of regression: an instrument that de-modernized your economy and your country, sending it back to a humble, agricultural past, and locking it into a prison of impoverishment from which there was little hope of ever escaping.

There was little mistaking the air of crisis surrounding the euro in the early days of summer, 2009. While much of the media's attention was understandably distracted by the soccer World Cup a few thousand miles away in South Africa, the grim realities of the euro's predicament were being hammered home every day.

A few days after its downgrade, Moody's reported on the fragility of the Greek banking system. The Greek banks had received a massive 90 billion euros in funding directly from the European Central Bank, the ratings agency reported. Cyprus-based Moody's analysts Constantinos Kypreas and Mardig Haladjian wrote in their report: "The high reliance on ECB funding is neither desirable nor sustainable long term."[8] Indeed not. There were two implications, neither of them very comforting. One was that the wholesale markets remained closed to the Greeks. Banks normally fund themselves by borrowing money from each other. In the case of Greece, that money had dried up. The global banks weren't extending credit to their Greek counterparts anymore, for the simple reason they didn't think they'd get it back. At the same time, Greek depositors were fleeing their own country's banks. There had been plenty of anecdotal evidence that wealthy Greeks were shifting their money offshore. Cyprus, Malta, and Switzerland were the preferred destinations. Now the physical evidence was starting to come through. Capital, the lifeblood of a functioning free-market economy, was leaving the country at an alarming rate.

The financial system was now on life-support from the European Central Bank. That was fine for the time being. If the capital markets wouldn't give the Greeks any money, the central bank would step in and do the job instead.

But it raised a difficult question. How would they ever get back to normal again? Or would Greece have to remain a patient of the ECB, kept forever in the continent's convalescent ward by its northern-European neighbors?

Worse, there was no sign that the euro's troubles were confined to Greece. Over the middle of June, the spreads between German and Spanish government bonds rose to a record high since the euro was launched. As we saw in the case of Greece, it was that one simple number—the difference between the price of a German bund and the price of each other euro member's bonds—that warned of the catastrophe to come. The Spanish newspaper *El Economista* reported that the International Monetary Fund, the EU, and the U.S. Treasury were putting together a credit line of as much as 250 billion euros for Spain. If true, that would be an extraordinary and scary admission not only that Spain could no longer afford to pay its own bills, but also that the European Union couldn't afford to bail it out and that the country had been left with no choice but to turn to the Americans for help. The story was swiftly denied by European Union spokesmen in Brussels, but it was written with enough credibility for it to move the markets.

Elsewhere, the noises were just as gloomy. John Monks, the former head of Britain's Trades Union Congress, disclosed in the British papers that European Union Commission President José Manuel Barroso had set out an "apocalyptic" vision during a private briefing for trade union leaders across Europe. Barroso sketched out a possible scenario in which the crisis-hit countries in southern Europe could fall victim to military coups or popular uprisings as interest rates soared and public services collapsed because their governments had quite simply run out of money. According to Monks, Barroso said: "Look, if they do not carry out these austerity packages, these countries could virtually disappear in the way that we know them as democracies. They've got no choice; this is it."[9] There may have been an element of grandstanding rhetoric in that warning. Trade unions throughout the continent were planning protests and strikes against the cuts to public spending all across Europe. A warning of the dire consequences of failing to accept the austerity measures might well help persuade people that there was no alternative. But that didn't mean there wasn't an element of truth in the warnings. Portugal, Spain, and Greece had been dictatorships as recently as the 1970s. It was ridiculous to pretend that these were nations where democracy had deep roots. Freedom had been swept away by economic crisis in the past. There was no reason to imagine that it couldn't ever happen again.

Indeed, the more people looked at it, the less secure Europe's single currency, and Greece's place within it, was starting to appear. Speaking at an investment conference, Theodora Zemek, head of fixed-income investment at the massive French-owned insurance and financial services conglomerate Axa, put forward a view that, even a few months earlier, would have been unthinkable anywhere within the mainstream European investment community. The end of the euro, at least in its current form, was in sight.

"The markets are very nervous because they can see that there is a fatal flaw in the system and no clear way out," she argued in a lecture on June 14. "We are in a very major crisis that has even broader implications than the credit crisis two years ago. The politicians have not yet twigged to this." According to Zemek, the rescue had bought a "maximum" of 18 months respite before deeper structural damage hits home, with a "probable" default by Greece setting off a chain reaction across southern Europe. "It would be the end of the euro as we know it. The long-term implications are at best a split in the euro-zone, at worst the destruction of the single currency. It is not going to end happily however you slice it." She went on to argue that the U.S. currency union was successful because Washington has overriding legal powers over the 50 states that make it up. "It is a precondition for the system to work but it doesn't exist in Europe and the bond markets are starting to figure this out. We are looking at a noble experiment on the brink of failure," she concluded.[10]

Plenty of other voices were reaching much the same conclusion. Jim Rodgers is a legend in the investment world. The co-founder of the Quantum Fund with his higher-profile partner, George Soros, he has an uncanny ability to figure out which way the wind is blowing. He argued that the bailout of the Greek economy, while it may have worked in the short term, meant that the euro was now doomed. "That's not the way it's supposed to work," he said, speaking at the Rafael Del Pino Foundation in the Spanish capital Madrid on June 16, 2010. "I don't think it's good for Europe, and I don't think it's good for the world to bail out people who have failed."[11] Like many other players in the capital markets, he saw the Greek rescue as a turning point, one that set the euro on a different, and, over time, very dangerous path. "Debasing what has been a strong currency and making it weaker and weaker is in the end going to destroy the euro," he said.

Indeed, right across the continent, the protests at the costs the euro was imposing on the continent's economy were becoming louder. Arctic explorers report that as you trudge across that frozen sea, you can hear groaning and creaking as the currents in the ocean beneath you shift the giant plates of ice around. The very ground on which you walk is moving noisily, sometimes throwing up new walls of frozen water, other times quite literally collapsing. The euro–zone economy felt something like that as 2010 wore on. In Italy, in June, a hundred leading Italian economists wrote to the leading daily newspaper *Il Sole*, arguing against the terrible damage the single currency was doing to that economy. "The grave economic global crisis, and its links to the euro–zone crisis, will not be resolved by cutting salaries, pensions, the welfare state, education, research . . . ," they wrote. "More likely, the 'politics of sacrifice' in Italy and in Europe runs the risk of accentuating the crisis in the end, causing a faster rise in unemployment, of insolvencies and company failures, and could at a certain point compel some countries to leave monetary union."[12]

To the Italian economists, the crisis was not just caused by a few profligate Greek politicians. It had its roots in the very design of the euro itself. "The fundamental point to understand is that the current instability of monetary union is not just the result of accounting fraud and overspending. In reality, it stems from a profound interweaving of the global economic crisis and imbalances within the euro–zone," they wrote. Adjustment mechanisms that were meant to stabilize the imbalances between northern and southern Europe had quite clearly failed.

This is the deeper reason why market traders are betting on a collapse of the euro–zone. They can see that as the crisis drags on this will cause tax revenues to fall, making it ever harder to repay debts, whether public or private. Some countries will progressively be pushed out of the euro-zone, others will decide to break away to free themselves from a deflationary spiral. . . . It is the risk of widespread defaults and the re-conversion of debts into national currencies that is really motivating bets by speculators.

■ ■ ■

So does Greece stand any realistic chance of recovering from the predicament in which it now finds itself? The answer to that is simple: No. "The key risk for Greece's public debt dynamics is that the economy suffers a greater-than-expected decline in nominal GDP and the economy veers towards a debt–deflation spiral, notwithstanding the authorities' best efforts to fulfill their fiscal targets," argued the ratings agency Fitch in an assessment of the Greek economy published in May 2010.[13]

There were two key problems, and the Fitch report accurately nailed both of them. The first was that the cuts in public spending kept depressing demand and pushing up unemployment. That in turn would depress tax revenues even further, making the debt burden even harder to control. That one was fairly widely accepted by economists and policymakers.

But the second was even more worrying. It was that debt became a kind of monster, growing in size all the time and devouring more and more of the economy as each year passed. "In the absence of a re-profiling of official maturities and/or a further IMF/EU program, Fitch estimates gross fiscal funding needs will jump to over 30 percent of GDP in 2014–2015," the report argued. "Paradoxically, therefore, even if the program is successful, the sovereign stands to be even more exposed to market risk than it was before."[14]

It is worth pausing to consider what precisely is being forecast there. Unless even more IMF or EU money was handed across to the Greeks, the size of the debt mountain was going to keep on growing and growing until, within a few short years, just keeping up the payments on that debt was going to consume a third of everything the Greek economy produces. Did anyone suppose for a moment that that would be sustainable? A country can't pay those kinds of debts and expect its economy to survive in any tolerable shape.

It is not just the government's finances that are in a mess. So is the banking system. The Greek banks held vast quantities of government debt on their books, and the rest of the global banking system, fearing that a default on those debts was inevitable at some stage, was understandably nervous about lending any more to the Greek banks. As we have already seen, they were forced to rely more and more on the European Central Bank to remain afloat. "Shut out of the interbank markets and unable to issue medium and long-term debt at reasonable cost, one can only describe the funding position of the Greek banking system as precarious," argued the London-based research institute Lombard Street Research in a report of the state of the Greek financial sector published in 2010.

You might think that the teams of European Union and International Monetary Fund officials who had descended upon Greece by the summer of 2010 might have come up with some clever ideas for rebuilding the economy. After all, austerity by itself was never going to fix this crisis. Greece would have to cut, that much was certainly true, but it would have to grow as well. And yet, at times the plans for a recovery of the Greek economy seemed close to comical. In mid-June, Prime Minister George Papandreou was in New York, and was interviewed on the Fox Business Network. It probably seemed a good idea at the time. He was in the world's main financial capital, and anything he could do to persuade the markets to back his country would help. And the U.S. State Department estimates there are three million U.S. citizens of Greek descent. So maybe some of them could be persuaded to invest in their ancestral homeland and help steer its economy through difficult times.

On the questions about the bailout, Papandreou played it straight. The European Union was backing his country a hundred percent, he insisted. The solidarity of euro-zone nations was proving effective. There was no need for anyone to worry about default.

All that was true enough. As we've already established, Greece was on life-support. No one was planning to withdraw it imminently. Like a patient in a coma hooked up to a drip-feed in a well-equipped hospital, there was no real risk of death any time soon. It could stagger on. The real issue, however, is whether the patient can ever emerge from a vegetative state.

On Fox, the interviewer, Nicole Petallides, wanted an answer to precisely that question. How could Greece start growing again? "As prime minister of this country, that is my main purpose, not only to pay back the loans, but to be a competitive economy," answered Papandreou.

> And Greece has great potential, which we haven't used. Greece has a tourist industry which can really thrive and even become more attractive. We're now moving into niche tourism—high-quality tourism. Greece is a safe country. It's a beautiful country, a hospitable country. I would like to make that plug on Fox News.[15]

A safe country? A beautiful county? They were perfectly valid points, but hardly the foundation for an economic fight-back.

What else did the prime minister have in his locker? Not much. "Secondly, Greece has great potential for renewable energy," he told an increasingly baffled interviewer.

> We have the highest wind energy potential in Europe and we haven't developed that and that's going to be a very important industry. There is the Mediterranean diet, which, again, we haven't developed as much, but it's a brand name in itself and Greece is the center of this Mediterranean diet, from olive oil to—to fruits and vegetables and—and this is something which we can have a niche market in.[16]

Wind energy? Anyone who actually knows anything about the industry knows that wind power may be a way of cutting carbon emissions, and making politicians feel they are doing something about the environment, but it isn't a serious, big business. The windmills are too expensive to build and maintain to make it a long-term, viable source of energy. And the Mediterranean diet? Well, it sounds like a good basis for a feature piece in a women's magazine. And no doubt all that olive oil is great for combating heart disease. But as a strategy for resurrecting a major euro-zone economy, and for eventually repaying the country's 300 billion euros of debts or at least meeting the interest payments on that enormous sum, it was laughable.

The closer analysts looked at Greece's predicament, the harder it was to find anything very positive to say about it. Carsten Brzeski, an economist with the Dutch bank ING, looked at the potential for Greece, and indeed the other Club Med nations, to export their way out of trouble, and concluded it just didn't exist. "While exports account for more than 50 percent of GDP in Ireland and around 35 percent in Germany, they barely make up 20 percent of GDP in Portugal, 15 percent of GDP in Spain and only 5 percent of GDP in Greece," he noted in a report published in June 2010.

> While net exports have been an important growth driver in Ireland since the early 1990s, growth in Spain, Greece and Portugal has been driven almost exclusively by domestic demand.[17]

That was fine so long as low euro-zone interest rates meant lots of money was flowing into the country, and so long as governments could borrow unlimited sums from the capital markets and spend the money freely on welfare programs. Domestic demand would grow from all the foreign capital shipped into the country. But once those taps got turned off, there would be nothing to replace it.

"To regain competitiveness a country needs to follow more deflationary policies than the rest of the euro-zone," argued Brzeski.

> Simply put, this means that countries such as Greece, Portugal and Spain would have to go through a protracted period with lower wage increases than in Germany. The German inclination for low wages clearly complicates such a task. In addition, historical evidence shows that the magnitude of the required adjustment is huge and almost unprecedented.[18]

Precisely so. The only way for Greece to become competitive again was to cut wages, and keep on cutting wages, at such a fast rate that they could eventually get them significantly below what people were earning in France or Germany. It is what is known in the jargon of economics as an *internal devaluation*: A country effectively devalues its currency by slashing wage costs rather than by reducing the value of its currency. In more everyday language, it might be called "doing it the hard way."

The trouble was, there was very little evidence that Greek society was in any shape to accept austerity on that scale. As recently as November 2009, the Greek government was still planning to increase public-sector wages by 1.5 percent in 2010. The European Commission forecasts that labor costs will rise by 6.7 percent between 2009 and 2011, even though Greece's largest union for non-state workers agreed to a pay accord in mid-2010 that included a pledge to freeze salaries that year. At the end of July 2010, the government had to mobilize the army to deliver fuel to gas stations, amid a truck drivers' strike that was paralyzing the country during the crucial tourist season. The drivers were protesting about an IMF-inspired plan to open up restrictive practices. There was simply no evidence to suggest that Greeks were willing to accept the kind of prolonged austerity that would make their economy competitive with Germany's again.

Or even that it would work if they did.

■ ■ ■

Perhaps the greatest tragedy for Greece was that, for all the austerity, for all the cutbacks, and for all the punishment it was taking in the international markets, all it was really doing was buying itself some time. "The 110 billion euros bail-out agreed by the European Union and the International Monetary Fund in May only delays the inevitable default and risks making it disorderly when it comes," argued U.S. economist Nouriel Roubini in an article in the *Financial Times* in June 2010.[19]

Roubini is widely credited as one of the few economists who foresaw the credit crunch. In forecasting that the International Monetary Fund European Union rescue package wouldn't work for Greece, however, he was hardly going out on the same kind of limb. It was obvious to just about everyone that the Greeks had about as much chance of getting out of this as Athens did of seeing a white Christmas. It just wasn't going to happen and everyone knew it. In June, Bloomberg polled a random sample of 1,001 subscribers to its terminal, who by and large are precisely the same people who make up the global financial community. Of those, 73 percent thought that a Greek default on its debts was likely sooner or later. All those reassurances from Frankfurt and Brussels about how they would stand behind the country had convinced hardly anyone.

The logic was simple enough. If you compared Greece with Argentina, a country that collapsed into a chaotic default on its debts in 1998–2001, the maths didn't look very encouraging. At the start of that crisis, Argentina's budget deficit was 3 percent of GDP; in Greece it was more than 13 percent. Argentina's outstanding stock of public debt was 50 percent; in Greece it was already 115 percent by 2010 and rising all the time. Argentina had a current account deficit of 2 percent of GDP; in Greece it was 10 percent of GDP, and no one could really remember the last time the trade balance had been in the black. As Roubini put it succinctly, if slightly harshly, "If Argentina was insolvent, Greece is insolvent to the power of two or three."[20]

Indeed so. Argentina didn't manage to hold out against the inevitable collapse, and neither will Greece. Even if you assumed that the austerity plan works, and there is no real reason to suppose that it will, then Greece's public debt would still keep on rising. By 2016 its outstanding debts were forecast to rise to 145 percent of GDP. If the economy were still stuck in recession, as it almost certainly would be, those kinds of debts would be unsustainable, for all the reasons explained above. Investors who managed to get out early would be able to use the European Union and International Monetary Fund money to liquidate their positions. But the stabilization program, put together at such huge cost for all the rest of the euro-zone nations, wouldn't have done much more than provide an exit route for some of the banks and hedge funds speculating in Greek paper, and would have done so at enormous cost. For the Greeks themselves, and for the euro as well, it would have achieved precisely nothing.

Whichever way you sliced the numbers, they just kept pointing toward default. As economist Christopher Smallwood pointed out in a study for Capital Economics, with real interest rates of 5 percent and zero growth in the economy, it would not be good enough for Greece just to cut the deficit. It would have to run a budget surplus of around 8 percent of GDP just to keep its debt-to-GDP ratio stable. Yes, a *surplus*. Greece had never run a significant budget surplus in its entire history. To imagine it could do so in the middle of an inevitably severe recession was complete madness. "In other words, it is not sufficient merely to balance the budget, hugely difficult though that will be; it will be necessary to continue with the programme of fiscal tightening far beyond that," argued Smallwood. "A default by Greece is therefore virtually unavoidable in the absence of a resumption of vigorous economic growth, of which there is no prospect as long as it remains a member of the euro-zone."[21]

Despite all the official denials, it looks as if a Greek default is unavoidable at some point. It might happen in 2011 or 2012. The country might even manage to hang on until 2013. A good rule in life, however, is that truth can't be hidden forever, and since the truth is that Greece has borrowed far more money than it can currently afford to pay back, sooner or later it will have to own up to that.

There is no point in imagining, however, that a default will fix any of Greece's problems by itself. It will still be locked into a currency union with northern Europe, with which its economy is fundamentally uncompetitive. Although it could theoretically fix that by savagely cutting wages, that doesn't appear realistic. The Greeks were taking to the streets over even the relatively modest cuts to public spending announced early in 2010. There was nothing in the country's history, economy, or political system to suggest it was willing to endure the kind of grinding austerity for a generation or more that would be necessary to make its industry competitive with Germany and France within a currency union.

Nor in truth was there anything to suggest it would work anyway. Economics is always a dynamic system. When you look at any particular solution, you have to think not just about what you will do, but how everyone else will respond to what you do. So if the Greeks cut their wages to make their economy more competitive again, it is pointless to suppose that people in Hamburg and Lyons and Eindhoven will sit around waiting to be thrown out of work by the new hyperefficient Greek factories. They will cut their wages as well.

In reality it is a trap, and one from which there is no escape—except, that is, by getting out of the euro.

The trouble was, the rules of the euro didn't envisage anyone ever leaving. Once you were in, you were in, and you were meant to stay in whatever the cost might be. Once you stepped through the door marked "Single Currency," they shut it behind you and threw away the key.

And yet, as we have already seen, the rules of the euro had already been torn up once during this crisis. There was no reason to suppose they couldn't be torn up again.

Chapter 11

How to Break Up a Single Currency

*I*t is January 2012. Europe is in the grip of a cold, harsh winter. The continent has suffered a financial catastrophe, far outstripping the collapse of Lehman Brothers four years earlier. The new Greek drachma has just collapsed in value by 80 percent. The Portuguese, Spanish, and Irish currencies have all fallen by 50 percent and inflation in all those countries has roared up past double digits.

Amid chaos in the capital markets, the euro has broken apart. Both the weak and strong states are suffering from violent downturns as the single currency finally unravels, although each in its own way. Output drops in every country by between 5 percent and 9 percent. Germany faces a "deflationary shock," as the resurrected deutschmark soars in value, closing down factories as they become suddenly uncompetitive. The U.S. dollar shoots up to 85 cents against the equivalent of the deceased euro with a "temporary overshoot" nearer to 75 cents. As a result, the United States slides into deflation, threatening the world's biggest economy with a double-dip recession. Eastern Europe feels the shockwaves from its more prosperous neighbors, with export markets collapsing and its economies contracting by 5 percent in 2011 alone. Even the UK, which prided itself on having stood aside from the euro when it was first introduced, sees a 3 percent drop in GDP the second severe recession in five years as its companies lose orders from their main markets. Sterling has soared in value as a refuge from the chaos on the other side of the English Channel, hitting the nation's exporters. And the big financial institutions of the City of London, *the most profitable part of the British economy, all suffer terrible losses on their portfolios of bonds and equities as the money markets collapse.*

Money has started to flee toward the safe-haven countries. Yields on 10-year U.S., German, and Dutch bonds have fallen to nearly 0.5 percent, by far the lowest ever seen, but that is distorting their asset markets and risks creating another dangerous asset bubble. In the Club Med countries, yields haven risen viciously, soaring to between 7 and 12 percent, even though some of those nations have been forced to reintroduce capital controls, restricting the freedom of citizens and investors to take money into and out of the country.

That was the scenario sketched out in July 2010 by Mark Cliffe, chief economist at the Dutch bank ING, in a note prepared for the financial group's clients called "Quantifying the Unthinkable." He wasn't actually making a concrete set of predictions but merely trying to give one version of what the collapse of the euro might look like. "This is perhaps something that policymakers may care to reflect upon when they blithely talk of exit from EMU as being a policy option," Cliffe concluded in the report.[1]

The message was a simple one. A collapse of the euro would be an economic catastrophe on a huge scale. It would dwarf the financial crisis of 2008 triggered by the bankruptcy of much of the banking system. Even what the report termed a "stage-managed" exit from the euro by the Greeks, while less cataclysmic in its impact, would still risk a collapse of confidence in the currency and turmoil on the foreign exchange markets so extreme and so chaotic that economies would be left battered and bruised for years to come. As the ING team was keen to point out, it was sometimes easy to suppose there was a quick and simple solution to the euro-zone's troubles. Simply start unpacking the single currency and take everyone back to where they had been a decade earlier. But that option was not going to be easy or straightforward, either. Whichever way you looked there was big trouble ahead.

Even though it was just sketching out possible future scenarios (and all predictions in the financial markets have to be taken with a heavy pinch of salt), the ING report was significant in one respect. By the late summer of 2010, the breakup of the euro was being seriously discussed for the first time among Europe's banks, fund managers, and increasingly among policymakers as well. Others scenarios were being kicked around. In another attempt to peer into the crystal ball, Morgan

Stanley speculated that it would be a run on a series of Mediterranean banks in 2013 that would trigger the final split-up of the euro-zone. The details were not that important. What mattered was that what had once been a fringe subject of interest only to a few cranks and eccentrics had, as the full horror of the predicament facing the Greek economy sank in, started to edge into the mainstream. Some commentators noted how it was strange, and possibly more than a coincidence, that the European Central Bank in December 2009 had published a working paper with the title "Withdrawal and Expulsion from the EU and EMU: Some Reflections," which in dense euro-legalese spent 50 pages looking at precisely how a member state might choose to leave single currency, or indeed get kicked out by the rest of the club. It was part of the conversation in a way that it hadn't been just a few months earlier. And that in itself was a big change.

When the European Union decided to conduct stress tests on the continent's banking system in the summer of 2010, to look at whether they had sufficient financial strength to withstand whatever market storms might blow their way, it decided not to include the explicit scenarios of the euro collapsing or of one of its members defaulting on its debts. "The euro cannot allow a default and therefore it's nonsense doing a stress test based on that," complained José Manuel Gonzalez-Paramo, the Spanish board member on the ECB, at the time the stress tests were announced. But other leading finance ministers and central bankers weren't taking such a hard line. Wolfgang Schäuble, the German finance minister, raised the possibility of a country leaving the euro-zone in an article he wrote for the *Financial Times* in March 2010. Amid a survey of the different possible solutions for the countries struggling to keep pace with the demands of a monetary union, he threw in the incendiary line: "Should a euro-zone member ultimately find itself unable to consolidate its budgets or restore its competitiveness, this country should, as a last resort, exit the monetary union while being able to remain a member of the EU."[2] It was the first time a senior member of the German government—or indeed any euro-zone government—had openly raised the possibility of a country leaving the single currency, and no doubt reflected the options that were being discussed in Berlin. Once an exit from the euro-zone had been put on the table, it was going to be hard to get it off again. Some commentators were already noting the way that Jürgen Stark, the German board member of the ECB and one of the few people who had opposed Jean-Claude Trichet's decision to start buying high-deficit country bonds, had a framed sheet of deutschmarks on his office wall. They were starting to ask if he kept them there because he thought they might come in handy some day.

There were good reasons for thinking that the euro-zone might well have to be dismantled. As we have seen in the previous chapter, the Greeks are now stuck in a deflationary trap from which there was unlikely to be any escape. What was true of Greece was true of the other peripheral members of the euro-zone as well, even if not in quite such an extreme form. Spain, Portugal, Ireland, and Italy, despite the fact that governments there, as we have seen, had been running significantly lower deficits, were all trapped in the same deflationary trap as the Greeks. Their economies were shrinking, there was little prospect of any return to growth, and governments were struggling to keep under control deficits that were already way too big. In a country such as Ireland, the contraction of GDP meant that by the summer of 2010, prices were actually falling by 3 percent a year. Portugal was close to the same point. When prices start falling, then the debt problems become even more acute, because of course while the total amount you owe remains the same, wages and prices, which provide the money to repay that debt, start to fall. Even if you keep up the payments, your debt mountain keeps on growing every year. You have to run faster and faster just to stay where you are.

It is such a grim prospect that it would be very odd if reasonable people weren't looking around for an alternative. If there were some other way of managing your economy, one that didn't involve years of grinding austerity and constant sacrifices, it would be crazy not to at least think about it.

But could the euro really be fixed? Or would it just have to be taken apart?

■ ■ ■

By the summer of 2010, plenty of people were coming forward with potential solutions for the crisis in the euro-zone. The trouble was, none of them looked very likely to work.

The most obvious, as plenty of economists and indeed politicians kept pointing out, would be to transform what started out as a monetary union into a fiscal union. Right from the start, as we saw in Chapter 1, it had been argued that a single currency inevitably meant there would need to be some way of transferring money from the richer countries to the poorer ones, just as there is within regions of the same country. It wasn't often stated in public, mostly for fear of frightening public opinion, which all across Europe was a lot more suspicious of proposals for more integration than the political elite was. But after the crisis broke, it was starting to be voiced more and more in public. "Member states should have the courage to say if they want an economic union or not," argued the European Commission's president, José Manuel Barroso, in a lecture on May 12, 2010. "Because without it monetary union is not possible."[3]

"We are clearly confronted with a tension within the system, the infamous dilemma of being a monetary union and not a full-fledged economic and political union," argued European Council President Herman Van Rompuy on May 25, 2010, in an article published by the British newspaper, *The Daily Telegraph*. "This tension has been there since the single currency was created. However, the general public was not really made aware of it."[4]

To the European elite, the answer to the crisis of the euro was clear enough. The EU had to take another step forward toward the creation of something that would look very like a single European government, certainly in the economic sphere. To some degree, as we have already seen, that had already happened. The bonds issued as part of the rescue package implied some pooling of economic sovereignty. And by demanding to see budget plans before they were placed before national parliaments, the EU had already strengthened its power for managing the single currency. But it would, on this analysis, need to go further still—not just supervising national tax and spending plans but setting them as well.

For many of the more enthusiastic believers in European integration, it was what they had wanted all along. Many saw that the euro was incomplete, that it required central fiscal powers, and viewed the single currency as a clever device for bouncing the continent into taking that decisive step. Once the euro had been launched, the risks of dismantling it would be so horrendous that most members would agree to go along with a centralized economic government for the single currency, even if somewhat grumpily, for fear that the alternative was even worse. And yet, now that they were here, it wasn't as easy as they might have imagined. In reality the obstacles to creating a fiscal union looked formidable.

The economic logic was clear enough. All the high-deficit countries faced years of grinding deflation. Government spending was being cut. Consumer demand, now that cheap and easy credit had been turned off, was stagnant. Exports were never likely to revive because their industries had been made uncompetitive by the euro. If you happened to be the finance minister for the euro-zone, sitting in an office in Brussels, the way you would fix this crisis was clear enough. You would use the tax revenues from states such as Germany or the Netherlands that were doing reasonably well, and you would spend lots of money in the high-deficit countries. That is roughly what happens in the United States. If Florida runs into a depression, federal funds can be diverted toward that state. Economic differences between the regions can be evened out by a big-spending central authority. At the same time, our Brussels-based finance minister would cut taxes in the successful countries. That would boost demand and start to reduce their trade surpluses. As their surpluses came down, the high-deficit countries could export more, again boosting their economies.

The nations in crisis would get a stimulus from the stronger members of the euro, both through higher public spending and through higher exports. Problem solved.

There were some flaws in the theory. For example, countries like Greece export virtually nothing that the rest of the world wants to buy. Spain has devoted a couple of decades to turning itself into one massive building site, and not to building export-orientated factories. So even if the Germans did massively increase their spending and bring their trade surplus down, they would probably be buying stuff from China or Japan or the United States, not from Greece or Spain. The euro-zone is not a closed economic system that trades only with itself, and you can't assume that reducing one nation's surplus will make any impact on a neighbor's deficit. It doesn't work like that.

Even so, the macroeconomics of that plan are not too bad. A fiscal union would go a long way toward fixing the problems caused by a monetary union.

The trouble was with the politics—and indeed with the culture of the different euro-zone countries. There was simply no agreement around a single economic government for the euro-zone. The Germans, as we have already seen, had already protested at the prospect of having to pay for the debts of the Greeks, and potentially for other high-deficit countries as well. None of the euro-zone countries looked willing to give up their own sovereignty on the scale that would be required to create a fully functioning fiscal union.

And even if you could create agreement around how a single economic government would work, what sort of policies would it follow? It wouldn't be easy to get agreement around that, either. There was no point in pretending that the Germans, for example, would be willing to run huge budget deficits for years to come in an attempt to boost demand in the peripheral countries and get their own trade surplus down. Frugality and financial responsibility are too deeply ingrained within that country's national character.

Arguing for a fiscal union is like coming up with a plan to save the euro that requires the French to stop eating cheese, or the Spanish to start eating their evening meal at seven. It might be feasible enough in theory. In the real world it is not going to happen, so what is the point in discussing it?

The alternative was for the existing rules to be enforced more seriously. The German finance minister had set out the principles for the economic government of the euro-zone quite clearly in his article for the *Financial Times*. All the euro-zone countries should redouble their commitment to the Growth and Stability Pact and get their budget deficits down to 3 percent of GDP as quickly as possible. Countries with huge trade deficits would have to get those back into balance by driving down real wages, even if it involved "a long, process period of adjustment." Emergency assistance would be available to euro-zone states that ran into trouble, but it would have to come with a "prohibitive price tag" to stop any members supposing that this was an easy way out of their troubles. And, finally, as already noted, if a member state found itself unable to meet those conditions, or found the price too high a one to pay, then it should exit the single currency while remaining a member of the European Union.

There was not much sign of a move toward a fiscal union there. In reality what the Germans were proposing was a revamped Stability and Growth Pact, but this time with sharper teeth.

There were some serious ideas being kicked around to make that happen. In June 2010, Olli Rehn, commissioner for Economic and Monetary affairs, said the entire European Union budget should be used to penalize "fiscal miscreants," that is, the countries that break the Growth and Stability Pact. In particular, nations that consistently broke the 3 percent deficit limit should lose their agricultural subsidies (which still account for the bulk of the EU's central spending). That proposal was clearly directed at the high-deficit countries, all of which receive a high percentage of the EU's farming subsidies. Greece, for example, accounts for only 2 percent of the EU's farmland, but consumes 6 percent of agricultural spending. Between them, Italy, Spain, Greece, and Ireland account for 37 percent of agricultural subsidies in the EU. It was a well-fashioned weapon—the fiscal equivalent of one of those Pentagon smart bombs that are designed just to take out the enemy soldiers while leaving your own men standing.

And yet in reality both alternative positions were ridiculous. There was no point in economists and European Union officials lecturing everyone that what the euro needed was a fiscal union. Clearly, no one seriously wanted that, certainly not in Germany and probably not in France, either, if you tested popular rather than elite opinion. There was no political will to make it happen. At the same time, however, there wasn't much point in telling Greece, Spain, and Portugal they had to submit to years of grinding austerity to make their economies competitive with Germany once again. It would involve years of zero growth and stagnant wages. Unemployment would soar: One estimate by Capital Economics suggested that the process of making Greece competitive within the euro-zone again would involve unemployment rising to at least 15 percent of the workforce, and in Spain up to 30 percent of the workforce. Even then there would be no real guarantee of success.

Nor was there much point in just insisting that the Germans increase their domestic demand to help rescue the euro-zone. For much of 2010, that was what everyone was telling them to do. Before the Group of 20 summit in Canada, held in June 2010, President Obama scolded countries cutting government debt as another recession threatened. U.S. Treasury Secretary Timothy F. Geithner called for "stronger domestic demand growth" in European countries that have trade surpluses, such as Germany. Earlier in the year, French Finance Minister Christine Lagarde had argued that Germany had to cut its trade surplus as part of a coordinated effort to reinflate demand and salvage the peripheral economies within the euro-zone. "German trade surpluses, bolstered by low labor costs, may not be sustainable for other countries in the euro region," she said in an interview with the *Financial Times* in March 2010. Germany should pump up its domestic demand to assist other euro countries, she insisted.[5]

Naturally enough, it fell on deaf ears. German export strength was "the right thing" for her country, Angela Merkel replied in a lecture in Berlin in June. She recounted a phone conversation with President Obama in which she had to remind him that Germany was determined to balance its books no matter what. Cutting government spending, she said, defending the nation's latest austerity package, is "absolutely important for us."

That was just about that, then. To the Germans, telling them to weaken their own competitiveness to help out the euro-zone made about as much sense as insisting that Brazil could play in the soccer World Cup only if they had only nine men on the field. You couldn't strengthen the euro-zone economy by making its strongest economy weaker. That was the economics of the insane asylum. Instead, the only solution the Germans were willing to contemplate was for the weaker nations to gradually pull themselves up by their bootstraps. It worked for Germany and it would work for everyone else as well, just so long as they were willing to make the effort.

Between those two positions it is hard to find any serious way of salvaging the euro. It clearly doesn't work the way it is now: The Greek bankruptcy is proof of that. And while there are ways of reforming it so that it would work better—either by creating a genuine fiscal union or by enforcing the Growth and Stability Pact better or by massively boosting demand in Germany through big deficits—no one is ever going to agree to those solutions.

If you can't reform the single currency, then you can only dismantle it. But how?

■ ■ ■

The first and most obvious answer is to organize what some analysts now refer to as a *stage-managed* breakup of the euro-zone. Fairly obviously, the last thing anyone wants to see is a chaotic and disorderly breakup of the single currency. The more carefully it is managed the better it will be for everyone. It is, of course, likely to be easier said than done. Everyone always says that it is better if marriages end in a well-ordered and amicable way, particularly if there are children involved, but as any divorce lawyer will tell you, that is not usually how it works out in practice. A monetary union, unfortunately, is likely to be similar to a marital one, at least in that respect.

Is it possible to break up the single currency? One objection is that there is no provision in any of the treaties establishing any rules for a member to leave. While true, that hardly seems an overwhelming obstacle. Plenty of currency unions have been broken up before. As we have seen, the Latin Currency Union of the nineteenth century was bought to an end in the early twentieth century without too much disruption. After the Soviet Union broke apart, national currencies were recreated very quickly in the former Soviet states. If you can merge currencies, it isn't going to be much more work to demerge them. Nor does it matter very much that there aren't any rules for it in the treaties. Just write a new treaty. After all, the rules governing the euro were hastily rewritten during the trillion-dollar weekend. There is no reason they can't be rewritten again to make it possible for members to make a dignified exit.

The issue isn't legalistic. It is economic and political. If a country genuinely wants out of the single currency, then that is clearly possible.

There would, of course, be challenges. It couldn't be done overnight. If Greece was to revert to the drachma, it would take time to print up the notes and mint the coins. Prices would have to be adjusted into the new (or rather, old) currency. The impact on the banking system would have to be accounted for. Since the new drachma would without question devalue sharply against the euro as soon as it came into being, a lot of money would exit the country ahead of its introduction. There would have to be some transitory help from either the International Monetary Fund or the European Central Bank to keep the Greek banking system afloat while the new currency settled down. They are, however, largely keeping the Greek banking system afloat now, so that wouldn't make much difference.

There would, as well, be the issue of its debts. Most of Greece's borrowing is abroad. Again, assuming the "new drachma" devalues sharply against the euro, anyone holding Greek debt would lose a lot of money once it was converted into drachma. You could, of course, force the Greeks to repay it all in euros. That might seem fair: They borrowed the money in euros, so there is no reason why they shouldn't repay it in euros as well. But it would bankrupt the country, because the costs of its debt would soar and so defeat the purpose of the exercise. In reality, if Greece left the euro, the move would have to be accompanied by a partial default and a restructuring of its debts. Then again, since most investors are expecting Greece to default anyway, it shouldn't be too hard to negotiate. By 2010, most holders of Greek debt had already bought it at a heavily discounted price and weren't expecting to be repaid at par.

The key point is that although there are considerable technical challenges to breaking up the euro-zone, none of them are insuperable. In fact, while challenging, they are not nearly as challenging as trying to fix the single currency.

So what is the best way of going about it?

Probably the simplest and most obvious solution is for Greece to leave the single currency. For all the reasons discussed throughout this book, euro membership has been a catastrophe for Greece, taking its economy backward, making it dependent on EU and IMF support, and leaving it facing years of pain and austerity. It neighbor and great rival, Turkey, which remains outside the EU and of course the euro, has been showing it a clean pair of heels. The Turkish economy has grown much faster in the last decade, and it has a better credit rating: Indeed, while Greece's credit rating was being cut, Turkey's was being upgraded (humiliatingly, the Turkish lira rose in value by 21 percent from March 2009 to March 2010—the year that Greece was collapsing). It is so obvious that Greece would be better off emulating Turkey than trying to merge its economy with Germany that at a certain point even the political elite in Athens should be able to grasp this simple point. When they do, they will surely try to negotiate their way out. And when that step is taken, it is hard to see that they will meet much opposition. It would be a brave—not to say foolish—German chancellor who tried to veto a Greek request to have the drachma back.

Another possibility, and one that the U.S. investment bank Morgan Stanley has suggested, is that Germany leaves the euro. The bailout package for Greece "set a bad precedent for other euro-area member states and makes it more likely that the euro-area degenerates into a zone of fiscal profligacy, currency weakness and higher inflationary pressures over time," Joachim Fels, chief global economist at Morgan Stanley's London office, argued in a note to his investors published in April 2010. "If so, countries with a high preference for price stability, such as Germany, might conclude that they would be better off with a harder but smaller currency union."[6]

It would certainly be relatively easy for Germany to get out of the euro. It wouldn't have to worry about capital fleeing the country, nor would it have to worry about the impact on its outstanding debts. Germany has one of the strongest economies in the world, and the new deutschmark would be a lot stronger than the euro; so its debts, insofar as they are denominated in other currencies, would become less burdensome, not more so. Admittedly, life would get a bit tougher for Germany's mighty export machine. The deutschmark would rise steeply in value against the old euro (which would also fall pretty sharply once the Germans had quit). Even so, German companies have always exported more on quality than price. The country lived with a strong currency all through the 1980s and 1990s. It would soon do so again.

Moreover, a German exit would quickly produce huge benefits for the Germans. Most obviously, they wouldn't have to subsidize southern Europe any more. But, and in economic terms probably more importantly, inside the euro-zone Germany has been running huge trade surpluses, sometimes running as high as 8 percent of GDP and seldom less than 5 percent. That is largely the result of having a currency that is too weak for the underlying strengths of the German economy (and keep in mind that in the first few years of its life the euro was extremely weak). The surpluses, however, are not really of any benefit to the Germans. They are a kind of subsidy to the rest of the world. With a restored deutschmark, the currency would appreciate until gradually the surpluses were eliminated. That would mean that everything that the country imports would get a lot cheaper and so would all those foreign holidays that Germans love to take. Ordinary people would improve their living standards fairly rapidly.

The problem with that option is this: What would happen to a euro without Germany in it? It would be a currency union dominated by France and Italy. It is hard to see the Dutch wanting to stay part of that. Or the Austrians. Nor does it seem very likely that the countries of Eastern Europe, which are all due to join the euro in due course, would want to sign up for a monetary union with two countries with such a mixed record of managing strong currencies. In reality a German exit would very quickly lead to the breakup of the entire euro–zone.

There are other possibilities. One would be to split the euro–zone up into two blocs, a northern euro and a southern euro. In effect the high-deficit countries, which are all in the south (apart from Ireland), would form one currency bloc, while the lower-deficit countries would form another. The key problem with the euro, as plenty of analysts have pointed out, is that it is not a natural currency area. The economies that make it up are too diverse. When the single currency was launched it was thought that sharing a currency would draw them together, but there has been very little sign of that happening. If anything, they have sailed even further apart. The solution? Create two euros. One would include Germany, France, the Benelux countries, Finland, and Austria. The other would include Italy, Greece, Spain, Portugal, Cyprus, and Malta. Morgan Stanley has already given that southern currency a provisional name—the *medi*. A few nations might be hard to place: Ireland, Slovenia, and Slovakia don't fit obviously into either camp. But they could be offered a choice. The southern currency would depreciate sharply against the northern, but otherwise all the advantages of having a currency that straddles several countries could be maintained. The two new currency areas, however, would be far more natural than the old single one.

There would be clear advantages on both sides. The southern euro would devalue sharply and would be a far weaker currency. There would be none of the problems of trying to keep up with a hypercompetitive Germany. And yet at the same time the currency would be a stronger one than any of the countries could manage on its own.

Likewise, there would be plenty of benefits for the northern euro countries. They would no longer have to subsidize their weaker southern neighbors. They could move toward a closer political union without any of the problems that come from trying to merge fundamentally incompatible political and social systems. The German issue would still remain. The figures show clearly that all the countries inside the euro have lost competitiveness against Germany since the single currency was launched, including France, Austria, and the Netherlands, although not quite so dramatically as Spain, Italy, and Greece. One suggestion has been to create three euro-zones, one for northern Europe, one for southern, and a separate one that consisted of Germany all by itself. At this point, however, the argument starts to verge on the ridiculous. If you were going to create three euros, you might as well go whole hog and bring back all the national currencies. In fact, given the problems the euro has created for just about every country within the single currency, going straight back to the national currencies might well be the simplest and quickest way to clear up the mess.

There is one other possibility: competing currencies. When the euro was being debated in the 1990s, the British floated the idea of *parallel* currencies. You would have the euro *and* the national currencies, and both would be accepted as legal tender in each of the member states of the European Union. Companies and individuals could choose which currency they wanted to strike a deal in. Countries would get back most of the advantages of having their own currencies. They could devalue when they wanted to. But the euro would survive. Initially it would be mainly a currency for big business, for the capital markets, and for tourists. But if the euro-area economies did finally converge, the euro might gradually push out national currencies. The difference would be that it would happen naturally when the market was ready, rather than being forced on economies that couldn't cope. It didn't fly at the time, mainly because it was seen as a British ruse for scuttling the whole single-currency project. But in fact it had plenty to be said for it.

Now, it will certainly be objected that the euro has to be preserved to keep the European Union together. That will certainly be the standard line from the Brussels-based elite over the next few years. Indeed, it was heard frequently during the trillion-dollar weekend, when, in the opinion of at least a few of the participants in the negotiations, the single currency was just a few hours away from collapse. "We must save the euro to save the European Union," was the cry that went up.

When Angela Merkel was trying to sell the Greek rescue package to a skeptical German Parliament, she slipped straight into that familiar, comfortable rhetoric. "It is a question of survival," she told the Bundestag. "The euro is in danger. If the euro fails, then Europe fails. If we succeed, Europe will be stronger."

But why? No matter how many times you say it, it doesn't sound any more convincing. The European Union and the euro are *not* the same thing. Three of the longstanding members of the EU—Britain, Denmark, and Sweden—have remained outside the euro since the currency was launched. It is very hard to argue that they have suffered as a result. Likewise, the majority of the new members from Eastern Europe have yet to join the single currency. It hasn't stopped them from being full members of the European Union.

In fact, if the UK had been a member it would have, without question, destroyed the single currency. Britain went through an extreme property and banking credit bubble in the past decade, despite having consistently higher interest rates than those set by the ECB. If the ECB had been running its monetary policy, it would have boomed and then crashed in a very similar way to Ireland and Spain, except on a far larger scale. It is doubtful whether the euro will survive the damage the Irish and Spanish booms will inflict on it. It certainly wouldn't have survived the damage inflicted by a British collapse as well.

In the light of that it is very hard to argue that breaking up the euro would mean breaking up the EU. It will certainly change its character in ways that will be explored in more detail in the next chapter. But it certainly needn't be the end of the EU—just a particular *version* of it.

Indeed, breaking up the euro might paradoxically strengthen it. After all, by any reasonable measure the single currency has been a failure. It hasn't made the economies of Europe converge: If anything, they have moved further apart over the past decade. It hasn't promoted growth, except of the most unsustainable and unbalanced kind: crazy credit booms in Spain and Ireland, reckless public spending in Greece, and massive, pointless trade surpluses in Germany. Nor has it shielded its members from financial instability: In fact, the euro has created instability, visiting a wholly self-made crisis on the European continent. It is a *cause* of instability, not a cure for it.

Looking forward, there are years of terrible austerity for the high-deficit countries, accompanied by big cuts in living standards and rates of unemployment that will make it virtually impossible for an entire generation of Greeks, Irish, or Spanish to make careers for themselves. In Germany, the Netherlands, and France, there will be simmering resentments over the bailouts. Years of *Bild* front pages shrieking about lazy Greeks living well on German taxes will take an inevitable toll on what was until now the most pro-European of countries. Does that strengthen the EU? It doesn't sound like it.

For most of its existence, the EU justified its existence by tangibly improving people's lives. They could travel around the continent without showing their passport, go and live and work or study in neighboring countries without having to ask for anyone's permission, and sell goods and services throughout a vast free-trade zone without having to pay any tariffs or fill in any forms. Perhaps most importantly, the EU made the two great wars that blighted the twentieth century look like ancient history: Like Roman gladiatorial contests, they were interesting to read about, but not anything you could imagine happening in your lifetime. There were plenty of things ordinary people could take note of about the EU, and conclude that for all its occasional ridiculousness, the pomposity of its bureaucrats, and the waste and extravagance to which it was sometimes prone, it was a force for improving their lives, not making it worse.

The way it is arranged now, the euro threatens all of that. In the next decade it will turn the European Union into a dark, oppressive force. It will be demanding cuts and austerity for its members, imposing taxes they don't want to pay, and lengthening recessions that already look severe enough. More and more anger will be turned on Brussels and Frankfurt as people come to realize they are trapped in an economic straightjacket that only a rather vague idea of "European solidarity" is preventing them from escaping. It will quite clearly be an institution that makes ordinary people's lives worse. Slowly but surely that will undermine its public legitimacy and support.

For that simple reason it is ridiculous to claim that saving the euro is about saving the European Union. Precisely the reverse is true: To save the EU, the euro needs to be dismantled.

But what would be the best way of unraveling the euro? Neither Greece leaving nor Germany leaving makes much sense. In either scenario, what remained would be just as unbalanced and dysfunctional as before. It wouldn't fix any of the underlying problems of the single currency. And it would involve almost as much chaos and confusion as unraveling the whole project.

Creating two or three different euro blocs, as discussed above, would make more sense. There is a chance that the groupings that emerged would work better. They would be optimal currency areas, to use Robert Mundell's phrase, which the euro-zone as it was created in 1999 never was. But it would still be a hugely complicated undertaking, with little guarantee of success. In the circumstances in which Europe's political and business elite have already decided to ditch the euro it seems unlikely that anyone would be in the mood to have another try at a complicated monetary experiment. One consequence of the euro being dismantled would be that schemes to merge currencies would disappear from everyone's agenda for a couple of generations at least. The subject would become taboo. So although there might be some advantage to creating minor euros, it is very hard to see there being any political energy left behind monetary experiments for a very long time to come.

In reality, the most rational option would be competing currencies. Return to the national currencies, recreating the deutschmark, the franc, the lira, and so on. The EU would be preserved in the same form in which it exists today. There would be the same free movement of goods, money, and people around the member states. There would be the same cooperation on security, policing, trade, agricultural, and environmental issues. There would just be no more euro. True, there would be a period of intense disruption. But once the recreated currencies settled down there would be a burst of prosperity. The deflationary shadow that the euro is casting over Europe would have been lifted. The Greeks, the Spanish, and the Irish could set about rebuilding their economies with new, lower exchange rates. The Germans would be importing a lot more, lifting their neighboring economies.

Within a year, freed from the shackles of the single currency, the whole continent would be growing at a fast clip again. Deficits would be falling. Everyone would be feeling better about the economy again.

There would, however, be advantages to keeping the euro as a *financial* currency. Businesses could price their goods in euros if they wanted to and sell stuff to each other in that currency. The financial markets could use it to price stocks and shares and to issue bonds. It could be used at airport terminals, and on the high-speed trains that now shoot across borders, and in the tourist resorts where people find it troublesome to keep converting from one currency to another. You would maintain a European Central Bank, jointly owned by all the central banks of the countries that make up the EU, with its own reserves, capital, and the power to issue currency. And, most importantly, the euro would remain legal tender in every EU country (although there needn't be any compulsion for people to accept it if they didn't want to). It would be backed by the capital of the ECB, drawing on the capital of the national central banks. It would float on the foreign exchange markets, allowed to find its own level, but the ECB would be mandated to maintain it as a strong and stable store of value.

There would be two big advantages. First, it would impose a discipline on individual countries. Right now, government-controlled central banks have a monopoly on creating money. No one else is allowed to do it. But you don't need to have learned very much about economics to know that all monopolies are bad for the customer. The temptation is always there for governments to run up big debts and then get the central bank to inflate their way out of trouble. That was certainly true of countries such as Italy and Greece before the euro was introduced. When there is only one currency that is legal tender, they can get away with that. If there were an alternative, individuals and businesses might well switch to that instead. The simple existence of alternative currency would deter governments from behaving irresponsibly. Run the currency well, and people will use it. Run it badly, and they will go elsewhere. In short, the central bank would have to compete for customers' loyalty, just as any other business in a free market has to.

Second, within the core euro-zone countries it might gradually displace national currencies. It is certainly possible to imagine that happening in the Netherlands, Belgium, and Austria. They might well be followed by some of the Eastern European countries. Latvia and Lithuania might easily decide it wasn't worth the hassle of running their own currency. They could just use the euro instead. The Czech Republic and Slovakia might well follow that lead, even if the Czechs are usually about as skeptical of European schemes as the British are.

The point is that it would have happened naturally. The currency could grow from the bottom up instead of being imposed from the top down. It would be adopted by individuals and businesses that were ready for it and could be safely ignored by others. And a huge amount of work went into creating the infrastructure of the euro: the notes and coin, the payment system, the cash registers, the central bank. It would be worth trying to salvage some good from the experiment—just so long as it does not involve crucifying the entire European economy for a generation.

Don't expect the dismemberment of the euro to be discussed in public for some years yet. Europe's leaders will fight to preserve the currency until the last moment. They've already tried one massively expensive rescue package, and that has bought them some time. It hasn't fixed any of the underlying problems, however. The next crisis will roll around in due course, and then another crisis after that. Each time, the same rhetoric about saving the euro will be deployed.

And yet, when grand projects fail, they always do so quickly. The Berlin Wall collapsed overnight. The British and U.S. armies promised they were in Iraq for the long haul, until suddenly they weren't there anymore.

It will be the same with the euro. The leaders of the EU will insist again and again that the single currency has to be preserved. They will fight the markets and clamp down on speculators, throwing a trillion dollars at the problem, then two trillion, and then three trillion in a vain attempt to see whether there is some sum of money huge enough to make a monetary union across European borders work.

And then, one day, in 2, or 5, or possibly 10 years, they'll realize that nothing will ever fix it. And the euro will be dismantled far more quickly and smoothly than anyone would have imagined.

Chapter 12

The Global Economy after the Single Currency

On June 10, 2010, hedge fund manager George Soros took the podium at the International Institute of Finance spring conference in Vienna. At 79, Soros was looking older than many people would have remembered him from the days when he was a colossus in the world economy in the early 1990s. But his mind was as fresh as it ever was and his analysis just as acute.

"We have just entered Act II of the drama," he told his audience of bankers, fund managers, and policymakers.

> When financial markets started losing confidence in the credibility of sovereign debt, Greece and the euro have taken center stage, but the effects are liable to be felt worldwide. Doubts about sovereign credit are forcing reductions in budget deficits at a time when the banks and the economy may not be strong enough to permit the pursuit of fiscal rectitude. We find ourselves in a situation eerily reminiscent of the 1930s.[1]

The financial crisis, Soros insisted in his lecture, was far from over. The architects of the euro-zone faced a massive task. They had to find a way to help the countries that had run up huge deficits get their budgets back into balance. And at the same time they had to find a way to fix the flaw in the system that had allowed the crisis to develop in the first place.

Soros is a man to whom the markets listen, particularly when it comes to great macroeconomic fault-lines. Over a career of four decades he was one of the founders of the hedge fund industry and one of its most brilliant practitioners. His skill was always in the way he could identify huge contradictions in the way the world's financial system is managed. In the early 1990s, he spotted that the *exchange rate mechanism*, the precursor to the euro, had been designed in a way that allowed for far too little flexibility and judged, correctly as it turned out, that its flaws were so severe it had no chance of surviving. He famously made a billion dollars for his fund when Britain pulled the pound out of the ERM back in 1992. His technique has always been a simple one: Ignore the platitudes of presidents, finance ministers, and central bankers, particularly when they are insisting that a particular outcome is unthinkable. In economics, the unthinkable happens surprisingly often and usually quicker than you think. Bet big on that and you'll usually make money.

So would the euro survive? And if it didn't, what would that mean for the global economy? Soros addressed precisely that issue a couple of weeks later at a conference in Berlin. In a speech at the city's Humboldt University, and in an opinion-page piece for the *Financial Times* that was published the following day, he laid the blame for the crisis squarely on the German government and people. "The euro is in crisis and Germany is the main protagonist," he argued. "Unfortunately Germany does not realize what it is doing. It has no desire to impose its will on Europe; all it wants to do is to maintain its competitiveness and avoid becoming the deep pocket to the rest of Europe."[2]

In effect, he argued, the German insistence that the rest of the euro-zone become more like Germany would ultimately lead to the breakup of the single currency and in time of the European Union as well. "By insisting on procyclical policies, Germany is endangering the European Union," Soros said in the lecture. "I realize that this is a grave accusation but I am afraid it is justified. To be sure, Germany cannot be blamed for wanting a strong currency and a balanced budget but it can be blamed for imposing its predilection on other countries that have different needs."[3]

The deflationary policies being imposed on the euro-zone, he argued, went against everything that had been learned from Great Depression of the 1930s. They could well push Europe into a pro-longed stagnation or outright depression, creating the risk of strikes, political turmoil, and social unrest. "In a worst-case scenario, the EU could be paralyzed or destroyed by the rise of xenophobic and nationalist extremism," he argued.[4]

To Soros, it seemed that the only way out was for the Germans to at least consider quitting the euro.

> The restored Deutschmark would soar, the euro would plummet. The rest of Europe would become competitive and could grow its way out of its difficulties but Germany would find out how painful it can be to have an overvalued currency. Its trade balance would turn negative, and there would be widespread unemployment. Banks would suffer severe losses on exchange rates and require large injections of public funds. But the government would find it politically more acceptable to rescue German banks than Greece or Spain. And there would be other compensations; German pensioners could retire to Spain and live like kings, helping Spanish real estate to recover.[5]

There were part of Soros's speech that you could agree with or not, depending on your own mix of opinions. As the preceding chapters have made clear, this book certainly agrees that the euro is finished. The fault-lines exposed during the Greek crisis were too severe to be fixed and certainly not by the ramshackle rescue package cooked up in Brussels over the trillion-dollar weekend. It would better for the system to be broken up wholesale rather than just for Germany to leave, for the reasons argued in the previous chapter.

But everyone can look at the facts and the arguments on both sides of the debate and reach their own conclusions. The interesting point about Soros's lecture was this. The big thinkers in the financial markets, by the middle of 2010, were starting to look beyond both the euro and the sovereign debt crisis.

And they were asking a simple, yet important question: What would the global economy look like after the single currency had been consigned to the history books? And after the sovereign debt crisis had traveled its course?

■ ■ ■

Russian President Dmitry Medvedev knows how to stoke a controversy. As the euro was struggling to cope with the fallout from the Greek crisis, the Russians were watching from the sidelines with grim satisfaction. At a certain point it became clear that they might well step in to declare that the game was finally over.

In an interview with the *Wall Street Journal* in the middle of June, Medvedev was asked if the emergency could threaten the single currency. "One cannot rule out this danger because a unique situation has emerged," he told the paper. "I don't exaggerate the threat, but it can't be underestimated. We very much hope the measures to support the euro and support the economy bring results; we're very interested in stability in Europe."[6]

That may sound an innocuous enough answer. But it was far from it. Other leaders around the world were dismissing talk of the euro collapsing as fanciful speculation. The Russian leader, by contrast, was quite happy to discuss it. In effect, Medvedev had made himself the first world leader of any importance to acknowledge openly the possibility that the euro would not survive much longer. Like Soros, he was starting to think about the consequences of its collapse.

It was the second time in matter of weeks that the Russian government had intervened in the debate on the euro. Only a few days earlier Alexei Ulyukayev, first deputy chairman of the Russian central bank, said that the country might start adding Canadian and Australian dollars to its international reserves, after growing more and more worried about the fluctuations in the value of Europe's single currency.

That mattered. Russia, sitting on vast quantities of valuable oil and other raw materials, has more than $450 billion in currency reserves, the third largest in the world. U.S. dollars account for 47 percent of Russia's reserves, while euros make up 41 percent, British pounds 10 percent, and Japanese yen 2 percent, according to figures published by the Russian central bank. Over the years the percentage of Russian reserves held in euros had been steadily increasing. So the Russians had been one of the major buyers of the euro in the foreign exchange markets. And they had been one of the few major countries starting to put it on an equal footing with the dollar.

Now they were talking about downgrading it in favor of relative pipsqueaks, such as the Canadian and Australian currencies. It wasn't so much a slight as a slap in the face. And one presumably calculated to hurt. But there was another intention as well—to start to push the ruble as a global currency. A couple of days later, at a conference in St. Petersburg, Medvedev made that point even more clearly. "Only three, five years ago it seemed like a fantasy to create a new reserve currency," he said. "Now we are seriously discussing it."[7]

There were two significant points to make about the Russian intervention. The first was that Russia has always had an ambivalent attitude toward the European Union. One theory of the creation of the EU holds that it was simply a response to Soviet ambitions during the Cold War. As the Soviet Union menaced Western Europe in the years after World War II, it made sense for those countries to band together to present a united face to the enemy. But once that threat had melted away, as it did after the fall of the Berlin Wall in 1989, there wasn't much purpose to the thing anymore.

From the Russian perspective, the European Union had always been a rival, a counterweight to its own influence. On that analysis, anything that was good for the EU was bad for Russia, and vice versa. If the euro went down, that would make Western Europe weaker. It had never bothered to hide its fury at the EU expanding to include members of what the Russians arrogantly refer to as the "near-abroad," countries such as Estonia and Lithuania that were part of the Soviet Union and that Russia regards as part of its natural sphere of influence.

If the euro were going to collapse, Moscow would be quite happy with that—with the one simple proviso that it wanted to get its own money out of the currency before it happened.

But the second and perhaps more interesting point was that by the summer of 2010, the world was starting to move on from the euro. Politicians, investors, and central bankers had looked at the mess that had been made of the Greek crisis and decided that this was not a currency with much of a future. It might be a year, five years, or maybe ten, but the end appeared to be in sight. They were starting to take that into their calculations and to make plans accordingly.

Dmitry Medvedev might have been the first world leader to say it in public. Plenty of others were thinking about it in private.

But if the single currency does collapse, what kind of impact will that have? How will investors react? How will governments? And what kind of difference will it make to the world economy?

■ ■ ■

Perhaps the most significant consequence of a collapse of the euro, if that is what happens, will be the impact it has on Germany and in turn on the European Union. As we have already seen, the Germans don't like the bailout of Greece. They are nervous that it will inevitably lead to yet more rescue packages and they are openly wondering whether this is a deal that can ever be in their interests.

"Although France and Germany managed to paper over their differences in the run-up to the June EU summit, the Germans are in no real mood to compromise," argued Katinka Barysch, deputy director of the Centre for European Reform, in a report published in June 2010.

> Perhaps for the first time since the Second World War, they are allowing themselves to be defiant and proud. Their export-oriented, stability-obsessed economic model is not up for discussion. Their participation in the euro-zone is becoming more conditional.[8]

As we saw in Chapter 4, Germany has changed from the introspective, guilt-ridden country the world became familiar with after World War II. Its self-confidence has been restored. In part, that was a story of how the weight of history was gradually receding into the distant past. It was also a matter of the changed geopolitics of Europe. In the Cold War, Germany was a frontline state. The Red Army battle plans always assumed a massive tank invasion of West Germany as the opening salvo of a war that was hot rather than cold. NATO troops were stationed throughout the country to deal with precisely that threat. For West Germany, enthusiastic membership in the EU and NATO weren't optional. They were a matter of national survival. They couldn't fight the Soviet Union on their own. But with the collapse of communism, Germany was no longer faced with a hostile frontier. It was surrounded by friendly neighbors with whom its was on good terms, and that was enabling the country to think in different ways. Membership in the EU was more of an option, something you could belong to or not depending on how it worked out for you. And the same was true of the euro as well.

"However, it was exactly because Germany did not always behave like the UK and France that European integration moved forward and European solutions were possible," argued Katinka Barysch in her 2010 report.

> The risk is that the euro-zone crisis is bringing a latent sense of frustration and disillusionment with the EU to the boil. With the German media in frenzy and Merkel's government weakened, German euro-scepticism may now take hold. Even if the euro crisis can be contained, it is difficult to see how the EU could make progress on anything—whether it is services market liberalisation or a common energy policy—with a reluctant, grumpy and inward-looking Germany at its heart.[9]

That is very true. The euro was meant to act as a catalyst for the modernization of southern Europe. It would be an instrument for transforming those economies. That was the plan, and, as we have seen, it has failed about as comprehensively as any plan can. Yet, ironically, it seemed by 2010 to have acted as a catalyst for something quite different.

The debate over the Greek rescue package has crystallized German doubts about the single currency, and shifted it, perhaps decisively, in a more anti-EU and anti-euro direction. The levels of public hostility in Germany to the bailout caught most of the European elite by surprise. They were used to the British public being instinctively opposed to any further steps toward European integration. They had grown to accept that the French would occasionally erupt into anti-European protests and that the Irish would routinely vote against new treaties a couple of times before ratifying them. But at least they could usually count on the Germans being on their side. No longer, it seems. And since Germany is the largest country in the EU, and the country that pays the largest share of the bills, that opposition will be harder to deal with.

That at the very least will change the EU, and radically so. There will be no more talk of further schemes for European integration. The euro was meant to be a step toward the closer integration of the continent. It now looks more like a full stop than a stepping stone. The EU for the next decade will be an introverted, inward-looking organization mainly preoccupied with sorting out the catastrophic mess it has made of the single currency and in no mood for any more ambitious schemes. It will retreat from the rest of the world, talking mainly to itself.

Naturally, it will struggle and struggle to save the euro. Losing battles get fought for a surprisingly long time: Indeed, the bitterness of inevitable defeat often lends them an added ferocity. But, for all the reasons discussed in the previous chapter, it will not ultimately succeed. "The euro was adopted really for political purposes, not economic purposes, as a step toward the myth of the United States of Europe," said the great liberal economist Milton Friedman in a lecture in 2001, just as the single currency was being launched in its physical form. "In fact I believe its effect will be exactly the opposite."[10]

As in so many other matters, Friedman was right on the money. The first and most obvious casualty of the Greek crisis is the ending of a half-century during which the states of Western Europe, led by Germany and France, moved to a closer economic and political union. The EU is not about to emerge as a global superstate to rival the United States or, in a couple more decades, China. The euro was an attempt to create a single European entity that could compete with any in the world. But it hasn't worked, and it won't be tried again for a very long time. The EU will turn into something far more modest (and be far better for it)—a vehicle for free trade, individual liberty, and cooperation on issues too big or too global in nature to be fixed within one set of borders. Stripped of its pretensions it will be a far more effective organization.

But what will be the consequences for the global economy? There will be three that really matter.

First, and perhaps most importantly, there will be a period of intense upheaval in the currency markets. For a time there, the euro really was a contender to become a globally preeminent currency and perhaps even supplant the dollar. That was partly because it was the money of one of the world's biggest economic blocs. But it was also because investors were increasingly disillusioned with the dollar. The vast trade and fiscal deficits run up by the U.S. government and the casual attitude of the Federal Reserve toward tolerating asset bubbles make it an unreliable store of value. Investors were casting around for an alternative, and latched gratefully onto the single currency.

Initially, as the euro is laid to rest the money markets will flee back to the dollar. It will be the only game in town. But all the doubts about the dollar will still be there and they will be just as valid as ever. A return to a global economy dominated by the dollar as the world's strongest currency simply isn't possible.

Over the next five years investors will start to cast around for an alternative. There isn't any clear candidate yet. It might be gold. It might be the basket of global currencies proposed by the International Monetary Fund. It might be the yuan if the Chinese decide to assert their newfound economic strength by increasing the power of their currency. It might well be some combination of commodities. It could even be something that no one has really thought of yet.

Once the answer emerges the currency markets will start to calm down. But there will be an intense period of uncertainty, characterized by wild swings of prices and sentiment, before that point is reached.

Second, Europe will recover quickly. The collapse of the euro will be accompanied by predictions of calamity, of imminent economic collapse, and of a dark, rapid descent into economic chaos. The political elite, which has never had much of a feel for how the markets behave, will struggle and struggle to keep it alive even as the evidence of the single currency's destructive impact on the euro-zone economy becomes more and more apparent. Hundreds of billions will be thrown at ever-more desperate attempts to shore up the currency. Each time a fresh, vastly expensive rescue package is mounted there will be terrifying warnings that the only alternative is bankruptcy—after all, how else can the cost to taxpayers possibly be justified?

At some point, however, they will give up the fight. All losing armies quit the field of battle eventually and this contest between the markets and the euro-zone governments will be no different. There will be a mood of nervousness as the single currency is taken apart. All those warnings of calamity in the euro collapses will have made people think they have stepped over an abyss.

But in fact the results will be pleasantly surprising. There will be a rough year as the old currencies are restored. Stock markets will plunge, bond yields will spike, and confidence will plummet—for all the reasons explored in earlier chapters.

But after a short period of nervousness, economies will bounce back quickly. Italy will lead the way. Of all the major euro-zone economies, the Italian had suffered the most. The country was never suited to a monetary union with Germany and it was not in the right shape structurally to benefit from the credit boom that the other Club Med countries enjoyed. The country had been through a decade of recession and austerity even before the sovereign debt crisis struck. But before it signed up to the euro, Italy was doing pretty well. Once it emerges from an illogical monetary union it will start to grow again, and fast.

It will be joined by France soon afterward. The franc will devalue slightly once it is restored, but not dramatically. A modest devaluation, however, should be enough to set the French economy back on a path to decent growth once again. A strong currency has made French labor uncompetitive, with its unemployment rarely dropping below 8 percent at any point in the past two decades. To leave almost a tenth of your workforce in permanent idleness is a huge drag on any economy. As the franc comes down in value the French economy will start to create jobs again, and all the people with jobs will have money to spend, creating yet more demand and more growth. The country will look a lot more like the high-growth nation of the 1950s and 1960s than the low-growth laggard of the past 30 years.

Even the Club Med countries will come back faster than anyone expects. It depends on the precise way that the euro is taken apart. The more orderly the process and the more that debts get written off in the process, the easier it will be for countries to make swift recoveries. Spain will bounce back fastest. The debt bubble did enormous damage but it also modernized the nation's infrastructure, and with its own currency once again and with control of its own interest rates it will be able to start growing at a rapid clip. Ireland with its low taxes and free-market approach to economics will recover just as quickly: The painful austerity drive embarked on by the government will leave it with one of the leanest, lowest-cost governments in Europe, which, coupled with its low tax rates, will be a huge advantage once it can get its own currency back again.

Even Greece should do okay so long as the bulk of its debts are renegotiated. The crisis has forced some measure of modernization on the Greek economy, although it has been too little and too late for it to survive within the single currency. But the reforms of the bloated public sector, the ending of restrictive practices, and the changes to the pension system, pushed through by the IMF and the EU under the threat of bankruptcy, will in time make it more competitive. Ironically, while the Greek political establishment believed that joining the euro would be the catalyst for the modernization of their economy, it will in fact be getting kicked out of the single currency that will do far more to drag Greece into the twenty-first century.

Even Germany will prosper. The sharp upward revaluation of the deutschmark will hurt its exporters. But they will recover from a strong currency the way they always have in the past. The recreated Bundesbank will be the rock around which the other European currencies revolve, and will have vastly increased its power and prestige as the world's foremost guardian of monetary discipline and price stability. Indeed, like a turbo-charged Swiss franc it may well become a safe haven for investors nervous about the turmoil that will still be raging through the currency markets. And freed from its obsessive kowtowing to Brussels, Germany will start to act more independently. The country's natural role is as a bridge between Eastern and Western Europe. Economically, it can only go from strength to strength in that role.

Indeed the dismemberment of the euro will be one of the great buying opportunities of the twenty-first century. The old European economies will get a bounce in growth and their companies will be expanding once again. Liberated from the shackles of the euro, there will be very little to hold them back. Stocks will embark on a decade-long bull run. Within five years, everyone will be wondering what all the fuss was about—and why they just didn't get rid of the euro as soon as it became apparent that it wasn't working very well.

Third, the age of austerity will bite. The sovereign debt crisis swirled around Greece. But that was simply because the country was the most obvious victim: It had a government hopelessly addicted to state spending and locked into a crazy currency union. It was an accident waiting to happen from the moment it signed up for the euro. But that doesn't mean that if there hadn't been a Greece, or if its government had signed up for a suicidal economic policy, the crisis wouldn't have struck somewhere else.

At its root, the crisis was not really about Greece. It was about the massive buildup of government debt and the addiction of most of the developed world to spending more than they could afford.

Take a comparison with the credit crunch. It may have started with the collapse of Lehman Brothers, but it was a mistake to think it was just about one investment bank taking on too much risk and collapsing under the weight of its own stupidity. It was about a whole financial system that was drowning under too much debt. Lehman was a symptom, not a cause, and saving the bank would not have averted the crisis. It would have simply exploded somewhere else.

It's the same with Greece. Sure, the country behaved with willful, crazed irresponsibility. But don't be fooled into thinking that if the Greeks had stuck to the rules of the euro and done more to encourage genuine growth there would have been no sovereign debt crisis. Like Lehman, it was the flashpoint, but the crisis would have simply exploded somewhere else.

At root, the sovereign debt crisis is an extension of the credit crunch. As George Soros put it, it was simply the second half of the drama. If that crisis was about too much consumer debt recycled through the banking system, this one was about too much government debt recycled through the bond markets. As we saw earlier, for at least three decades governments all across the developed world have been steadily increasing their indebtedness, spending more than they can raise in revenues, even as they are facing ever-rising fiscal challenges. The sovereign debt crisis was a way of making a simple point, but forcefully enough that it would be listened to. You cannot carry on spending more than you earn forever. It isn't sustainable. At some point, you will need to fix that or face a collapse in confidence and a deep recession.

The only real cure is a long spell of what, by the standards of the past three decades, will feel like relative austerity. Governments will have to learn to live within the means of the countries they govern.

Voters will need to learn to elect leaders willing to do that, or else, like the Greeks, live under what in reality amounts to an economic dictatorship imposed by the bond markets and the International Monetary Fund. Taxes will need to rise. Spending will need to fall. Budgets will have to be tightened. Working lives will have to be extended and retirements postponed. Promises will have to be reined in.

Investors will need to learn to navigate their way around that; so will companies and governments. In the wake of the credit crunch, governments tried to fix what was essentially a debt crisis with more debt. They tried to replace excessive consumer spending with excessive government spending, as if the cure for extravagance could be yet more profligacy. Needless to say it hasn't worked. Going forward, the threat of collapse of confidence on the bond market will be an effective discipline. Austerity will reign, both for consumers and governments. The developed world won't be able to spend its way out of the crisis. The money is all gone.

What will that mean in practice? Markets will change. In most of the developed world the boom sectors have been retailing, leisure, and financial services. It has all been about protecting, distributing, and enjoying wealth but not about creating it. The emerging nations have done the manufacturing while the developed world has done all the spending. There will need to be a long process of rebalancing as the emerging economies consume more and the developed world makes more stuff. The sovereign debt crisis will be the catalyst for that process, but it will last for a long time. To steal a phrase from Winston Churchill, it's the end of the beginning, nothing more.

Industries will change shape. Banking and financial services will inevitably get smaller as there is less capital to recycle around the world. The leisure economy will start to shrink. Incomes in the developed world will remain under pressure, but the difference will be that they will no longer be puffed up with cheap and easy debt, so stagnant living standards will feel a lot more painful. Companies that contract to the government are going to suffer. So are regions that depend heavily on government spending (usually the poorer parts of most countries or the places where the votes for the governing party are most concentrated).

But it is important not to be too gloomy. The long run of economic history shows that irrational pessimism is wrong just as often as irrational exuberance, if not more so. Over the medium term free-market economies get richer rather than poorer, and there is no reason to expect that to change now. Manufacturing will rebalance between the developing and developed world. There are already signs that globalization is to some extent being reversed. It doesn't make much sense for everything to be manufactured in China and then shipped expensively to Europe or America to be bought in gleaming shopping malls with money borrowed from the Chinese. More things will be made locally and wages will even out between Asia, Latin America, India, the United States, and Europe. That will be painful for a while in the nations where living standards will have to come down: Any kind of averaging out is uncomfortable for the people who were above the mean. But once the adjustment is made the global economy will look a lot better balanced and a lot healthier as well.

And new industries will be created. Again, the historical record shows that during hard times entrepreneurs are busily creating the wealth of the future. In some ways the crisis we have just witnessed—the credit crunch followed by the sovereign debt crisis—is not so much a rerun of the 1930s, which started with a stock market collapse, as the 1870s. The financial panic of 1873—which started with the failure of a U.S. bank, leading to the collapse of the Austrian bourse, which led in turn to a global wave of bankruptcies—ushered in a decade known to economic historians as the Long Depression. But it was also a period of intense innovation, even if economies were contracting overall. In the United States, Thomas Edison was setting up General Electric and wondering if there might be a market for light bulbs. In Germany, Deutsche Bank was started as a new type of industrial bank, eventually financing the mighty manufacturing giants of the Ruhr. Much the same was true of the 1930s, a period of furious technological innovation, during which most of the industries that were to dominate the next three decades were hammered into shape. The chemicals and plastics industries were just getting going. Companies such as RCA were investing in television, and IBM in automating office work. Again, in the turbulent 1970s, marked by hyperinflation and currency collapses, the personal computer industry was being created by entrepreneurs such as Bill Gates and Steve Jobs.

No doubt it will happen again. The next decade will be turbulent. The sovereign debt crisis will take years to resolve. The demise of the euro will be slow and painful. But at the same time new industries will be created and new wealth created. It will be a lot easier to spot the destruction of the old way of doing things and it will attract a lot more headlines. But that doesn't mean that under the surface a new economy isn't being created. And in the long run it is the creation of new industries and new ways of organizing the economy that will be the most important trend to watch.

■ ■ ■

In closing, what lessons should be learned from the sovereign debt crisis and the failure of the euro? There are three that really count.

1. Don't put politics before economics. The greatest mistake made with the design of the euro was to make it a currency that was primarily political. It was designed as an instrument for creating a single European state.

True, there were some good economic arguments in favor of creating a common currency between some of the nations of the European Union. Fluctuations in exchange rates do inhibit trade and make selling goods and services across borders more expensive, even if options and futures make it far easier for businesses to cope with that and automated cash machines mean it is relatively hassle-free for tourists to cross from one currency zone to another. There was a point to the exercise.

But from an economic point of view you wouldn't have come up with this currency union. You might have merged the Netherlands, Germany, and Austria (and thrown the Swiss franc into the mix as well, if you felt like it). Or you could have merged British and Irish currencies (which were, of course, shared for many years), or the Italian and Spanish. Any one of those might have formed an optimal currency area. Or you could have created the euro as a separate currency and let it take root naturally over many decades.

But a rushed, forced union between Ireland, Portugal, and Greece, along with Germany and France, and then bringing in places such as Malta and Slovakia? There can hardly be an economist on the planet who thought that was an optimal currency area. These were economies with vastly different characteristics. Their industrial strengths, labor markets, welfare systems, and monetary traditions had almost nothing in common. The attempt to force them into a monetary union was in reality an attempt to spring them into a political union.

But economies don't bend to ideological will, no matter how determined it might be. You have to get the economics right first, and then worry about the politics afterward. If you wanted a political union among the states of the European Union—and there is nothing ignoble about that as an ideal—it would have been far better to concentrate on creating the shared democratic structure first. Perhaps then some of the currencies could be merged piecemeal—the deutschmark and the Dutch guilder, for example, followed by the French franc and the Spanish peseta.

That way you might have got to the euro in the end, perhaps in 50 years' time. But the single currency that was launched in 1999 was a step too far and too soon. It tried to force the pace of history—and that is always a project that ends in disaster.

2. Let the markets decide. One point is important to keep in mind about the Greek crisis and the way that in time it will destroy the euro. There was an alternative. The euro could have been saved even as late as May 2010. How? By letting Greece go bust.

The treaties were, after all, completely clear. The euro was not a transfer union and there was never any obligation for the other members of the euro-zone to come to the rescue of the Greeks. The markets had complacently assumed that they would, and the politicians who always believed the euro was a vehicle for closer political union wanted it to, but there was never any necessity to do so. Instead, Greece could simply have announced that it was no longer able to pay back all the money it owed and said it was restructuring its debts.

What were the banks and the bondholders who owned Greek debt going to do then, exactly? Send tanks into central Athens and demand their money back? Of course not. They would have no choice but to sit down and negotiate. They might have been offered 50 cents back on every euro, a significant loss but hardly catastrophic.

Sure, there would be problems. The Greek banks would be in trouble and the European Central Bank would have had to step in with emergency funds to keep them afloat. Other European banks might well have faced major losses on their holdings of Greek bonds. If so, they might well need financial assistance also. And the price of borrowing would soar for all the other Club Med countries. It wouldn't have been a cost-free policy.

And yet it was better than any of the alternatives. Once Greece was bailed out it created what in economics is known as a *moral hazard*. In simple English, there was no incentive for anyone to play by the rules. Why not just break them as the Greeks had done and then wait for the bailout? The rules of the euro had to be torn up, turning it from a hard to a soft currency and undermining the credibility of the currency, probably fatally. And for all the reasons we have seen, it wouldn't even have fixed the problem.

By contrast, a default would have created a far stronger euro. It would have been a sturdy anti-inflationary currency, a recreation of the old deutschmark. There is a gap in the market for such a currency and the euro could have filled it. True, it might have made life difficult for the Club Med countries, but over time they would have adjusted.

But if you wanted to save the euro, you had to leave Greece to go bust. As soon as you bailed the country out the currency was doomed. Europe's political leaders should have realized that from the start. They should have let the markets drive the process, rather than the other way around.

3. Be intensely suspicious of grand schemes that don't allow for error. The euro was in many ways a utopian scheme. It was a grand project for creating a political union. For most of its history, however, the European Union had built itself through modest, incremental steps. From the creation of the European Iron & Steel Community in 1951 onward, it had slowly integrated different aspects of the European economy and political system. One layer was built upon another. Nothing was done in a rush. Most importantly, there was always space to backtrack, to renegotiate any treaty that didn't get passed, or to reform any structure that didn't appear to be working out.

The euro broke with that tradition and disastrously so. It assumed that massive changes could be wrought in the main economies of Europe within the space of a few short years. It assumed that new systems could be thrown up overnight and centuries of tradition thrown away with not much more than the shrug of a shoulder. It was revolutionary in its ambition but also in its implementation: All revolutionaries assume, always wrongly as it happens, that massive change can be steered from the top, suddenly and completely, with little resistance.

And yet the great flaw with most revolutionary utopian schemes is that they assume everything will go according to plan. In the real world that is precisely what doesn't happen. Even the best-worked-out scheme usually goes wrong fairly quickly.

The architects of the euro assumed that all the nations signing up for the single currency would stick to the Growth and Stability Pact. The possibility that they might just ignore it was conveniently brushed under the carpet; nor was any thought given to what solutions might be at hand if the Pact was broken. The possibility of asset bubbles in the peripheral nations was not taken into account, nor was there any mechanism for bursting them once it became clear that that was precisely what was happening.

In short, the euro didn't leave any room for error. The perfection of the plan was one of its key assumptions, and so was the honesty and straightforwardness of everyone participating in it. Once it collided with the real world, of course, that meant it was doomed from the start. It joins a long list of schemes undone by the arrogance and hubris of their designers.

Finally, the demise of the euro and the sovereign debt marks the start of the great rebalancing of the global economy between the West and the East. You could argue that the West's intellectual and economic dominance of the world started in ancient Athens. Maybe it finally died in modern Athens as well.

Economic power has been shifting from the West to the East for two generations now. The pace ebbs and flows, but the direction of change never varies. That subject is worth a dozen separate books, but it is still worth pausing to consider some of the statistics. The combined U.S. and European Union share of world GDP fell from two-thirds in 1990 to just about 50 percent in 2009, according to Deutsche Bank calculations. There is no reason not to expect that trend to continue. Indeed it might well accelerate as the developing countries create consumer markets of their own rather than just manufacturing so much of the stuff the West buys. The United States and the European Union between them accounted for 75 percent of global stock market capitalization in 2001, but were down to 50 percent in 2010. The number of listed companies from the BRIC nations was just 2 percent of the global total in 2001. It is 22 percent now. Last year, more than half of the world's IPOs were in China alone. Likewise, Asia's share of the total investment banking revenue pool rose from 13 percent in 2000 to more than 20 percent in 2009. Management consultants McKinsey predicted in 2001 that this fundamental long-term economic rebalancing will leave the traditional Western economies with a lower share of global GDP in 2050 than they had in 1700.

And so on and so on. On whichever statistical measure you care to take, the BRIC nations are rising in importance and the traditional industrial powers are in relative decline. Nor should attention be confined to Brazil, Russia, India, and China, or the Asian tigers such as South Korea and Taiwan. By 2010 it was clear that countries such as Turkey, with a population of nearly 80 million, and Indonesia, with a population of nearly 250 million, were also transforming their economies and taking decisive steps toward joining the club of developed industrial nations. Those two countries alone are a market that is bigger, in population if not yet in wealth, than the United States.

What is the relevance of that to the sovereign debt crisis? Simply this. For close on three decades, but accelerating in the past 10 years, the developed world has been gradually caught up with, and in some ways eclipsed, by the emerging economies. It is, and remains, for the developed countries a period of relative economic decline.

One consequence of that has been that real wages have been under pressure. Earnings have been stagnant in most of Europe and the United States for the broad mass of the working and middle classes for much of the past decade. These have been lean years, not years of plenty, and they are likely to remain so.

But we successfully disguised that through debt. We turned them into years of plenty not by producing more but by borrowing more. As we have already seen, much of the prosperity in the Western world over the past decade was largely illusionary, based on building up more and more debt.

First consumer debt exploded until it was brought to a shuddering halt by the credit crunch. Then government debt exploded as a way of keeping the party going, until the sovereign debt crisis brought that to an end as well.

It wasn't just the Greeks who were burying their heads in the sand. We all were.

But the limits of debt have been reached. Perhaps the most lasting impact of the sovereign debt crisis will be to force the developed world to finally realize it has been joined by a new set of economic powers. It will have to learn to live with that.

It doesn't mean anyone will necessarily be worse off. Economics isn't a zero-sum game. There are no recorded instances of a nation getting poorer because another one got richer. That's not how it works. But the global labor market has become a lot more competitive, wages are going to be under pressure, and every dollar or euro or pound is going to be a lot harder to earn in a world where three billion people are competing for every piece of work rather than just one billion.

Most significantly, Europe and the United States won't be able to just borrow themselves out of trouble any more, nor paper over the failing of their own economies with more and more debt. They are bust. And like all bankrupts they will have to slowly and sometimes painfully pay down their debts and find new ways of making a living.

Notes

Introduction   May Day in Athens

1. Quoted in "Greece's George Papandreou Announces €140bn Bailout Deal," *The Guardian*, May 2, 2010.
2. Quoted in "Merkel Says She Was Right on Greece, Winning 'Unthinkable' Cuts." *Bloomberg News*, May 2, 2010.
3. Giorgos Delastik. *To Ethnos.* May 3, 2010.

Chapter 1   Now We Are Ten

1. Jean-Claude Trichet, Lecture, European Parliament, January 13, 2009. Available at www.ecb.int.
2. Ibid.
3. Jean-Claude Trichet, Speech, Bratislava, January 8, 2009. Available at www.ecb.int.
4. Jeffrey Frankel and Menzie Chinn, "The Euro May Over the Next 15 Years Surpass the Dollar as Leading International Currency," *International Finance* 11 (2008).
5. From *Actes et Paroles* by Victor Hugo, published in 1855.
6. Otmar Issing, from *The Rise of Europe's Economic Government* (London: Open Europe, 2010). Available at www.openeurop.org.uk.
7. *Die Welt*, December 17, 1996.
8. T.R. Reid, *The United States of Europe* (New York: Penguin Press, 2004).
9. Wim Duisenberg, from *The Rise of Europe's Economic Government* (London: Open Europe, 2010). Available at www.openeurop.org.uk.
10. From European Union, *EMU at Ten: Success and Challenges of 10 Years of Economic and Monetary Union.* Available at http://ec.europa.eu.

11. Ibid.

12. Ibid.

13. Michal Rocard, quoted in *The Euro: The Politics of the New Global Currency* by David Marsh. (New Haven, CT: Yale University Press, 2009).

Chapter 2 How to Blag Your Way into a Single Currency

1. "Greece's Stumble Follows a Headlong Rush into the Euro," *New York Times*, May 5, 2010.

2. Ibid.

3. Fernand Braudel, *The Mediterranean and the Mediterranean World in the Age of Philip II, Volume I* (Berkeley and Los Angeles: University of California Press, 1995).

4. Carmen M. Reinhart and Kenneth S. Rogoff, *This Time Is Different: Eight Centuries of Financial Folly* (Princeton, NJ: Princeton University Press, 2009).

5. F. A. Hayek, *Choice in Currency: A Way to Stop Inflation* (London: Institute of Economic Affairs, 1976).

6. From "EC Finance Ministers Approve Greek Convergence Program," *Bloomberg News*, March 15, 1993.

7. Hans Tietmeyer. Speech by the President of the German Bundesbank, Prof. Hans Tietmeyer, delivered to the Boersen Executive Club, Copenhagen, March 14, 1997.

8. Hans Tietmeyer. Special address by the President of the Deutsche Bundesbank, Prof. Hans Tietmeyer, at the conference on The Challenge of the Euro for Emerging Markets, convened jointly by the National Bank of Poland and the European Economics and Financial Centre, Warsaw, February 12,1998.

9. Jean-Claude Trichet. Speech by the Governor of the Bank of France, Jean-Claude Trichet, on the fiftieth anniversary of the Land Central Bank of Rheinland-Palatinate and the Saarland, Mainz, Germany, June 2, 1997.

10. Robert Mundell, "The Euro: How Important?" *Cato Journal* (Winter 1999). Available at www.cato.org.

11. Romano Prodi, quoted in "Greece Asks to Join the Euro," *BBC News*, March 9, 2000.

12. Yannis Papantoniou, "Greek Euro-Zone Ambitions Tempered by Inflation Fears," *World News*, August 23, 1999.

13. Costas Simitis, "Greece Wants In on Euro Currency," March 9, 2000.

14. *Le Monde*. January 5, 2000.

15. Wilhelm Hankel, quoted in "Greece Prepares to Shed Europe's Oldest Currency for the Euro," *Bloomberg News*, December 31, 2000.
16. "Greek Bond Yields Fall to Record Lows After Country Joins Euro." *Bloomberg News*, January 3, 2001.
17. Yannos Papantoniou, Lecture to the London School of Economics. May 12, 2005.

Chapter 3   At Club Med the Party Never Ends

1. International Monetary Fund, *Report on the Spanish Economy 2008*. Available at www.imf.org.
2. *Economic Survey—Spain 2005* (Organisation for Economic Co-operation and Development, 2005). Available at www.oecd.org.
3. *Debt and Deleveraging: The Global Credit Bubble and Its Economic Consequences*. (McKinsey Global Institute, 2010). Available at www .mckinsey.com.
4. Matthew Lynn, "Three Lessons to Learn from the Irish Experience," *Bloomberg News*, January 19, 2005.
5. *Debt and Deleveraging: The Global Credit Bubble and Its Economic Consequences* (McKinsey Global Institute, 2010). Available at www .mckinsey.com.
6. *Completing the Euro-Zone Rescue*. (London: Centre for Economic Policy Research, 2010). Available at www.voxeu.org/reports/EZ_Rescue.pdf.
7. Ibid.
8. Ibid.

Chapter 4   The Story of the Swabian Housewife

1. Angela Merkel, quoted in "In Greek Crisis, a Window on German Psyche," *New York Times*, May 4, 2010.
2. Angela Merkel, quoted in "Merkel Makes Like Obama with German Stimulus Excluding Europe," *Bloomberg News*, March 25, 2009.
3. *Opting Out of the Great Inflation: German Monetary Policy after the Breakdown of Bretton Wood*. (European Central Bank, 2009). Available at WWW.ECB.INT.
4. Alan Walters, "The Most Powerful Bank: Inside Germany's Bundesbank," *The National Interest* (Spring 1994).
5. From "The Four Horsemen of the Acropolis: An Old Battlefront Returns in War on Euro," *Der Spiegel*, June 30, 2010. Available at www.spiegel.de.

6. Jürgen Habermas, "Germany's Mindset Has Become Solipsistic," *The Guardian*, June 11, 2010.

7. Jürgen Habermas, quoted from "A rare interview with Jürgen Habermas," *Financial Times*, April 30, 2010.

8. Jürgen Habermas, "Germany's Mindset."

9. Wolfgang Schäuble, "Why Europe's Monetary Union Faces Its Biggest Crisis," *Financial Times*, March 12, 2010.

10. *Debt and Deleveraging: The Global Credit Bubble and Its Economic Consequences* (McKinsey Global Institute, 2010). Available at www .mckinsey.com.

Chapter 5   Fixing a Debt Crisis with Debt

1. Gordon Brown, quoted in "Brown Says World Slump Will Intensify if G-20 Fails to Act," *Bloomberg News*, April 1, 2010.

2. Gordon Brown, quoted in "Brown Says G-20 Agreed on 'Plan for Recovery' (Transcript)," *Bloomberg News*, April 3, 2010.

3. Barack Obama, quoted in "Obama Says G-20 Summit Is 'Turning Point' for Economy (Update3)," *Bloomberg News*, April 3, 2010.

4. Richard Werner, quoted on The Big Picture blog. Available at www .ritholtz.com/blog/2010/06/the-first-quantitative-easing-1930s.

5. "The Lure of Liquidity" (Morgan Stanley, June 18, 2010). Available at www.morganstanley.com

6. Ibid.

7. Bank for International Settlements, *Annual Report 2009/2010*. Available at www.bis.org.

8. European Union, *The 2009 Ageing Report: Economic and budgetary projections for the EU-27 Member States (2008–2060)*. Available at http:// ec.europa.eu/economy_finance/publications.

9. Bank for International Settlements, *Annual Report 2009/2010*. Available at www.bis.org.

Chapter 6   Burying Your Head in the Greek Sand

1. Quoted from "Papandreou Defiance Began with Gun-to-Throat Arrest (Update2)," *Bloomberg News*, June 25, 2010.

2. Quoted from "Greek Socialists Unseat Center-Right Government," *New York Times*, October 4, 2009.

3. Standard & Poors's credit report, October 2009.

4. Quoted from "Greece Admits to Faking Data to Join European Union, NYT Says," *Bloomberg News*, September 23, 2004.
5. Karel De Gucht. Interview with El Pais, May 5, 2010.
6. Quoted from "Goldman Says 'Nothing Inappropriate' in Greek Swaps (Update1)," *Bloomberg News*, February 22, 2010.
7. Quoted from "Merkel Slams Greek 'Scandal' as Goldman Role Examined (Update3)," *Bloomberg News*, February 18, 2010.
8. Quoted from "Unwed Daughters in Greece Catch 'Time Bomb' in Pension Overhaul," *Bloomberg News*, June 18, 2010.
9. Quoted from "Wishing Greece Had Never Joined the Euro," *New York Times*, May 4 2010.

Chapter 7   The Debts Fall Due

1. Standard & Poors's credit report, December 7, 2009.
2. Quoted from "ECB's Trichet Says Greece Needs to Take 'Courageous' Decisions@," *Bloomberg News*, December 7, 2009.
3. Quoted from "Greece Commits to Cutting Budget Deficit Amid Rating Concerns," *Bloomberg News*, December 8, 2009.
4. Quoted from "Almunia Says EU Ready to Assist Greece in Budget Plan (Update1)," *Bloomberg News*, December 9, 2009.
5. Quoted from "Merkel Says EU Has 'Common Responsibility' for Greece," *Bloomberg News*, December 10, 2009.
6. Quoted from the Maastricht Treaty. Available at http://europa.eu/legislation_summaries/economic_and_monetary_affairs/institutional_and_economic_framework/treaties_maastricht_en.htm.
7. Quoted in "Greek Prime Minister George Papandreou: 'We Will Not Default on Our Debt,'" *The Daily Telegraph*, December 11, 2009.
8. Quoted from "Greece Struggles to Stay Afloat as Debts Pile On," *New York Times*, December 11, 2009.
9. Quoted from "Greek Finance Minister 'Clearly' Disappointed by S&P Downgrade," *Bloomberg News*, December 17, 2009.
10. Quoted from "Merkel Says EU States Responsible for Own Finances (Update1)," *Bloomberg News*, December 17, 2009.
11. Quoted from "Greeks Strike for 2nd Time Against Steps to Cut Deficit," *New York Times*, February 25, 2010.
12. *Bild,* February 12, 2010.
13. *Bild*, March 6, 2010.
14. *Bild*, March 4, 2010.

15. *Focus*, February, 2010.

16. Theodoros Pangalos. BBC. February 24, 2010.

17. Fitch Ratings. Report on Greece. April 9, 2010.

18. Quoted in "EU Sets Clock Ticking on Greece as Merkel Talks Near (Update1)," *Bloomberg News*, March 1, 2010.

19. Quoted in *Il Sole 24 Ore*, January 6, 2010.

20. Quoted in "Germany 'Won't Give One Cent to Greece': Minister," *AFP*, March 5, 2010.

21. Quoted in "We're Happy to Give the Greeks Anything, Just Not Money," *Der Spiegel,* April 3, 2010.

22. Quoted in "IMF Welcomes Greece's 'Very Strong' Fiscal Package (Update1)," *Bloomberg News*, March 3, 2010.

23. Quoted in "Greece Wins EU45 Billion Aid Pledge to Blunt Crisis (Update1)," *Bloomberg News*, April 11, 2010.

24. Quoted in "Merkel 'Buckled' on Greek Aid Terms, Lawmakers Say (Update1)," *Bloomberg News*, April 12, 2010.

25. *Bild*, April 28, 2010.

26. Quoted in "Papandreou Slammed by Unions, Opposition Over Bailout (Update1)," *Bloomberg News*, April 23, 2010.

27. Quoted in "Greece's Papandreou Requests EU, IMF Financial Lifeline: Video," *Bloomberg News*, April 23, 2010.

28. Quoted in "Merkel Tells Greece, Euro Region That Bailout Isn't a Done Deal," *Bloomberg News*, April 25, 2010.

Chapter 8   The Trillion-Dollar Weekend

1. Quoted in "Trichet Life Compass Points to Euro at Center of European Unity," *Bloomberg News*, June 7, 2010.

2. Quoted in "German Parliament Approves Greek Rescue," Associated Press, May 7, 2010.

3. Quoted in "Germany Backs Greek Aid as Merkel Urges EU Discipline (Update1)," *Bloomberg News*, May 7, 2010.

4. Quoted in "Lagarde Saving Europe Proves Being First Isn't What's Electable," *Bloomberg News*, June 21, 2010.

5. Quoted in "Systemic Crisis in Euro-Zone: Sarkozy," *AFP*, May 8, 2010.

6. Quoted from "How the Euro Rescue Package Came Together," *Der Spiegel*, May 17, 2010. Available at www.spiegel.de.

7. Ibid.

8. Quoted in "EU Crafts $962 Billion Show of Force to Halt Crisis (Update3)," *Bloomberg News*, May 10, 2010.
9. Ibid.
10. *Frankfurter Allgemeine*, May 10, 2010.
11. *Die Welt*, May 11, 2010.
12. *Boersen-Zeitung*, May 10, 2010.
13. Quoted in "Weber Defies Trichet Over Europe Bond Bailout as ECB Succession Approaches," *Bloomberg News*, June 17, 2010.
14. Quoted from "Bailout Plan Is All about Rescuing Banks and Rich Greeks," *Der Spiegel*, May 18, 2010.
15. Pierre Lellouche, quoted in "The French Question Euro Bailout," *Financial Times*, May 28, 2010.
16. Quoted in "Trichet Life Compass Points to Euro at Center of European Unity," *Bloomberg News*, June 7, 2010.
17. Quoted in "Europe Won't Let Euro Zone State Fail: ECB's Trichet," Reuters, June 19, 2010.
18. *The Rise of the EU's Economic Government* (London: Open Europe, June, 2010). Available at www.opeeurope.org.uk.
19. Quoted in "Hesitation by Leaders Drove Cost of Europe's Crisis Higher," *Washington Post*, June 16, 2010.

Chapter 9   Contagion

1. Quoted in "Spain Loses AAA Rating at Fitch as Europe Battles Debt Crisis," *Bloomberg News*, May 29, 2010.
2. Quoted in "'Portugal Will Be Next Victim of Banksters,' says Greek Deputy Prime Minister," Reuters, April 5, 2010.
3. Moody's Credit Report, July 13, 2010.
4. Quoted in "Irish Show Greeks Suffering Is Price of Admission to Euro Union," *Bloomberg News*, July 21, 2010.
5. Quoted in "Moody's Cuts Irish Rating on Debt Outlook, Bank Costs (Update2)," *Bloomberg News*, July 19, 2010.
6. Adele Bergin, Thomas Conefrey, John Fitz Gerald, and Ide Kearney, *Recovery Scenarios for Ireland* (Dublin: The Economic and Social Research Institute, 2010). Available at www.esri.ie.
7. Quoted from "Irish Economy Is Stabilizing After 'Near Free Fall,' IMF Says," *Bloomberg News*, July 14, 2010.
8. Quoted in David Marsh, *The Euro: The Politics of the New Global Currency* (New Haven, CT: Yale University Press, 2009).

9. Is Italy Europe's Ticking Time Bomb? (London: Capital Economics, July 5, 2010).

10. Ibid.

11. Morgan Stanley, Global Economic Forum, July 5, 2010. Available at www.morganstanley.com

12. Adam Smith, *The Wealth of Nations*.

13. Quoted in "Bernanke Delivers Blunt Warning on U.S. debt," *Washington Times*, February 25, 2010.

14. Niall Ferguson, "A Greek Crisis Is Coming to America," *Financial Times*, February 10, 2010.

Chapter 10   The Debt–Deflation Death Spiral

1. Quoted in "Greece Cut to Junk by Moody's on 'Substantial' Risks (Update2)," *Bloomberg News*, June 15, 2010.

2. Ibid.

3. *Imerissia*, June 16, 2010.

4. *To Vima*, June 16, 2010.

5. *Ta Nea*, June 16, 2010.

6. *Kathimerini*, June 16, 2010.

7. *Estia*, June 16, 2010.

8. Moody's Credit Report, June 16, 2010.

9. Quoted in "Nightmare Vision for Europe as EU Chief Warns 'Democracy Could Disappear' in Greece, Spain, and Portugal," *The Daily Mail*, June 15, 2010.

10. Quoted in "AXA Fears 'Fatal Flaw' Will Destroy Eurozone," *The Daily Telegraph*, June 14, 2010.

11. Quoted in "Jim Rogers Buys Euros, Says Bailouts Destroy Currency (Update2)," *Bloomberg News*, June 16, 2010.

12. Quoted in "The Euro Mutiny Begins," *The Daily Telegraph*, June 16, 2010.

13. Fitch Ratings, Report on Greece, May 2010.

14. Ibid.

15. Fox Business Network, June 21, 2010.

16. Ibid.

17. ING, Research report, June 2010.

18. Ibid.

19. Nouriel Roubini, "Greece's Best Option Is an Orderly Default," *Financial Times*, June 28, 2010.

20. Ibid.
21. *Why the Euro-Zone Needs to Break-Up* (London: Capital Economics, July 21, 2010).

Chapter 11   How to Break Up a Single Currency

1. *Quantifying the Unthinkable.* ING, July 2010.
2. Wolfgang Schäuble, "Maligned Germany Is Right to Cut Spending," *Financial Times*, June 23, 2010.
3. Quoted in "EU Budgetary Proposals Draw Immediate Rebuke," *EU Observer*, May 12, 2010.
4. Herman Van Rompuy, *The Daily Telegraph*, May 25, 2010.
5. Christine Lagarde, *Financial Times*, March 16, 2010.
6. Quoted in "Greece May Spur German Rethink, Morgan Stanley Says (Update1)," *Bloomberg News*, April 16, 2010.

Chapter 12   The Global Economy after the Single Currency

1. Quoted in "Soros Says 'We Have Just Entered Act II' of Crisis (Update2)," *Bloomberg News*, June 10, 2010.
2. George Soros, "Germany Must Reflect on the Unthinkable," *Financial Times*, June 24, 2010.
3. George Soros. Lecture, Humboldt University, June 23, 2010. Available at www.georgesoros.com.
4. Ibid.
5. Ibid.
6. Dmitry Medvedev, Interview with the *Wall Street Journal*, June 18, 2010.
7. Quoted in "Medvedev Promotes Ruble to Lessen Dollar Dominance (Update1)," *Bloomberg News*, June 19, 2010.
8. Quoted from Katinka Barysch, "Germany, the Euro and the Politics of the Bail-Out," Centre for European Reform, London, June 2010. Available at www.cer.org.uk.
9. Ibid.
10. Quoted in "They Said It . . . How the EU Elite Got It Wrong on the Euro," Open Europe, London, June 2010. Available at ww.openeurope .org.uk.

Acknowledgments

Thanks to Pete Baker for his expert editing, and to everyone on the team at John Wiley & Sons for helping to put the book together.

Thanks also to all the people who made time to help me understand the crisis in Greece and its implications for the global economy.

And thanks most of all to my wife, Angharad, and my three daughters Isabella, Leonora, and Claudia, for allowing me to disappear for much of the summer of 2010 to write this book.

About the Author

Matthew Lynn is an experienced financial writer and commentator. He is a business and economics commentator for Bloomberg Television and a columnist for Bloomberg News and *MoneyWeek* in the UK, as well as a regular contributor to the *Spectator* magazine in London. Before that, Lynn worked for 10 years at the *Sunday Times* in London as a business writer and columnist. As Matt Lynn, he is also the author of the *Death Force* series of military thrillers published by Hodder Headline.

Index